P9-BHX-165

REY
PENINSULA

COMPILED BY WORKERS OF THE WRITERS' PROGRAM OF THE WORK PROJECTS ADMINISTRATION IN NORTHERN CALIFORNIA

American Guide Series

AMERICAN CENTENNIAL EDITION

JAMES LADD DELKIN
STANFORD UNIVERSITY
CALIFORNIA

SECOND REVISED EDITION

AMERICAN GUIDE SERIES

NORTHERN CALIFORNIA WRITERS' PROJECT

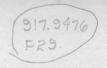

Original Preface to First Edition

Ever since the Monterey Peninsula made its literary debut in the sharply recorded observations of his visit which round-the-world traveler Compte de la Pérouse set down in 1786, journals, histories, plays, novels, and poems innumerable have dealt with the ancient capital of Spanish civilization on the Pacific Coast. In Richard Henry Dana's *Two Years Before the Mast*, in Bayard Taylor's *Eldorado*, in Robert Louis Stevenson's *Across the Plains*, and in Charles Warren Stoddard's *In the Footsteps of the Padres* are memorable vignettes of the Peninsula as it appeared to distinguished travelers at successive intervals throughout the nineteenth century. The Monterey region is the locale of Gertrude Atherton's *Patience Sparhawk* and *Splendid Idle Forties*, of Mary Austin's *Isidro*, of John Steinbeck's *Tortilla Flat*. It appears in the stories of Bret Harte and the autobiography of Lincoln Steffens. Of its wild beauties George Sterling has sung in *The House of Orchids* and other poems; Robinson Jeffers, in all his books: *Tamar, Roan Stallion, Dear Judas, Give Your Heart to the Hawks, Thurso's Landing*.

To these—and many, many more volumes which comprise the literature of the region—*Monterey Peninsula*, this guide, is the latest addition; the first comprehensive guidebook to see print since the appearance in 1875 of a volume known as the *Handbook of Monterey and Vicinity*.

In the preparation of this volume the Northern California Writers' Project was aided by Mary Greene, Curator, Old Customs House Museum; Bertha D. Hellum, Librarian, Monterey Public Library; Elizabeth Niles, Librarian, Ralph Chandler Harrison Memorial Library, Carmel; the Reverend Michael O'Connell, Carmel Mission; Mrs. Clay Otto, Curator, Carmel Art Association Gallery; Dr. Harold Heath, Professor Emeritus, Stanford University; by Frederick Bechdolt, Mrs. M. M. Gragg, Herbert Heron, James Hopper, and Nellie K. Smith; and by many other individuals and organizations of the Monterey Peninsula, for whose generous cooperation we wish to express our thanks. We are indebted to the Monterey History and Art Association for its interest and assistance. The availability of research data gathered by two other WPA Projects, the Historic American Buildings Survey and Monterey Historical Survey Projects also has been of great aid.

3

A GUIDE TO THE MONTEREY PENINSULA

The woodcut illustrations by Mallette Dean and photographs by Sibyl Anikeyev were provided by the Northern California Art Project, for whose cooperation we are indebted to the State Supervisor, Joseph Allen.

The compilation, writing, and editing of *Monterey Peninsula* have been done under the supervision of Margaret Wilkins, State Editorial Supervisor, and Paul C. Johnson, State Research Supervisor, with the aid of Wallace Boyle and Lawrence Estavan. For the field work and much of the writing, Gail Hazard, Eleanor Irwin, and Lillian Ross deserve credit; for a large part of the final draft, Charles Coppock. In the writing, Sydney S. Greenleaf, Cora Vernon Lee, Cornel Lengyel, Gladys Pittman, and Basil D. Vaerlen also have shared. The index was compiled by Max Loewenthal.

WALTER McELROY, *State Supervisor*
Northern California Writers' Project.

Contents

5

III. SHORE AND VALLEY

IV. APPENDICES

Illustrations

7

A GUIDE TO THE MONTEREY PENINSULA

ILLUSTRATIONS

9

A GUIDE TO THE MONTEREY PENINSULA

MISSION COURTYARD
            California Mission Trails Association
MISSION TOWER . . . .   Howard B. Hoffman
            Northern California Writers' Project
TOR HOUSE, CARMEL . . . .   Sibyl Anikeyev
            Northern California Art Project
PACIFIC GROVE, MUNICIPAL POOL
            Call-Bulletin Library
LOVERS' POINT . . . .   Howard B. Hoffman
            Northern California Writers' Project
COPPER BAS-RELIEF, CARMEL . . . .   Howard B. Hoffman
            Northern California Writers' Project
CARMEL VALLEY FARM . . . .   Sibyl Anikeyev
            Northern California Art Project
SHACK IN PALO COLORADO CANYON . . .   Sibyl Anikeyev
            Northern California Art Project
RAINBOW BRIDGE, BIXBY CREEK
            California Highways, Examiner Reference Library
SANTA LUCIA MOUNTAINS
HOPKINS MARINE STATION
            Dr. Walter K. Fisher

General Information

INFORMATION SERVICES

Monterey: California State Automobile Assn., 520 Fremont St.
Chamber of Commerce, 585 Munras St.

Pacific Grove: Chamber of Commerce, Forest and Central St.

Carmel: Any realtor.

POST OFFICES

Monterey: 565 Hartnell St.

Pacific Grove: Lighthouse Ave. and Park St.

Carmel: North Dolores near Sixth.

RAILROAD STATIONS

Monterey: Southern Pacific, Del Monte and Adams Sts.
Pacific Grove: Southern Pacific, Briggs St. W. of 19th St.

BUS STATIONS

Monterey: Pacific Greyhound, 260 W. Franklin St. Bay Rapid
Transit, 216 Del Monte Ave.

Pacific Grove: Pacific Greyhound, 612 Lighthouse Ave.

Carmel: Pacific Greyhound and Bay Rapid Transit, 6th and Dolores Sts.

LOCAL BUSES

Monterey to Oak Grove and Del Monte (from Franklin and Alva-
rado Sts.); to Presidio and Asilomar (from Franklin and Alvarado
Sts.); to Pacific Grove (from Alvarado St.); to Carmel (from Bay
Rapid Transit Depot, 216 Del Monte Ave.); to East Monterey
(Seaside) (from Cooper House, Polk and Munras Sts.).

AIRPORT

Monterey Airport, 3 miles E. of Monterey, for United Air Lines.
Usually four flights daily; two to San Francisco, two to Los Angeles.
Planes may be chartered.

A GUIDE TO THE MONTEREY PENINSULA

TAXIS

Monterey: 25c, 35c, and 50c zones; to Pacific Grove, 50c and 75c; to Carmel, $1.00. Meter, 40c per customer mile.

Pacific Grove: To Carmel, $2.00.

TRAFFIC REGULATIONS

Pedestrians have right-of-way on all street crossings. Speed limit 25 m.p.h. in cities, 15 m.p.h in Presidio.

HOTELS

This list includes only hotels whose daily rates are not less than $1.00.

Monterey: Del Monte. Federal, 331 Alvarado St. Kimball, 235 Alvarado St. Mission Inn, 456 Tyler St. Monterey, 406 Alvarado St. Royal, 342 Alvarado St. San Carlos, Franklin and Pacific Sts. Serra, Del Monte Ave. and Tyler St.

Pacific Grove: Asilomar Resort, Asilomar Blvd. and Sinex St. Centralia, 612 Grove St. Del Mar, 603 Lighthouse Ave. El Carmelo Inn, 643 Lighthouse Ave. Forest Hills, Forest Ave. and Gibson St.

Carmel: Carmel Inn, San Carlos near Seventh. Forest Lodge, Santa Fe Ave. and El Camino Real. La Playa, on El Camino Real near 8th St. La Ribera, 7th and Lincoln Sts. McPhillips', 5th and San Carlos Sts. Pine Inn, Ocean Ave. Lobos Lodge, Ocean and Monte Verde. Colonial Terrace, Carmelo and 12th. Holiday Inn, Bayview and Martin Way.

Pebble Beach: Del Monte Lodge, 17-Mile Dr.

Carmel Highlands: Highland Inn. Peter Pan Lodge.

Big Sur: Big Sur Lodge.

Carmel Valley: Del Monte Guest Ranch, San Clemente Dam. Rancho Carmelo. Robles del Rio Lodge.

TOURIST COURTS

Monterey: Anchor, Fremont Extension and Cañon del Rey. Cypress Court, 665 Pacific St. David Avenue Court, Lyndon St. and David Ave. Pine Oak Court, 2149 Fremont St. Casa Munras, Fremont and Munras St.

GENERAL INFORMATION

Pacific Grove: Bide-a-wee, Asilomar Blvd. Carlway, Sinex St. and Asilomar Blvd. Ideal, Lighthouse Ave. and Asilomar Blvd. Knights Cottage Court, 482 Bennett St. Mikel's Cottages, 210 Ridge Rd. Municipal Camp Grounds, Alder and Sinex Sts. Pine Grove Court, Lighthouse Ave. and Grove Acres. 17-Mile Drive Cottage Court. 1000 Sinex St.

Carmel: El Rio Carmelo, Carmel River Bridge. Carmel Cottage Court, Carpenter and 2nd Sts.

DUDE RANCHES

Del Monte Guest Ranch, San Clemente Dam. Carmel Dude Ranch. Rancho Carmelo, and Robles del Rio in Carmel Valley.

RESTAURANTS

Monterey: Bing Sing Chan, Washington and Del Monte; Chinese. Betty's Seafood, Fisherman's Wharf. Biff's, Fremont St. at El Estero; Italian dinners. Cademartori's (Casa Serrano), 412 Pacific St. First Brick House, 351 Decatur St.; Spanish dinners. La Fonda, Mission Inn, 456 Tyler St.; Mexican dinners. My Attic Café (Casa Sanchez), 414 Alvarado St. Pop Ernest's, Fisherman's Wharf; Seafood. San Carlos Hotel Sidewalk Café, 200 W. Franklin St. Tortilla, 154 Calle Principal; Mexican. Mike's Seafood, Fisherman's Wharf.

Pacific Grove: Del Mar Café, Hotel Del Mar, 603 Lighthouse Ave.

Carmel: Aztec Lounge. Blue Bird, Ocean Ave. Ella's Southern Kitchen, Dolores St. near Ocean Ave. Normandy Inn (sidewalk café), Ocean and Monte Verde Aves. Whitney's, Ocean and San Carlos Aves. Russian Inn, Ocean and Dolores. Asia Inn, Dolores near Ocean. Pine Inn, Ocean Ave. Sade's, Ocean and Lincoln.

NIGHT CLUBS

Monterey: Blue Bell, 375 Alvarado St.; dinner, dancing, floor show. Blue Ox, Fremont Extension. Knotty Pine, Lighthouse and Dickson Aves.; dinner, dancing, floor show. San Carlos Hotel, 200 W. Franklin St.; dinner, dancing.

THEATERS

Monterey: State Theater, 417 Alvarado St.; and Monterey Theater, 221 Alvarado St.; for motion pictures. First Theater, 202 Pacific

13

St., for "little" and amateur productions. Rio Theater, Seaside and Del Rey.

Pacific Grove: Grove Theater, 612 Lighthouse Ave., for motion pictures.

Carmel: Carmel Theater, Ocean Ave. and Mission St.; and Playhouse, Monte Verde Ave. and 9th St.; for motion pictures. Forest Theater, Mountain View and Santa Rita Aves.; and Sunset School Auditorium, San Carlos Ave. and 9th St.; for stage productions.

RADIO STATIONS

KDON, 1210 kc., Monterey Peninsula Herald Building, 498 Washington St.

NEWSPAPERS AND PERIODICALS

Monterey: Monterey Peninsula Herald, 498 Washington St., daily.
Monterey Trader Press, 408 Tyler St., weekly.
Pacific Grove: Tribune, 305 Forest Ave., weekly.
Carmel: Pine Cone, Dolores St. near Seventh, weekly.

LIBRARIES

Monterey: Monterey Public, W. Franklin and Van Buren Sts. New Monterey Branch Library, Prescott and Laine Sts.

Pacific Grove: Pacific Grove Public, Central Ave., between Fountain and Grand Aves.

Carmel: Harrison Memorial, Ocean and Lincoln Aves. Wishing Wells Rental Library, Lincoln near Ocean Ave.

ART COLLECTIONS AND MUSEUMS

Monterey: Cooper House Museum *(open irregular hours; donation expected),* Polk and Munras Sts., primitive art. First Theater *(open 1-5),* Scott and Pacific Sts. Mexican Idol, 226 Calle Principal; native Mexican art. Lial's, Margaret *(open 2-5),* Alvarado and Munras Sts. Monterey High School, S. end of Larkin St.; murals. Offices of the City of Monterey *(open 9-5),* cor. Madison and Pacific Sts.; early and contemporary Monterey art. Old Customs House *(open 1-5),* Calle Principal at Fisherman's Wharf; primitive and

GENERAL INFORMATION

contemporary art.Oliver Art Gallery *(open 9-6)*, 120 Calle Principal; contemporary Monterey art.

Pacific Grove: Museum of Natural History *(open 10-4 except Mon.)*, Forest and Central Aves.; marine exhibit. Pacific Grove High School Library *(open 8-5)*, Forest and Sinex Aves.; WPA murals. Pacific Grove Public Library *(open 10-9)*, Central and Fountain Aves.

Carmel: Carmel Art Association Gallery *(open 2-5)*, 6th and Dolores Sts. Carmel Art Institute, Robles del Rio. Harrison Memorial Library *(open 11-9)*,, Ocean and Lincoln Aves.; paintings by California artists, etchings by Haden, Rembrandt, Schongauer, Meryon, and Durer. Seven Arts Gallery, Lincoln and Ocean.

CONCERT HALLS

Monterey: Casa Alvarado, Alvarado and Munras Sts.; for schedule inquire at Lial's Music Store.
Carmel: Sunset Auditorium, San Carlos Ave. and 9th St.
Pacific Grove: Monterey Peninsula Community Concert Association, Chamber of Commerce, Forest and Central Sts.

SPORTS

Badminton: Mission Ranch Club, Carmel, Asilomar, Pacific Grove.
Baseball: Monterey Ball Park, Franklin and Adams Sts. Pacific Grove Baseball Park (night baseball), Pine Cone Dr. and Dennett Street.

Basketball: Monterey and Pacific Grove High Schools; in season.
Bowling: Monterey Bowl, Franklin and Pacific Sts.
Boxing: Presidio, Monterey.

Chess: Chess Club, American Legion Hall, Carmel; each Thurs. Girl Scout Hall, Junipero and Fountain Aves., Pacific Grove; each Mon.

Fishing: Fisherman's Wharf, Monterey, for surf and deep-sea fishing; boats for latter leave at 7:30 a.m. daily (fare includes bait and tackle). Municipal Beach Pier, Pacific Grove, for surf and deep-sea fishing; boats for rent.

Golf: Pebble Beach Golf Course. Cypress Point Golf Club; guest cards available. Monterey Peninsula Golf and Country Club. Pacific Grove Municipal Golf Course, 19th St. and Jewel Ave.

A GUIDE TO THE MONTEREY PENINSULA

Hiking: Information at Monterey Chamber of Commerce, 585 Munras St., or at Big Sur Ranger Station.

Horse-racing: Monterey County Fair, Monterey; fall.
Horseshoe-pitching: Pacific Grove City Park, Forest and Central Avenues.

Riding: Pebble Beach Riding Stables, Pebble Beach. Betty Green Stables, 4th and Junipero Aves., Carmel. Highlands Stables, Carmel Highlands. Jack's Peak Riding Stables, Aguajito, Monterey-Carmel Highway.

Roller Skating: El Estero, Del Monte Ave. at El Estero; free outdoor skating in summer. Rollerdrome, Del Monte Ave., Monterey. Skating Rink, Grand and Lighthouse Aves., Pacific Grove.

Swimming: Public beaches at Monterey (municipal wharf), Pacific Grove, Asilomar, and Carmel. Monterey High School; free. Pacific Grove Municipal Beach and Plunge, foot of 17th St. Pebble Beach Pool; guest cards available. Rancho Carmelo.

Tennis: Monterey High School (free); Monterey Peninsula Country Club (card only); and Cypress Point Club (card only). Pacific Grove Municipal Courts (free), Ocean View and Monterey Aves., and Gibson Ave. and 14th St. Municipal Courts, Junipero St., Carmel; night playing; equipment for rent.

Trapshooting: Del Monte Gun Club; instructor.

CHURCHES
Only centrally located churches of most denominations are listed.

Monterey: Baptist, Prescott Ave. and Lane St. Catholic, Royal Presidio Chapel, 550 Church St. Chiesa Evangelica Italiana, 319 Pacific St. Christian Science, Madison and Larkin Sts. Japanese Presbyterian, 695 Pearl St. Latter Day Saints, 582 Hawthorne St. Presbyterian, 404 W. Franklin St.

Pacific Grove: Catholic, St. Angela, 321 Central Ave. Christian, Central and Carmel Aves. Christian Science, Central and Fountain Aves. Congregational, Central Ave. and 14th St. Episcopal, St. Mary's-by-the-Sea, Central Ave. and 12th St. Lutheran, 160 Monterey Ave. Methodist, Lighthouse Ave. and 17th St. Mormon, Pine Ave. and 11th St. Pentecostal, Pine and Grand Aves.

MONTEREY CYPRESS ROOT

ON THE SEVENTEEN-MILE DRIVE

GHOST TREE

WHERE SEVEN OCEAN CURRENTS MEET

LONE CYPRESS

MOUNTAIN HOMESTEAD

GENERAL INFORMATION

Carmel: Catholic, Mission San Carlos del Rio Carmelo, Santa Lucia Ave. and Carmel River. Christian Science, First Church, Monte Verde Ave. and 5th St. Church of the Wayfarer (Community), Lincoln between 7th St. and Ocean Ave. Episcopal, All Saints, Monte Verde between 7th St. and Ocean Ave.

Calendar of Events

NOTE: "nfd" means *no fixed date.*

Winter	nfd	Del Monte	High Goal Handicap (Polo)
	nfd	Carmel	Kite Festival
Spring	nfd	Presidio	Sunrise Easter Service
	nfd	Del Monte	Dog Show
June	nfd	Monterey	Monterey Birthday Party
	nfd	Monterey	Flower Show
Summer	nfd	Pacific Grove	Concerts: School of Music
July	nfd	Carmel	Bach Festival
	3-5	Pacific Grove	Water Carnival
	nfd	Carmel	Shakespeare Festival
Aug. or	nfd	Pebble Beach or	State Amateur Championship
Sept.		Del Monte	Golf Tournament
			State Amateur Handicap
			Championship (Golf)
Sept.	nfd	Monterey	Monterey County Fair
			Montery County Horse Show
Fall or Winter	nfd	Pacific Grove	Butterfly Festival

18

I. The Peninsula

The Natural Heritage

Midway down the long stretch of the California coast, the Monterey Peninsula rises out of the sea, southern horn of the great crescent of sandy shoreline that sweeps around Monterey Bay. On the Peninsula's northern rim, looking across the wide waters of the Bay, lies Monterey, second oldest settlement of Alta California and for more than four decades its capital. "The Bay of Monterey has been compared," wrote Robert Louis Stevenson, ". . . to a bent fishing-hook . . . Santa Cruz sits exposed at the shank; the mouth of the Salinas River is at the middle of the bend; and Monterey itself is cosily ensconced beside the barb." From the town the Peninsula's shoreline of white sand and dark rocks edges northwest toward windswept Point Pinos, dips abruptly south to rugged Cypress Point and then southwest to Pescadero Point, where begins the inward-curving sweep of Carmel Bay. Across the water, hemming in Carmel Bay on the south, rises Point Lobos, a spray-dampened and craggy pile of tree-grown rocks. Between Monterey and Carmel Bays stretch the Peninsula's 25 square miles of rolling dunes, low hills, flat-topped ridges, and twisted trees, edged by rugged cliffs and boulders and marvelously white beaches.

First sighted by Juan Rodríguez Cabrillo just 50 years after the discovery of America, Monterey Bay's "noble harbor" remained a persistent legend for more than two centuries until it was found again and converted to man's use. It was the search for this harbor, to be a haven for the rich galleons of Spain in their trade with Manila, that led to the discovery of San Francisco Bay, to the establishment of missions, presidios, and *pueblos* in northern California as outposts of empire against other land-hungry nations. The Monterey Peninsula rose at first as the site of the old capital of Spanish and Mexican California, where all politics and mission business of importance transpired, and it fell as an American possession when the Gold Rush denuded it of its population and took business and politics farther north. But like Rome the Peninsula left the heritage of a rich civilization. It left its mission and presidio and scores of historic adobe buildings preserved, despite neglect through the Dark Ages which fell on Monterey in the middle of the nineteenth century and lasted almost until the beginning of the twentieth.

THE NATURAL HERITAGE

The Peninsula has been called the "Cradle of California History"; but its historic charms were all but forgotten until its rediscovery as a tourists' and home-owners' paradise, prized for its sunny climate, the beauty of its pine-clad hills, its cypress-shaded sea cliffs and glistening beaches. As the "Circle of Enchantment"—so named by twentieth-century boosters who have made the most of its attractions, both past and present—Monterey was put back on the map.

The cities and resorts, elaborate hotels and exclusive golf courses, and the luxurious residences of the Peninsula are strung around its ocean edge in the shape of a U. There are three municipalities— Monterey, Pacific Grove, and Carmel-by-the-Sea. At the northern neck of the Peninsula is the Hotel Del Monte, one of the oldest, best known, and most expensive of California's resort hotels. Monterey, tourist and fishing center, largest of the Peninsula's three municipalities, spreads to the west, and beyond it lies Pacific Grove, originally a Methodist retreat, now a quiet family town, retaining traces of the religious and moral scrupulousness of its founders. Along the Peninsula's southern coastline are Del Monte Lodge, the Monterey Peninsula Country Club, and Pebble Beach, with their golf courses and polo fields. Southward is Carmel-by-the-Sea, habitation of artists and pseudo-artists, whose peculiar architecture is the result of each owner's being allowed to build according to his whim (as long as he doesn't cut down a tree!), the weird houses twisting and tumbling over one another, their roofs round or sharp or flat and vaguely rambling in the most unexpected places. Beyond it lies old Carmel Mission itself.

Scenically, the Peninsula is concentrated California. Here is the full, loose sweep of Monterey Bay stretching north from Point Pinos toward Santa Cruz, with its blue oval harbor; here are the dunes of fine white sand, shifting or chaparral-covered, the shoreline of granite cliffs, broken and rugged and battered by conflicting ocean currents; and here the twisted and tortured cypresses that are native to no other spot in the world, the pines to which the cypresses give way as one travels inland, the oaks which follow the pines. Cypress and pine are in fact symbols of Monterey: the cypresses lurch along the rocky headlands; the pines dot the hills, blending into forests of madrone and redwood. The hills are the pasture lands—the low "unfinished" hills as Stevenson called them, their flanks dissected by ravines—rising abruptly southward from the Peninsula's northern tip to attain an elevation of approximately 800 feet two miles south of Monterey.

21

A GUIDE TO THE MONTEREY PENINSULA

The Peninsula itself is but a small part of Monterey County's 5,600 square miles of foothills and mountains, of narrow canyons and valleys, stretching along the coast for 125 miles with an average width of 45 miles. Beyond the Peninsula to the south and southwest rise the brown foothills and blue peaks of the Santa Lucia Mountains, covered with pine and chaparral. They stand as a barrier against the storm winds of the Pacific, rising above sea level from 800 to 5,000 feet, in their wildest parts untapped by highway or road. Highest elevation is Santa Lucia Peak (5,844 alt.). The range extends southwest from Carmel in an unbroken line until it merges with the Mount Diablo Range—a rugged mass with an average breadth of 18 miles, founded on granite, bearing iron ore, coal, gypsum, and some gold. Much of it lies within the Monterey division of Los Padres National Forest, a 322,273-acre reserve drained by the Carmel River, set aside for recreation and water conservation purposes. So deep and narrow are the canyons cleft from the sheer western slopes that often the branches of tall trees scrape the canyon walls on either side. Behind the eastern slopes of the Santa Lucia, paralleling the coast, are sheltered the large, rich Salinas Valley and the smaller but fertile Carmel Valley, both drained by rivers of the same names. The Salinas River is California's third largest. East of the Salinas Valley, running southward a hundred miles, rises the Gavilan Range, Monterey County's eastern boundary.

"The one common note of all this country," observed Robert Louis Stevenson, "is the haunting presence of the ocean." "Everywhere," he wrote, "even in quiet weather, the low, distant, thrilling roar of the Pacific hangs over the coast and the adjacent country like smoke above the battle." Walking along the beaches, he noticed the myriads of sea birds, the marine life of every description. "Crowds of ducks and sea-gulls hover over the sea. Sand pipers trot in and out by troops after the retiring waves, trilling their song as they go. Strange sea-tangles, new to the European eye, the bones of whales, or sometimes a whole whale's carcass, white with carrion-gulls and poisoning the wind, lie scattered here and there along the sands."

The Bay of Monterey abounds in fishes and marine creatures of all sizes, from an occasional visiting whale to tiny silver-sides that swim about the piles of wharves in brilliant flashes just under the surface of the water. Octopi, sea lions, and abalone live among the rocks near shore. Life along the bottom of the bay is bright and varied. Crabs of all colors—drab, gray, pink, or dark red, flat-topped, thick-clawed and armoured, beautiful or hideous—crawl between fronds of seaweed. There are oysters and clams—big and little —mussels, cockels, and scallops; sponges and sea snails. Shrimp and lobster wander among gay starfish, passing gardens of anemone that look so innocent yet prove so fatal to their prey, passing the large illuminated jellyfish that sting so painfully with their long tentacles. On the surface of the water algae float about in great brown and purple patches, huge serpent-like streamers riding with graceful ease, while other forms grow from the rocks along the shore in feathery masses like tropical islands in the midst of a hurricane.

The California sardine, most prolific fish in the bay waters, occurs in schools or shoals. Second in commercial importance are the Pacific mackerel and the California pilchard. Aside from these, the fishing fleet brings in chiefly albacore, anchovies, flounders, grayfish, halibut, herring, kingfish, perch, pompano, rock-fish, salmon, sand dabs, sea bass, skates, sole, and sharks. Of the sharks five species appear, ranging from 4 to 20 feet in length; they are prized for their livers, from which a substitute for cod liver oil is manufactured. Octopi are caught, dried, and exported to China by the ton, as are jellyfish, preserved in alum and salt.

The rocks off the shore are the homes of large heards of sea lions (sea wolves to the Spanish settlers). Two varieties live here, the Steller and the California sea lions. Of these the former is larger in size and less uniformly dark in color, his voice a deep and prolonged roar that sounds clearly above the roar of the surf. The voice of the California sea lion is shriller, more of a howl, ending in a hoarse coughing bark. At night when the tide is out and the sea quiet, the calling of both species can be heard far inland, a continuous roaring. In 1938, in the kelp beds along the coast south of Carmel, the southern form of the sea otter reappeared. These animals, ruthlessly slaughtered in the first half of the nineteenth century, when Yankee traders carried their pelts across the Pacific to market them in Canton, were believed to be extinct. Like seals they are highly gregarious, congregating in herds and remaining near their chosen feeding ground over a long period of time. When not feeding the animals float on the surface. The three herds noted in 1938 were estimated to number from four to five hundred individuals. They produce young, one at a time, usually every second year; they have prime fur, deep and soft, and the long white-tipped hairs give the skin a frosted appearance and enhance its value. The former range of the sea otter extended from the Pribiloff Islands off Alaska to Lower California.

Inland from the seashore, wooded slopes and canyons harbor

23

A GUIDE TO THE MONTEREY PENINSULA

varied kinds of animal life. In recent years, two almost extinct species have reappeared here, the California condor and the snowy egret. The brown pelican finds in this region his northernmost nesting grounds. Most common birds include the blue-jay, dive, flycatcher heron, jay, dove, magpie, pigeon, quail, thrasher, and woodpecker. Birds are bewildering in their variety: a larger number of species is said to be found here than in any other region of the State. In the back country, sportsmen haul in from the rivers black bass, sunfish, and occasionally rainbow trout. Through the wilder fastnesses of the Santa Lucia Mountains, parts of which are among the most inaccessible regions in the country, roam mountain lions, deer, coyotes, rabbits, opossums, skunks, coons, and some bears. Even the wild boar is here, imported from Russia.

The slopes of the Santa Lucias are covered largely with chaparral, pine, fir, oak, and madrone. The chaparral grows rank and high (30 feet or more)—a dense thicket of thornlike branchlets and leathery leaves. The Santa Lucia fir, limited to this, its natural habitat, has a slender, spire-shaped crown, thick with bristling foliage. Redwoods, growing here in their southernmost stand, tower from canyon depths among white-barked, gnarled sycamores. The union of the sycamore —typical of the low flat semiarid regions of southern California— with the redwood indicates the character of the region as a transition zone, as does the union of the yucca and the redwood lily. Rearing its crown of sword-shaped evergreen leaves on a tall stalk, the yucca lifts its clusters of white blossoms to the heights of a man's head or higher. On inaccessible ridges the redwood lily grows seven feet high crowned with rare, fragrant bloom, shading from white through pink to red-purple. Wild lilac covers the hills with its smoky blue color. On the hills or along the seashore are found 150 other varieties of wild flowers—poppies, lupines, Indian paintbrushes, wild iris, and others less well known.

Of all the Peninsula's growing things, none have brought it so much fame as its pines and cypresses. Over the whole Peninsula grow the Monterey cypress *(Cupressus macrocarpa)*, with twisted branches and dark green foliage that forms a spreading crown, and the Monterey pine *(Pinus radiata)*, dark green with sturdy branches and fissured bark, almost black. In its native state the Monterey cypress grows only on the headlands about Carmel Bay, never more than 350 feet from the sea; but, although incapable of extending itself naturally, it has been transplanted to other parts of the State, where it grows in hedges, windbreaks, and parks. The young trees, pyramid-shaped, are symmetrical; the older ones, grotesque with their umbrella-shaped tops and gnarled branches. Where they stand exposed to the sea winds, their tops are flattened, their branches bent sprawling to the ground. Most striking feature of the wind-broken trees is their boardlike trunks, only six to nine inches thick but one to nine feet broad. The normal life span of the Monterey cypress is 200 to 300 years. Many of the trees are found growing from the cliffs, from which, one by one, they finally tumble into the sea. The Monterey pine, native to Monterey and adjoining counties, grows rapidly (from 60 to 90 feet within three years) to a great size, often attaining a height of 100 feet and a girth of from four to six feet. Its bark is deeply ridged and furrowed, cleft into irregular plates that roughen the trunk's surface from its base to a point higher than a man's head. The Monterey pine—also known as the "beach pine," since it thrives in sandy soil near the ocean—is prized chiefly for its watershed protection and its use as firewood. The Bishop pine and the Gowan cypress, both limited in range like the Monterey pine and cypress, also flourish over the Peninsula, which the botanist Jepson has called an isolated arboreal island because it shelters four cone-bearing trees of limited distribution. The dark, thick foliage of the pines and cypresses creates an impression of deep shade resting over the Peninsula's whole landscape, a darkness in sharp contrast to the blue-green water and white foam of the sea. The "kind of wood for murderers to crawl among," Stevenson called these forests with their "long aisles of pine-trees hung with Spaniard's Beard."

So famous are the Monarch butterflies—which visit the Peninsula every year by the millions to spend the winter among the pines near Point Pinos—that Pacific Grove has passed an ordinance declaring it "unlawful for any person to molest or interfere with in any way the peaceful occupancy of the Monarch butterflies on their annual visit to Pacific Grove." (With permission of the chief of police, a home owner may evict them from his property, but anyone else who ventures to disturb them risks a $500 fine or six months' imprisonment.) The Monarchs, large golden-brown and black butterflies, which are thought to spend their summers in western Canada or southern Alaska, arrive every year in late October or early November, flying like a dark ribbon across the sky. The main migration is preceded by scouts who arrive about two weeks earlier to select the best winter quarters. By the thousands the butterflies gather on one small group of pines near the Point Pinos lighthouse and on many trees throughout the area, clinging together with folded wings on cold or foggy days so that they almost hide the foliage. When the sun shines, they fly about, feeding chiefly on milkweed. So appreciative is Pacific Grove of their yearly visits that it has placed the Monarch on the seal of its chamber of commerce and adopted "Follow the butterflies to Pacific Grove" as its municipal slogan.

Climatically, the Peninsula is lucky. The sea keeps the temperature moderate at all seasons, never extremely hot or extremely cold; and the nights are cool. The temperature varies less than 10 degrees the year round, ranging usually from about 53° to about 61°. Rainfall, usually heaviest in January, averages only 18 inches a year. Early settlers were sometimes plagued by droughts, through which they often lost crops and cattle, but modern irrigation and water systems, such as the San Clemente Dam in the Carmel River, have long ago solved this problem. In spring the rolling hills back of the Peninsula are carpeted with rich green; in summer they are scorched to a golden brown. Autumn colors the whole country with riotous hues, reds, tans, and greens predominating.

Throughout the summer fog drifts in from the Pacific to cool the valleys; for three months, July to September, it is apt to lie over the Peninsula, shielding it from the worst of the heat. Robert Louis Stevenson described the "vast, wet, melancholy fogs" moving in from the ocean: ". . . they crawl in scarves among the sand-hills; they float, a little higher, in clouds of a gigantic size and often of a wild configuration; to the south, where they have struck the seaward shoulder of the mountains of Santa Lucia, they double back and spire skyward like smoke. . . . It takes but a little while till the invasion is complete. The sea . . . has submerged the earth. Monterey is curtained in for the night in thick, wet, salt, and frigid clouds, so to remain till day returns; and before the suns rays they slowly disperse and retreat in broken squadrons to the bosom of the sea."

Of the climate, *Alcalde* Walter Colton, resident of Monterey from 1846 to 1849, wrote: "Nov. 28. It is now near the close of that month which in other climates is often one of the most unpleasant in the year; but here it has been one of unrivaled brilliancy. The sky has been almost without a cloud, the winds have slept, and the soft air has lain on the landscape like a golden slumber. . . . Feb. 6. We have another rain . . . nature . . . calls up no thunder, throws out no lightning; she only squeezes her great sponge, and that as quietly as a mermaid smooths her dripping locks. Feb. 20. The day is not far distant when a trip to California will be regarded rather as a diversion than a serious undertaking. It will be quite worthwhile to come out here merely to enjoy the climate for a few months. It is unrivaled perhaps in the world."

Long before Colton, however, the praises of Monterey had been sung. The very first white man to land after Cabrillo's discovery, Sebastián Vizcaíno (1603), was also the first booster, and his description of the terrain reads like that of a high-pressure press agent. In a letter to his king, he stated that the place was "the best port that could be desired, for besides being sheltered from all winds, it has many pines for masts and yards, and live oaks, and water in great quantity, all near the shore." And at another time he wrote, "The land has a genial climate, its waters are good, and it is very fertile, judging from the varied and luxuriant growth of trees and plants; for I saw some of the fruits . . . which are larger than those of Spain. Though Padre Juan Crespí was later to call the bay "a little cove" and to say, "The pines are very dilapidated . . . and I did not see a single one on the whole Point that would do for masts or spars for these ships," Vizcaíno's flowery vision would not vanish.

Many a traveler since has echoed Vizcaíno's tribute. The first foreigner to visit Spanish California, the Frenchman, Jean-François Galaup, Comte de la Pérouse (1786), on an official world tour for his government, stopped 10 days at Monterey and praised the land but criticised the missions. Captain George Vancouver, the Englishman who tarried in Monterey for 50 days in 1792, described in his *A Voyage of Discovery*, published six years later, a walk from the Presidio to Mission San Carlos: "The road between lies over some steep hills and hollow valleys, interspersed with many trees; the surface was covered with an agreeable verdure; the general character of the country was lively, and our journey altogether pleasant." Richard Henry Dana, in *Two Years Before the Mast* (1835), has left a familiar description of the approach to Monterey from the sea: "We made land at Point Pinos, which is the headland at the entrance to the Bay of Monterey. . . . We came to anchor within two cable lengths of the shore, and the town lay directly before us, making a very pretty appearance, its houses being plastered . . . the soil is as rich as a man could wish; climate as good as any in the world; water abundant, and situation extremely beautiful." General John Charles Frémont too observed the Peninsula in his California travels of 1846 and recorded this impression in his *Memoirs of My Life:* "I went into camp beyond the town, near the sea, on a flat among firs and pines toward the top of the ridge fronting the bay. This was a delightful spot. Before us to the right was the town of Monterey with its red tiles; to the left the view was over the ships in the bay and on over the ocean where the July sun made the sea-breeze and the shade of the pine trees grateful."

Best known perhaps of all is Stevenson's classic description, from *Across the Plains* (1879): "Thus the ancient capital of California faces across the bay, while the Pacific Ocean, though hidden by low hills and forest, bombards her left flank and rear with never-dying surf. . . . On no other coast that I know shall you enjoy, in calm, sunny weather, such a spectacle of Ocean's greatness, such beauty of changing colour, or such degrees of thunder in the sound. The very air is more than usually salt by this Homeric deep. Inshore, a tract of sand-hills borders on the beach. Here and there a lagoon, more or less brackish, attracts the birds and hunters. . . . A great faint sound of breakers follows you high up into the inland cañons, the roar of water dwells in the clean, empty rooms of Monterey as in a shell upon the chimney. . . . You pass out of the town to the southwest, and mount the hills among the pine woods. Glade thicket, and grove surround you. . . . But the sound of the sea still follows you . . . and when at length you gain the summit, out breaks on every hand and with freshened vigour, that same unending, distant, whispering rumble of the ocean. . . . The whole woodland is begirt with thundering surges . . . "

Best-known treatment of Monterey in literature since Stevenson's time is probably John Steinbeck's present-day description of the city and some of its inhabitants in his novel *Tortilla Flat:* "Monterey sits on the slope of a hill, with a blue bay below it and with a forest of tall dark pine trees at its back. The lower parts of the town are inhabited by Americans, Italians, catchers and canners of fish. But on the hill where the forest and the town intermingle, where the streets are innocent of asphalt and the corners free of street lights, the old inhabitants of Monterey are embattled as the Ancient Britons are embattled in Wales. These are the paisanos. They live in old wooden houses set in woody yards, and the pine trees from the forest are about the houses . . ."

An American place where history has deposited a rich residue of landmarks and social customs long outmoded, where industry and agriculture have endured the ravages of an unstable economy, the Monterey Peninsula harbors a complex regional culture that is saved from provincialism by the cosmopolitan character of its inhabitants and the vitality of its traditions. Fashionable vacation resorts for international society, its towns are equally hospitable to the fisherman and the soldier, the artist and the cannery worker, the "week-ender" and the tourist, the student of marine biology and the farmer from the inland valleys. The "Barbizon of California" the Peninsula's imaginative boosters have called it; and among their efforts to extol its climatic and commercial advantages they alternately praise and criticise both the progress and the natural beauty of their community. Such extravagant schemes as a recent attempt to have the capital of California restored to its original seat at Monterey reveal the Peninsula's veneration of its social and political heritage, yet its inhabitants are too progressive to neglect the exploitation of their natural and historic resources for the enrichment of their economy and their culture.

The Peninsula
Through Four Centuries

Capital of California under Spanish and Mexican rule, Monterey was for three-quarters of a century the stronghold of Hispano-Mexican civilization on the Pacific Coast. So firmly established were Old-World customs on the Monterey Peninsula that the culture of the padres and the dons survived the American occupation and persisted almost unchallenged by modern industry and civic progress until the close of the nineteenth century. Even today, despite its vacation resorts and the reputation of the city of Monterey as the "Sardine Capital of the World," the region remains a veritable museum of California social and political history. In numerous old public buildings and well-preserved adobe dwellings—some still inhabited by descendants of the original Spanish occupants—are enshrined the picturesque mementos and romantic relics of a vanished era. Though alert to the present and eager for a prosperous future, the Monterey Peninsula still clings to the glories of its past.

THE EPOCH OF THE EXPLORERS

Just 50 years after Columbus discovered the New World, Juan Rodríguez Cabrillo, a Portuguese sailing for Spain in search of a legendary "Strait of Anian" which would provide a sea route directly through the unexplored continent of North America, one stormy day in 1542 entered a bay whose white beaches and frothy waters described a gleaming crescent against a dark green range of mountains. The astonished navigator did not risk a landing on this strange and windblown shore, but before he sailed away he took possession of the rough cool country for "God and Phillip II" and gave to a projection at the southern end of the bay the lasting name of Punta de los Pinos (Point of Pines), Cabrillo was probably the first white man to see the Bay of Monterey, so named half a century later by another intrepid explorer.

Sebastian Vizcaíno, sailing north from Mexico in 1602 in search of pearl fisheries and an empire richer than the Peru that Pizarro found, put into the bay and found it calm. On December 17 Vizcaíno and his crew went ashore to celebrate thanksgiving mass under a big oak that grew close to the blue water. He found neither pearls nor an Indian empire but he wrote a glowing report of the "noble harbor" which he promptly named in honor of the then Viceroy of New Spain, Gaspar de Zuniga, Count of Monterey. "The land is of mild temperature," he reported, "and of good waters and very fertile . . . judging by the luxuriant growth of the trees and plants . . . for I saw some fruits from them, particularly of chestnuts and acorns, larger than those of Spain; and it is well populated with people, whose disposition I saw to be soft, gentle, docile and very fit to be reduced to the Holy Church . . ."

Vizcaíno's report was not acted upon, but it was published and from it grew the lengend of Monterey—particularly of the "noble harbor"—which a century and a half later brought the Spaniards again searching up the rocky coast of Alta California (Upper California). In 1765, José de Galvez came to Mexico as *Visitador-general* (Inspector-general), and his arrival accellerated the march of empire. Two others were associated with Galvez in what became a concentrated effort to settle the California to the north: Padre Junípero Serra, appointed to guide the Franciscans who were to replace the Jesuits in control of the missions, and Francisco de Croix, Viceroy of New Spain. Resolved to rediscover Vizcaíno's harbor, Gaspar de Portolá accompanied by Serra led an expedition in 1769 to San Diego, where they founded a mission. Portolá and a few soldiers, receiving Serra's blessing, continued the northwest march. They discovered San Francisco Bay and planted two crosses on the heights above Monterey Bay, but in neither place was Portolá certain that he had found Vizcaíno's fabulous harbor.

On return of the Portolá expedition to San Diego, Serra was convinced that Monterey Bay had actually been rediscovered. "You must go back," he declared, "and this time I will go with you." So in March, 1770, Portolá set out by land and Serra by sea. They found the crosses erected on the heights above the bay the previous year still standing, decorated with arrows, feathers, shells, and strings of sardines "still somewhat fresh." On June 3 they established a mission and a presidio. Portolá raised the standard of Carlos III, threw stones and pulled up grass—as was the Spanish custom when taking possession of new land. "We afterwards ate our dinner together on the beach . . . " Serra wrote. "The whole service had been accompanied with much thunder and powder." The mission, the second to be established in Alta California, was named San Carlos Borromeo.

31

Military command of the projected settlement was entrusted to Lieutenant Pedro Fages when Portolá returned to Mexico, and some members of his expedition remained to constitute Monterey's aristocracy of "oldest families." Crude temporary buildings, including a chapel, were constructed by the settlers on rising ground above the present site of the Royal Presidio Chapel. Attracted by the fertile Carmelo Valley beyond the southward hills, however, Serra in 1770 removed the mission to the place it occupies today, thus satisfying his desire to withdraw the neophyte girls beyond the covetous gaze of the soldiery. Perhaps a more important cause seems to have been Serra's anger at Governor Fage's refusal to subject his military command to the authority of the Church. Thus began at Monterey that feud between the State secular and the State sacerdotal which was finally to be won by Mexican civil authorities only after a half century of strife had disrupted Spanish rule in Alta California.

The growth of the mission system in this northern province of New Spain caused the removal in 1775 of the provincial capital from Loreto in Baja (Lower) California. The arrival of Governor Felipe de Neve the following year established the political importance of the settlement founded by Portolá and Serra. Early in this same year came the first official contingent of colonists from Mexico: 247 men, women, and children with more than 500 head of livestock, led by Colonel Juan Bautista de Anza across more than a thousand miles of deserts and mountains from the Presidio of Tubac in Sonora. The majority of these settlers remained at Monterey while Anza surveyed sites for a presidio and a mission on San Francisco Bay; and on his return to Monterey on April 14, 1776, they gathered in the plaza to bid fond farewell to their commander on his way back to Mexico. "I was deeply moved by their gratitude and affection ..." he wrote, "and I testify that from the beginning up to today I have not seen any sign of desertion in any of these whom I have brought from their country to remain in this distant place; and in praise of their fidelity I may be permitted to make this memorial of a people who in the course of time will come to be very useful to the monarchy in whose service they have voluntarily left parents and country, which is everything one can abandon." With such paternal sentiments Anza, handsome in plumed sombrero and flowing *capa* (cape), mounted his horse and rode away forever from the Presidio of Monterey. His settlers remained to become a mainstay of the new colony.

Governor Neve at Monterey proceeded to draw up the first civil code for Alta California; its plans for extensive colonization of the

LL SLOPES AND OCEAN

PASTURES BY THE SEA

CLINGING CYPRESS

ABIN IN THE SANTA LUCIAS

CYPRESS TRAIL, POINT LOBOS

BEACH AT CARMEL

SAND DUNE

territory, when finally carried out, determined the system of land tenure whose influence is visible in California even today. Like Pedro Fages he had his recurrent arguments with Serra over the issue of dual authority.

As *Padre-Presidente* (father-president) of the California missions, Serra devoted his great abilities toward the work of converting the Indians to Catholicism and the mission lands to vineyards, fields, and pastures for fat herds of cattle and horses. To Mission San Carlos Borromeo the friendly savages of the Monterey Peninsula were lured with bright trinkets, beads, and other gifts suitable for adornment of their bodies, which the climate permitted them to clothe or leave naked as they pleased. Gratefully the unsuspecting natives reciprocated with gifts of berries and other wild products on which they subsisted. Their mode of living was regarded with horror by the padres: no longer must these "gentiles" be permitted to live homeless, like animals among the pines, on acorns, roots, and grasshoppers—the men engaging in war with clubs and bows and arrows, the women tatooing their faces and wearing ornaments of bone and wood and sea shell. The inducements offered the Indians by Serra and his companions apparently had more immediate effect at Mission San Carlos than elsewhere, for as early as 1773 it contained more converts than any other mission in Alta California. Once within the mission's enclosure the neophytes were threatened with dire punishments if they ever reverted to their former mode of living. In 1776 Serra had reason to think he might "wear a martyr's crown" when the converts at the mission revolted against these stern restrictions, but the presence of a few soldiers from the presidio reconciled them to their fate. Thenceforth they submitted to a regime which entailed work among the herds and in the fields, the making of pottery and basketware, and the tanning of hides. From their labor grew the prosperity of the mission, regarded with increasing envy by the civil authorities of Monterey.

Remote from civilization as it was, the little town was not lacking in diversions; and these increased as the capital of Alta California grew commercially more accessible to the outside world. In 1785 arrived Doña Eulalia, wife of Governor Fages. Her trip from Baja California, made against her better judgment, nevertheless took the form of a triumphal march. Her first act upon arrival at Monterey was to give most of her clothes and her husband's to the Indians, whose nakedness shocked her. This impulsive generosity was stopped, however, when her husband informed her that in Monterey there were not shops from which she could replenish her wardrobe. Disgusted with the crude comforts and outlandish society of her new home, Doña Eulalia soon was stirring up trouble in an endeavor to bring about her repatriation to Mexico City. She accused her husband of infidelity and made extravagant demands which he could not fulfill. Almost everyone, including soldiers and padres, became involved in the turmoil. At one time the mission fathers, scandalized by her tempestuousness, were forced to hold her in confinement and even, it is said, to threaten her with stripes and handcuffs. Eventually the quarrel was composed, and the *Señora gobernadora* (governor's wife) returned to her husband's home. She did not give up her struggle to shake the dust of Monterey from her dainty feet, however, and in 1790 Fages petitioned to be relieved of his post. In the fall of that year Doña Eulalia and her children left Monterey, followed by her husband a year later.

Important events at Monterey were the twice-yearly visits of the supply ship from Mexico. When they came all was well; but when they sometimes failed to appear discomfort, hunger, and privation faced the community. To make matters worse the law commanded all vessels from Manila to touch at Monterey but forbade trading with them. In 1789 the arrival of the supply ship from Mexico was so long delayed that the town suffered actual need and its expectations were consequently heightened. When the lookout, at long last, came galloping in to report an approaching sail, the people rushed to the beach and the soldiers prepared to fire a salute of welcome. The wadding of one of the cannon blew out and fell, a flaming mass, upon the thatched roof of a nearby house. Instantly the presidio was on fire; the buildings were so weathered that they burned like kindling and before the flames could be extinguished about half the presidio structures had been destroyed.

Serra was a man of 57 when he came to Monterey. He was never one to spare himself. The long journeys necessary to visit the missions—from Santa Clara in the north to San Diego in the south—made on foot, had taxed his declining strength. The death in 1782 of his close associate, the explorer and diarist Padre Juan Crespí, saddened him and left him ill and lonely. He died in 1784 and was buried at Mission San Carlos where, before the altar on an August day, passed a long line of soldiers, sailors, colonists, and Indians.

Father Serra had been dead two years when the settlement's first foreign visitor, the French scientist Jean-François de la Pérouse, sailed into the bay on September 14, 1786. He was welcomed handsomely by the Spanish settlers and entertained by Governor Fages and Doña Eulalia. When the Californians tried to refuse payment for the many gifts they had pressed upon the visitors, he insisted upon settlement. Among other things, he left with the Californians a potato root, saying: "Our gardener gave to the missionaries some potatoes from Chile, perfectly sound; I believe this is not one of the least of our gifts and that this root will succeed perfectly around Monterey."

Captain George Vancouver of Britain's Royal Navy made his first of three visits to the Bay of Monterey in 1792. Though a foreigner to be feared, he was welcomed by the Montereños with naive enthusiasm. "On Sunday, December 2, in consequence of a polite invitation," he wrote, " I paid my respects to the Mission of San Carlos— situated about a league to the southeastward of the Presidio of Monterey. The road between lies over some steep hills and hollow valleys, interspersed with many trees ... the general character of the country is lively." He left a voluble record of his visit, observing among other things that stone was being cut for a new church, that 800 Indians were gathered around the mission, and that the "land was covered with an agreeable verdure."

José Antonio Romeu followed the harrassed Pedro Fages to the governorship; but unable to withstand the rigors of the office, he died within the year, and his lieutenant-governor, José Joaquín de Arrillaga, was chosen to complete his term. Viceroy Revilla Gigedo laid down qualifications for the new ruler-to-be of California: "The new governor ... must have the advantages of good talent, military skill, and experience, robust health for the greatest hardships, prudent conduct, disinterestedness, energy and a true zeal for the service ..." He chose Diego Borica, jovial, honest, and hard-working, who became civil and military governor in May, 1794.

Meanwhile, inept Spanish policy tightened trade restrictions so that when Captain Vancouver returned in 1793 he was received without festivals or inland excursions, though civilly enough. The first United States vessel, the *Otter* under Captain Ebenezer Dorr, touched at Monterey in 1796. The Californians feared piracy and the Yankees feared being jailed in the presidio's dark *calabozo* (prison). The issue was resolved amicably, however, when Governor Borica received the visitors hospitably but forbade them to wander beyond the vague limits of the town. The presence of several English stowaways aboard the *Otter* caused Captain Dorr considerable embarrassment, which he overcame by leaving a few of the Britishers at Monterey when he sailed away; the rest he put ashore near the mission, and these included one woman whose debarkation had to be encouraged at the point of a gun.

THE GOLDEN AGE

By the end of the eighteenth century in Alta California, the day of the first explorers and settlers was drawing to a close. The Presidio of Monterey and Mission San Carlos had been firmly established. Up and down the length of the land from San Francisco to San Diego stretched a line of missions, connected by a rough trail which the Spaniards called El Camino Real (The King's Highway). Life was becoming settled, if still isolated, and a new period was dawning, a period of great cattle ranches, of fiestas and balls, of politics enlivened with occasional gunfire. Of this Golden Age of Alta California, Monterey was to be the gay and exciting metropolis.

Besides the *rancheros* (ranchers) who lived in Monterey at the close of the eighteenth century, there was a military force of 80 officers and men equipped with dignity, an abundance of gold braid —and little else. The growing settlement extended inland toward the shady hills with little regard for street planning or property lines. Blue eyes and fair hair began to appear among the Indians and the Spaniards, occasionally at first but with increasing frequency, as the soft lazy years drifted by. At the request of Padre Lasuen some 20 skilled artisans had been brought from Mexico to Mission San Carlos at royal expense. These gave instruction to female neophytes which resulted in development of their native talents for weaving and dyeing of fabrics, fine embroidery, and other handicrafts of which some exquisite examples have been preserved. Male converts were taught to become expert herders of cattle, horses, and sheep; others became teamsters and butchers—Saturday being the regular day for slaughtering beef at the mission—and some developed skill as carpenters, blacksmiths, silversmiths, and tanners of fine leather for the making of those magnificent saddles and bridles which were the pride of the *caballeros* (gentlemen). Articles manufactured at the mission were offered in trade to foreign vessels for which Monterey was becoming a convenient port-of-call. Carrying heavy stacks of hides and leathern bags of tallow on their heads for a distance of half a mile, Indian and Spanish laborers loaded their wares on small boats which then carried the products for export out to ships anchored in the bay.

THE PENINSULA THROUGH FOUR CENTURIES

Defying the low opinion of the mission padres, the aristocratic *rancheros* on a few immense grants around Monterey lived lives of luxurious idleness and considered themselves a class above the rest of the population. Leaving their estates in charge of their wives, the work to Indian slaves, they rode with superb recklessness about the countryside and indulged in a round of gambling, political intrigue, and fandangos which exhibited a vitality they scorned to employ in commercial pursuits. So diligently did these proud families observe the tradition of Old World chivalry that they neglected the possibilities of trade and even accepted crude substitutes for butter and cheese when, with little effort or ingenuity, these dairy products could have been provided both for domestic consumption and for export.

Monterey's early social life followed the pattern of the great feudal estates of Old Spain. While the church and the military played an important part, it was the owners of the great ranchos and their families who set the tone of leisure-time activities—the pleasures, sports, festivities. Every saint's-day, every birthday, wedding, christening, or religious holiday was the occasion for a Mass and a fiesta. The death of a child caused great rejoicing, for the infant, uncontaminated by the sins of man, entered heaven at once; the funerals accorded children were gay with flowers, music and dancing, the firing of muskets, and frivolous songs. Dancing was a passion with the early Spanish citizens; they began as soon as they could walk and continued until the grave. Among the dances most popular were the *jota, bamba, los camotes, el Zarabe, el Burro, el son,* and the *contradanza.* Doña Alta Gracia Barcelona danced the *bamba* at the age of 96 without spilling a drop of water from the glass balanced on her head. Musicians were numerous, for almost every man and woman could play the guitar. A real celebration lasted three days, after which the guests rode home, often as far as a hundred miles.

Horesback-riding was the favorite sport. As Walter Colton remarked, "Nothing but a tornado or a far-striking thunderbolt can overtake the Californian on horseback." The love of riding developed many games of skill. A popular one was burying a live cock in the ground, leaving only his head exposed. At a given signal the rider would start from a distance of about 60 yards, advance at full gallop to lean from his saddle and pluck the fowl from the ground. Another game was racing beside a flying bull, grabbing his tail and, by a complicated twist of the wrist, throwing the animal to the ground. Horse races were held on the Calle Principal almost every day. Even

37

the *carretas* (long narrow cart) carrying women and children, often raced to church on Sunday mornings.

When the last Spanish Governor of the State, Pablo Vicente de Solá, arrived in 1815, a brilliant reception was accorded him. Even he was amazed by the celebration, which included fireworks, bear and bull fights, and an exhibition of equestrian skill by the soldiers. After a feast of native delicacies a gala ball given in the evening by the ladies of Monterey wound up the festivities. Solá paid the ladies a rather doubtful compliment when he praised their clothes because they were of the fashion popular in Spain 50 years before.

The bear and bull fight given on this occasion has been vividly described by Theodore Hittell. "After the banquet," he relates, "the Governor was invited by the comandante to witness a bullfight. . . . As soon as they were seated, two mounted horsemen dressed in the customary brilliant array of the Spanish bull-ring made their appearance; and as they advanced strings of bells attached to the trappings of their horses kept up a jingling accompaniment to all their movements. There was nothing in these to specially attract the governor's attention, nor was there in the fierce and savage bull that was soon afterwards brought forward, tossing his huge front and pawing the ground. Such spectacles he had often seen in Spain and Mexico. But he opened his eyes wide with wonder when he saw a grizzly bear, held by four mounted vaqueros each with a reata fastened to a separate leg, bound into the arena, struggling against his captors and snapping with such fury as to cause terror even in those accustomed to the sight. The governor turned with an inquiring look to the comandante, who replied that the bear was a specimen of the animals, abundant in the neighboring mountains, which often came down to regale themselves upon the cattle in the valley.

"Meanwhile the bull and the bear were fastened together by the feet with a stout chain of sufficient length to allow them considerable freedom of action; and then the reatas were thrown off, and the beasts confronted each other. The bull lowered his head and looked threatening, and the bear arose on his haunches as if awaiting the onset. But for ten minutes neither advanced. The spectators began to grow impatient. The vaqueros rode up and down and prodded the bull; and the bear, with a quickness and agility astonishing in a body so apparently unwieldy, avoiding the horns, threw himself with a grasp upon the bull's neck and both rolled over and over in desperate struggle upon the ground. The noise was terrific and the dust rose in clouds, while the onlookers shouted and yelled as they saw the fight was deadly and witnessed the flow of blood. Presently the bull, fatigued with exertion and hot with thirst, protruded his tongue, and the bear made an attempt by a change of position to seize it. But the attempt cost him his life. The bull was wary and on his guard and with a sudden plunge transfixed his enemy and with a tremendous effort threw him into the air. As the bear fell with a ghastly wound, the bull infuriated with his own injuries pursued his advantage; and with a second and deadly plunge closed the combat."

The raw material for this exciting sport was secured by the young blades of the town, who used to rope the bears on the beach; the grizzlies were drawn from the hills by the carcasses of whales, left to rot on the sand by the Portuguese whalers. But hunting at this time was more a necessity than a sport. Prowling mountain lions, coyotes, bears, were a constant menace to the livestock on the ranchos. Hunting parties were organized on a large scale.

Despite the rich pastoral atmosphere that enfolded the land in lazy splendor, trouble was ahead for the lotus-eaters of Monterey. Mexico, desiring to populate Alta California, sent north as colonists her undesirables, mostly petty offenders. This the proud and sensitive Californians resented as an affront to their patriotic devotion to the land which they had come to regard as destined for independence. Revolution was afoot in South America and the names of Bolivar, San Martin, and Mirand were quickening the pulses of the dissatisfied and the ambitious. In the Argentine, zeal for the new republican creed was spreading.

The United States, flushed with newly acquired independence, supported the colonists in their struggle against Spain. Many American ships, fitted out at Baltimore, were privateers on the fringe of international law. In 1818 the apprehensive Californians at Monterey were warned of the approach, from the Sandwich (Hawaiian) Islands of two ships ostensibly bringing independence from the south. On November 20 the vessels, the *Argentina* under Captain Hippolyte de Bouchard, who had served as sergeant major in the Buenos Aires navy, and the *Santa Rosa,* alias the *Cheka,* alias the *Baca,* alias the *Liberty,* under an Englishman, Peter Corney, were sighted off Point Pinos by an excited sentry; they flew the flag of Argentina. Peevish, despotic Pablo Vicente de Solá, last of the Spanish governors, had made some preparations, sending livestock and articles of value to the missions inland.

That night the *Santa Rosa* anchored close to the shore and the following morning fighting began. The *Santa Rosa* asked for supplies and was refused; there was a blast from the vessel's cannon and the Montereños replied when Corporal José Vallejo opened up with his improvised shore battery. Corney, it is said, lowered the *Santa Rosa's* flag, but Vallejo, ordered to cease firing, refused to obey. Then Joseph Chapman, an American, came ashore with two sailors and the three were promptly arrested.

A landing party from the *Argentina* advanced and Bouchard, under a flag of truce, demanded the surrender of Alta California. Solá says he told the captain there would be no surrender "while there was a man alive in the province." So Bouchard landed his entire force—the Spaniards said 400, but that was more than the total aboard both ships—and Solá, outnumbered, retreated to the Rancho del Rey near the present site of Salinas. The invaders remained in Monterey more than a week sacking the town and burning most of the buildings before they left on December 1. So ended the first invasion of the California coast. The damage was repaired and the Montereños settled down to what they hoped would be security and peace.

The movement toward a break with the Old World was, however, spreading throughout New Spain. In 1822 Governor Solá wrote to Governor Luís Antonio Argüello of Lower California saying he had received from Mexico "such documents as are printed in a country of dreamers, since independence is a dream." Two months later word reached him that the "dream" had come true; Mexico was independent of Spain and one Augustín de Iturbide called himself emperor. A hastily summoned convention at the Monterey presidio gave allegiance to the new government with surprising alacrity, and Solá was elected to the delicate mission of acting as envoy to Mexico.

Before Solá could depart, Augustín Fernandez de San Vicente came to Monterey as representative of the Emperor; he promptly called a *provincial diputación* (provincial legislature) and explained to the delegates that they could elect themselves to important posts. Only disturbing element was the stand taken by Padre Vicente Francisco de Sarría, who insisted he could not take the oath of allegiance "without violating prior obligations of justice and fidelity." He suspected, and not without reason, that the heyday of the missions was drawing to a close. An election was held in November and Luís Argüello, *comandante* of the San Francisco presidio, was chosen first Mexican governor of California. Solá, rejoicing in independence as vociferously as he had once condemned it, left for Mexico the same month.

PLOT AND COUNTERPLOT

The people readily swore allegiance anew, when the republic which succeeded Iturbide's *opéra-bouffe* empire in 1825 sent José María Echeandía to the north as governor of the two Californias. It made little difference what kind of government ruled in Mexico as long as they could carry on a trade which was profitable and necessary for their subsistence. Governor Argüello's few years had been comparatively quiet, but when his successor appeared the situation was strained. The soldiers had long been without pay and they had to be restrained from raiding the prosperous missions. Foreigners were touching the coast more frequently; many of the Californians had ambitions which were soon to bring on an era of political disorder.

Echeandía promoted this state of affairs when he established his capital at San Diego and refused to come to Monterey because he feared the climate. Matters came to a head in 1828 when the soldiers at Monterey revolted. They were persuaded to return to their places but in November of the following year they rebelled again, under the leadership of an ex-soldier, ex-convict named Joaquin Solís. The foreigners at Monterey, eager for peace and good business, supported the rebels, and the garrison at San Francisco joined the uprising. Echeandía and the rebels met at Santa Barbara in a battle—mostly of words—and the governor won. He advanced on Monterey, captured Solís and other ringleaders, and shipped them off to Mexico. Then, discovering that the Monterey climate would support his health, he decided to remain. When Manuel Victoria was appointed governor Echeandía refused at first to budge, and turned the office over to his successor in January, 1831, only after the latter had come to Monterey prepared to eject his rival from the capital.

Meanwhile more foreigners were arriving to settle in California. It was feared the British might seek to extend their holdings south of Oregon. The Americans were coming in ever greater numbers, some to trade, others to settle. Smuggling became profitable as import duties sometimes were as high as 100 per cent of the invoice cost of the cargo. Once a cargo from Honolulu valued at $20,000 was unloaded at Monterey during the night; in the morning duty was paid on the residue aboard ship at a valuation of $1,000.

Of the town itself, Richard Henry Dana, who visited it in 1836, later wrote: "Monterey, as far as my observation goes, is decidedly the pleasantest and most civilized looking place in California. . . .

The town lay directly before us, making a very pretty appearance, its houses being plastered. The red tile, too, on the roofs contrasted well with the white plastered sides. . . . In the center of it is an open square surrounded by four lines of one-story plastered buildings, with half a dozen cannons in the center; some mounted and others not. This is the Presidio, or fort . . . every presidio has a town built around it; for the forts were built by the Mexican Government and then the people built near them for protection. The Presidio here was entirely open and unfortified. There were several officers with long titles, and about 80 soldiers, but they were poorly paid, fed, clothed, and disciplined. . . . The houses here . . . are . . . built of clay made into large bricks. . . . These are cemented together by mortar of the same material, and the whole are a common dirt color; the doors which are seldom shut, open directly into the common room; there being no entries. Some of the more wealthy . . . have glass to their windows and board floors. . . . The better houses have red tiles upon the roofs . . ."

"But the Montereños," said Dana, "were idle, thriftless people, and can make nothing for themselves. The country abounds in grapes, yet they buy bad wines made in Boston and brought round by us, at an immense price . . ."

Governor Victoria, chastened by wounds to body and pride received in a skirmish with Echeandía's lancers near Los Angeles, climbed into bed at Mission San Gabriel and let it be known he wished to return to Mexico. The provincial legislature, in January, 1832, therefore elected Pío Pico civil governor; he resigned three weeks later when Echeandía refused to support him. Echeandía, it seemed, was in control but the Americans and British were becoming impatient with California revolutions and readily supported Augustín Zamorano, one-time secretary of Echeandía and Victoria at Monterey, who was soon recognized as governor. A foreign legion was organized under the English trader William E. B. Hartnell, for the purpose of defending Monterey. Proclamations were issued by both sides and the battle was declared a draw.

Then José Figueroa arrived from Mexico as new governor in January, 1833. Immediately he gave amnesty to all who had taken part in the revolt, and sent Mariano Guadalupe Vallejo, brother of the hero of the Bouchard invasion, to explore the Bay of San Francisco. The liberal Figueroa was an active force in colonization during his brief administration; he appointed William Antonio Richardson captain of the Port of San Francisco and ordered the establishment there of the pueblo of Yerba Buena, from which San Francisco has grown.

It was likewise during Figueroa's regime that the earliest known printing in California appeared; a proclamation of the governor to the soldiers at the presidio, printed at Monterey January 16, 1833.

Figueroa's predecessor in the governorship, Zamorano, himself turned to printing the following year, using the old Spanish press on which California's first newspaper would be printed 12 years later. Zamorano's first surviving specimen of typography is dated 1834; it describes his plant and lists his prices. Soon followed a 16-page pamphlet—the first book to be printed in California—containing the provisional regulations for the government of the province: *Reglamento Provincional para el Gubierno . . . de la Alta California.* Robert Ernest Cowan in his monumental *Bibliography of the History of California and the Pacific West,* 1510-1906, first issued in San Francisco (1914), located 12 books printed in California during the Mexican era, of which nine were published in Monterey and three in Sonoma. Four of these are of a political-military character, one devotional, and six school texts.

The lifting of trade restrictions by Figueroa—though import duties remained exorbitant—brought an influx of traders to Monterey from Boston and Honolulu, the latter being headquarters for the American whaling fleet in the Pacific. Though the British firm of McCullough, Hartnell, and Company, operating under contract with Mexican authorities, had practically a monopoly of the traffic in hides, there was still room for private individuals supplying cargoes for ships plying between the California coast and the ports of Peru and New England. Since all trade was carried on by barter, hides being the accepted equivalent of currency, profit depended on the ability of shipmasters and supercargoes to smuggle products into California ports with which to pay for hides and tallow. One of the most daring and successful of these Yankee evaders of customs officials was William S. Hinckley, who in 1836 formed a business partnership in Monterey with Nathan Spear and Jacob Leese. Transferring their activities to Yerba Buena shortly thereafter, these three American traders laid the commercial foundation of San Francisco and aided in the transfer of California to the United States by their relations with Consul Thomas O. Larkin and Mexican officials favorable to annexation.

The sudden arrival in Carmel Bay in 1833 of the *Beaver,* first steamship in Pacific waters, with her sails and great paddle-wheels, so startled the mission Indians that they fled into the hills; at Monterey, however, she was welcomed by the town's population from the shore as she rounded Point Pinos. Until 1891, when her teakwood hull was wrecked in stormy waters in Vancouver harbor, the *Beaver* came frequently to take on cargoes of hides and agricultural products at Monterey.

Rapid changes of governors followed the death of Figueroa in 1835. There was a lively scandal in Monterey during the three-month rule of Governor Mariano Chico in 1836. He had the audacity to appear at a public function with his mistress—who he claimed was his niece—and with a woman who even then was under arrest charged with adultery. Following this escapade things became so hot in Monterey that Chico hid aboard a ship and sailed away to Mexico at the end of July.

Juan Bautista Alvarado, a young man of 27, born in Monterey, came forward as leader of a new revolution. Supporting him were a fiery band of Mexicans, some Indians, and some Americans led by Isaac Graham, owner of a distillery in the Pajaro Valley. Alvarado marched his forces from one place to another, in the open, and returned them under cover to make his force appear much larger than it actually was. When finally he gave the order to fire on Monterey it was discovered there was only one ball to fit the cannon. This was dispatched and it hit the house of the governor. The battle ended and the opposing forces, under Nicholás Gutiérrez, surrendered.

Alvarado had not put down counter-revolution in the south and for some time he was occupied with military movements there. For a while he ruled as civil governor, Mariano G. Vallejo serving as military governor. In April, 1840, he turned on his erstwhile companion-at-arms, Isaac Graham, who with a number of others was deported to Mexico. The group was released only after Thomas Larkin had appealed in person to the American and British consuls at Mazatlan. The incident was recalled later when American immigrants in northern California feared expulsion from the territory and led them to suspect all Mexican officials of treachery.

Friction grew between Vallejo and Alvarado; the Indians released from the missions were growing bolder; foreigners were arriving in greater numbers; and the general opinion prevailed that California was destined for annexation either by Britain or the United States. Suddenly, one day in October, 1842, several American vessels appeared off Point Pinos, cleared for action. An armed force soon landed and marched to the Customs House, where the authorities

44

were informed that war existed between the United States and Mexico. Commodore Thomas Ap Catesby Jones, in command of the squadron, demanded surrender of the presidio. There were only a few ragged, unpaid soldiers to offer resistance, so the *comandante* with appropriate oratory told the invaders that everything in sight belonged to them. The flag of the United States promptly was raised, for the first time, in Monterey.

Thomas Larkin produced letters he had received from the East in which there was no mention of Mexican-American hostilities. Jones grew doubtful, conferred with Americans in the town, and after 24 hours told the *comandante* that it was all a mistake. The American flag was hauled down and the Mexican colors raised again over the town. Governor-to-be Manuel Micheltorena, safe at San Fernando, drew up and issued a brave document in which he declared his desire of battling the invader; but he returned to Los Angeles instead.

The rule of Vallejo and Alvarado ended on December 31, 1842, the latter leaving 25 cents in the treasury. In July, 1843, Governor Micheltorena took his army—comprised mainly of liberated convicts—and advanced on Monterey. The country was torn by civil strife despite the change of administration, and the Americans were coming over the mountain passes. Thomas Larkin received a notice from the American Secretary of State which he read with interest: "The future destiny of that country," it stated, "is a subject of anxious solicitude for the government and the people of the United States. . . . Whilst I repeat that this government does not under existing circumstances intend to interfere between Mexico and California, they would vigorously interfere to prevent the latter from becoming a British or French colony . . ."

At the same time, Louis Gasquet, acting consul for France at Monterey, was writing impassioned letters to his home office for a man-of-war to patrol the coast and for permission to swing the sympathies of the Californians toward an alliance with his country.

On January 27, 1846, Captain John Charles Frémont, making topographical surveys in California, arrived in Monterey to consult with Larkin, who had recently been made United States consul and confidential agent of the Secretary of State. Here he met José Castro and Juan Bautista Alvarado, to whom he protested that his men were not armed, that he had left them on the frontier, and that he wanted only to purchase supplies in order to continue on to Oregon. The Californians gave him supplies and he promised to confine his activities to the interior.

But within a few days Frémont was back in the Salinas Valley with his men. Castro ordered him away but he retreated only as far as the top of Gavilan Peak, where he erected barricades and remained for three days. Then he moved north, leaving Castro at San Juan and Monterey in comparative peace. But events moved rapidly. For on June 14 was announced the formation of the independent Republic of California—the "Bear Flag Republic."

On July 1 or 2 Commodore John D. Sloat arrived in the Bay of Monterey on the *Savannah*, flagship of the Pacific Fleet. Here he met the *Cyane* under Captain Mervine and the *Levant* under Captain Montgomery. For several days they remained in port, exchanging civilities with officials on shore and talking with Consul Larkin.

On the morning of July 7, Sloat finally made up his mind to act and sent Captain Mervine ashore to demand surrender of the town. No important officials were around; there were no troops and no ammunition. At 11 o'clock in the morning, the marines, 250 strong, marched through the town; they raised the flag of the United States over the Customs House and posted proclamations in Spanish and English declaring California to be American territory.

LOS GRINGOS

The Californians at Monterey received the American occupation with apathy, for they were disgusted with the old regime and its devastating politics. Of the population Walter Colton, an American who was appointed *alcalde,* in somewhat biased terms declared: "Here is the reckless Californian, the half-wild Indian, the roving trapper of the West, the lawless Mexican, the licentious Spaniard, the scolding Englishman, the absconding Frenchman, the luckless Irishman, the plodding German, the adventurous Russian, and the discontented Mormon."

Yale graduate, former editor of the *North American Review,* and now a naval chaplain, Colton was alien both by temperament and training to the people over whom he was to exercise authority, but he tried to be just at all times, though the native gaiety hurt his puritanical soul. The first few months of the occupation were difficult. A state of guerrilla warfare kept the troops hurrying from one spot to another. Renegade Indians lived by thievery. Food was scarce and expensive. Commerce was at a standstill. Colton levied heavy fines on gambling and liquor. In September he proclaimed that all smuggled liquor would be confiscated, one-half to the informant, one-half to the municipal fund. Penalties were imposed for selling liquor to any United States soldier, sailor, or marine. The money thus accumulated—and it was a sizeable amount, for the Californians were born gamblers—went toward the building of Colton Hall. Little as the Puritan zeal and thoroughness of Colton were to the liking of the Montereños, they could not but rejoice in having him as *alcalde* when, in the autumn of 1846, Frémont and about 40 of his trappers and freebooters arrived in town. "They were allowed no liquor," observed another visitor, Lieutenant Walpole of H. M. S. *Collingwood*. The town felt no scruples over this breach in Monterey hospitality.

In September, 1846, Colton impaneled the first jury in California. Isaac Graham, the Tennessee trouble-maker, accused Carlos Rousillon of stealing lumber, and Rousillon in turn accused Graham of slander. The trial was complicated by the fact that the jury was composed one-third of Mexicans, one-third of Californians, and one-third of Americans. The plaintiff spoke in English, the defendant in French, the witnesses in every language known to California. W. E. P. Hartnell acted as interpreter and apparently did his job well, for the jury deliberated only an hour before returning a verdict that pleased both sides. Rousillon recovered his character, and Graham his property.

This same *Alcalde* Colton introduced penal labor into California. "Nothing puzzles me so much," he wrote, "as absence of a penitentiary system. There are no workhouses here; no buildings adapted to the purpose; no tools, and no trades. The custom has been to fine Spaniards, and whip Indians. The discrimination is unjust, and the punishments ill suited to the ends proposed. I have substituted labor; and have now eight Indians, three Californians, and one Englishman at work making adobes. They have all been sentenced for stealing horses or bullocks. I have given them their task; each is to make fifty adobes a day, and for all over this they are paid. They make seventy-five, and for the additional twenty-five each gets as many cents. This is paid to them every Saturday night, and they are allowed to get with it anything but rum. They are comfortably lodged and fed by the government. I have appointed one of their number captain. They work in the field; require no other guard; not one of them has attempted to run away."

"The first newspaper published in California made its appearance," Colton wrote on August 15, 1846. "It is to be issued every

47

Saturday, by Semple and Colton. . . . The press was old and rusty—no rules, no lead—the type rusty and all in pi. No paper except tobacco wrapper . . ." This paper, the *Californian,* was printed on the press that Governor Figueroa had brought from Mexico in 1832 —the only one in California. Since the Spanish alphabet has no letter "w" two "v's" were used instead. Colton's partner, Robert Semple, was a Kentuckian who stood 6 feet 8 inches in his stocking feet.

Along with its first newspaper, Monterey acquired those other distinctive features of Yankee culture, the school and the library.

The first attempt at education following the American conquest came in 1847 when Mrs. L. C. Isbell was employed to teach 56 pupils in the upper story of the Customs House. She resigned after three months for lack of supplies and understanding; the pupils spoke only Spanish, Mrs. Isbell only English. The first convent was established in 1851 by three Dominican nuns: Saint Catherine's Academy, attended by about 150 pupils, many from other parts of the State.

The first public library in the State was founded in 1849, when several citizens formed an association, raised $1,500, and entrusted Walter Colton to purchase a collection of books. He selected a library of approximately 1,000 English, American, and Spanish books which he sent by way of Cape Horn.

The year 1847 was an eventful one. The governorship was in doubt until orders from Washington, D. C., named General Stephen W. Kearney civil and military head of the territory with Colonel Richard B. Mason second in command. In 1847 the first Pacific Mail steamship to reach the territory, the *California,* docked at Monterey to the delight of the citizens who gathered in a huge crowd at the wharf. Company F of the Third Artillery came to the town, bringing William Tecumseh Sherman, H. W. Halleck, and the Ord brothers. Monterey was growing rapidly. Since many of the arrivals distrusted the native adobe, lumber was shipped around the Horn. Bricks began to be kilned here and the chalk-rock was used increasingly. Ship carpenters went to work and New England-isms crept into the architecture. Most striking of the new buildings was the stone town hall going up under the *alcalde's* direction with funds derived in part from fines levied on those who had consumed too much *aguardiente.* Then suddenly the discovery of gold on the American River depopulated the town. "And here am I," complained *Alcalde* Colton, whose authority was ignored by the Argonauts

CITY AND PRESIDIO

MONTEREY IN 1849

THE PRESIDIO and PUEBLO of MONTEREY, UPPER CALIFORNIA.

Smith, Elder & Co. Cornhill

THE EARLY PUEBLO

MONTEREY TODAY

PURSE SEINE PATTERNS

FISHERMAN'S WHAR[

bringing social and economic upheaval, "who have been a man of some note in my day, loafing on the hospitality of the good citizens and grateful for a meal, though in an Indian wigwam."

In spite of the delays resulting from the rush to the mines, Colton Hall was ready for use in September, 1849, when the military governor, Bennet Riley, called a convention to assemble to adopt a constitution. Of the 48 delegates elected, many spoke only Spanish. For these W. E. P. Hartnell was official interpreter. The convention lasted six weeks; it drew up a constitution designed after those of New York and Iowa and decided that California should be a free State. Deliberations of the assembly were accompanied by almost continuous festivity ending with a grand ball at the home of Don Jacinto Rodríguez. Here the delegates refused categorically to return to Colton Hall to sign the constitution, so the document was brought to the ball and there the final signatures were placed upon it.

The literary globe-trotter Bayard Taylor, then a poet of 25, described the convention festivities in great detail. With the exception of Los Angeles, Taylor found that "Monterey contains the most pleasant society to be found in California. There is a circle of families, American and native, residing there, whose genial and refined social character makes one forget his previous ideas of California life." Taylor passed many agreeable hours in the houses of the native families. The favorite resort of Americans during the convention was that of Doña Augusta Ximeno, an accomplished lady "thoroughly versed in Spanish literature as well as the works of Scott and Cooper through translations. . . . I have been frequently surprised at the justness and elegance of her remarks on various authors. She possessed all those bold and daring qualities which are so fascinating in a woman when softened and made graceful by true feminine delicacy. She was a splendid horsewoman and had even considerable skill in throwing the lariat."

After the convention, a ball was given to the citizens of Monterey. Colton Hall was cleared, decorated with young pines from the forest and the American colors. Three chandeliers poured light on the festivities. Soon after eight o'clock, the hall was crowded with nearly all the city's residents. About 60 ladies were present and an equal number of gentlemen, in addition to the members of the convention. "The dark-eyed daughters of Monterey, Los Angeles and Santa Barbara mingled in pleasing contrast with the fairer bloom of the trans-Nevadian belles," Taylor noted. The variety of feature and complexion was equalled by the variety of dress. In the whirl of the waltz "a plain, dark, nun-like robe would be followed by one of pink satin and gauze; next, perhaps a bodice of scarlet velvet with gold buttons, and then a richly figured brocade, such as one sees on the stately dames of Titian." The clothes of the men were much less picturesque, but showed considerable variety. Scarcely a single dress that was seen belonged entirely to its wearer. "If the clothes had power to leap severally back to their respective owners, some persons would have been in a state of utter destitution. For my part I was indebted for pantaloons and vest to obliging friends."

The appearance of the company, nevertheless, was genteel and respectable, according to Taylor. "In one group might be seen Captain Sutter's soldierly mustache and clear blue eyes; in another the erect figure and quiet, dignified bearing of General Vallejo. . . . General Riley was there in full uniform, with the yellow sash he won at the Contreras; Majors Canby, Hill and Smith, Captains Burton and Kane, and other officers stationed in Monterey, accompanying him. . . . Conspicuous among the native members were Don Miguel de Pedrorena and Jacinto Rodríguez, both polished gentlemen and deservedly popular. Dominguez, the Indian member, took no part in the dance. . . . The most interesting figure to me was that of Padre Ramirez, who, in his clerical cassock, looked on until a late hour."

The music for this important celebration was furnished by two guitars and two violins. The musicians played three pieces alternately for the waltz, the contradance, and the quadrille. Each tune ended with a squeak, "something like the whistle of the octave flute in *Robert le Diable.*"

But Monterey's days as capital were numbered. The new constitution was ratified by popular vote, Peter H. Burnett was elected governor, and the seat of government was moved to San Jose.

DECLINE AND FALL

Monterey settled back to 25 years of comparative apathy. The discovery of gold marked a shifting of center and the beginning of a leisurely period of romantic isolation and decline of Monterey. Off the main routes of traffic, which were carrying hundreds of thousands of people and millions of dollars into California, the city became once more a sleepy village. Incorporated as a city in 1850, it repealed its act of incorporation and then re-enacted it three times in all—in 1851, 1853, and 1889—before it could make up its mind to retain the title and dignity of a city for good. No commercial development of note took place. Except for the whaling industry which flourished through the sixties—the Portuguese, especially, sought out the whales which were spouting in the Bay—Monterey's commercial activities provided a living for less than a thousand people. Almost the sole support of the town came from the surrounding ranchos, still large, over which grazed sheep and cattle. There was some growing of hay and grain and there were small orchards and vineyards; but no one dreamed of intensive cultivation. The old houses fell into disrepair. Monterey remained a Mexican village, speaking the language and carrying on in the tradition of another day. The mutually opprobrious term of "gringo" and "greaser" continued to be used, but in Monterey, so many more people spoke Spanish than English and so many families bearing English surnames were half Spanish, that Yankee intolerance of Latin speech and ways perforce gave way.

William Tecumseh Sherman had described the inhabitants in 1849 as the up-and-coming Yankees saw them. Said he, "There are some families that style themselves Dons, do nothing but walk the streets with peaked broad-brimmed hats and cloaks or serapes, which are brightly colored, checkered panchos, a colored shirt, silk or fancy pants slashed down the outside with fringe or buttons, shoes on their feet and a cigar in their mouth." Like many Americans, he did not see beneath the surface of Monterey into that compact, self-contained little aristocracy which, as the years rolled by, became ever more sure of itself.

When William H. Brewer, in charge of the United States Government Survey, visited the town in 1861, he found its inhabitants "more Mexican than I expected. . . . Spanish is still the prevailing language . . . more than half of the 'places of business' are liquor shops, billiard saloons, etc.—all the stores sell cigars, *cigarritos* and liquor. Stores are open on Sunday as well as other days, and that is the day for the saloons and bar-rooms to reap a rich harvest . . ." But it was largely a paper harvest. Within the town scarcely anyone had much ready money.

The decades of doldrums to follow meant the preservation of Old Monterey. Since expansion was no problem, the historic buildings were not torn down; the fires which swept other cities did no harm to walls of adobe. Of the 200 buildings standing in 1849, one-fourth remained nine decades later, epitomizing the evolution of the cultures of Spain, Mexico, and pioneer America.

When, in 1850, Walter Colton had resigned in favor of a town council, that body became the "Common Council of the City of Monterey" and its members, "aldermen." This legislative body passed several laws of minor importance: all dogs must be licensed; horseback racing was forbidden on the main street; slaughtering of cattle within one mile of Colton Hall was prohibited on penalty of a $5 fine; wells and pits must be protected by a fence or they would be filled at the owner's expense; all persons must, on a dark night, expose a lantern in some conspicuous place on their house or be liable to a fine of 50 cents for the first offense, $1 for the second. It thereafter adjourned and from July 26, 1853, to January 24, 1859, held no further meetings.

When the council met again, it was to consider the public debt. The city had land, but no money. It owed money—the sum of $991.50—to David Jacks, a Scots pioneer of 1849, and to his partner D. R. Ashley, for legal services in prosecuting its title to the land before the Board of United States Land Commissioners. It was forbidden by State law to sell its land, except at public auction. The aldermen deliberated. They came to a conclusion expressed in an instrument of conveyance dated February 9, 1859, which "granted, bargained and sold . . . all the lands . . . belonging to the City of Monterey" to the city's creditors for the sum of $1,002.50." The council thereupon discreetly adjourned and did not reassemble until 1865. The courts ruled the sale legal. So resentful against Jacks were the people that 20 years later, according to Robert Louis Stevenson, "the stage was stopped and examined three evenings in succession by horsemen thirsting for his blood. A certain house in the Salinas road, they say, he always passes in his buggy at full speed, for the squatter sent him warning long ago." Voluble Dennis Kearney, San Francisco teamster and demagogue, on a visit to Monterey advised that they "hang David Jacks."

In 1869 Jacks appeared on the scene again. The State Legislature had ceded the waterfront to a depth of 20 feet at low tide to the town. The city council leased the property for $1 a year to a company organized by Jacks, with the proviso that a "good, and substantial wharf" be built within six months. There was much talk of corruption and much grumbling at the size of wharfage and docking fees collected, but the wharf was a boon to Monterey.

Though the town's former maritime supremacy had been surrendered since the Gold Rush to San Francisco, cut off as Monterey was from the main current of California life, her port, at which coastwise steamers called four times a week, still kept alive a spark of commercial enterprise. They took on cargoes of agricultural products from Peninsula farms and from ranchos farther inland. Until about 1885 the port was headquarters for whalers operating in Monterey Bay, pursuit of the California grays and humpbacks having been organized in 1854 by Captain J. P. Davenport and a company of a dozen with a station on Point Pinos. Meanwhile a colony of Chinese fishermen in what is now New Monterey numbering about 80 persons—a "sober, honest set of men"—operated a fleet of about 30 boats. They fished, cured the catch, and collected abalone shells (worth $20 per ton) for shipment to San Francisco and thence to the mines and foreign ports. It was estimated (in 1875) that the export of dried fish from Monterey amounted to 100 tons annually.

When the Southern Pacific Railroad extended its lines through the Salinas Valley new settlers began to arrive. Some of the large ranchos were divided and planted to wheat and other crops. The building of a narrow-gauge railroad to Salinas in 1874 allowed the ranchers to ship their wheat to Monterey, where it was trans-shipped by steamer. By 1888 the county was the banner grain-producing area of California, the 2,300,000 bushels of wheat and barley harvested that year being the result of extensive planting of these grains which the padres had first introduced at Mission San Carlos a century before.

The machine age which might have been expected to follow the railroad's appearance in 1874 was slow to dawn. The *Monterey Argus* reported that the planing mill which a Mr. H. Prinz opened in this year had a capacity of 10,000 feet of good boards every 24 hours' working time. But a tax valuation sheet of 1879-80 is more reliable than the *Monterey Argus* as evidence of the place of manufacture in the economic life of the time. The assessment was at one-fifth of the real value.

Heavy machinery	$25,728
Sewing machines	35,580
Musical instruments	29,700
Total	$91,008

Monterey had shared so little in its county's increasing prosperity that fast-growing Salinas demanded—and won—the seat of county government in 1872. Colton Hall, which had served as the county courthouse, declining a step further in rank, was now used as a grammar school. Only the annex with its windows—barred none too well apparently, for the record says of more than one prisoner that he "broake out of jale"—still served its original purpose.

Beginning in the middle seventies, a few outsiders began to discover the beauty of Monterey Bay and the decaying charm of the old town. A Methodist bishop heard of the "salubrious pine-clad hills" and established (in 1875) "The Christian Seaside Resort" which became Pacific Grove; Charles Warren Stoddard, between voyages to Europe, Egypt, and the South Seas, found Monterey a peaceful place in which to work; Robert Louis Stevenson made the old Pacific capital memorable in his recollections of a three months' visit in the fall of 1879. To Stevenson it was a strange thing to find "in that world of absolutely mannerless Americans, a people full of deportment, solemnly courteous, and doing all things with grace and decorum . . . a strange thing to lie awake in 19th century America, and hear the guitar accompany, and one of these old heart-breaking Spanish love songs mount into the night air, perhaps in a deep baritone, perhaps in that high-pitched, pathetic, womanish alto which is so common among Mexican men, and which strikes on the unaccustomed ear as something not entirely human but altogether sad."

"I suppose the men *do* work sometimes," commented the visiting Englishwoman, Lady Duffus Hardy, a year or two later, "but I have seen them at all hours, shouldering the door-posts, smoking in sombre, majestic silence, while the wives sit on stools beside them, generally with bright-colored handkerchiefs pinned across their breasts . . ." Lady Hardy was impressed by the "conservatism" of the Montereños—"a dark, swarthy, lazy-looking race . . . [who] scarcely seem to have energy enough to keep themselves awake . . ." She found Monterey "only interesting from its association with the past. It is dirty, it is dusty, it is utterly devoid of all modern improvements. Streets! there are none to speak of, except, perhaps, a row of slovenly shops which have been run up by some demented genius the last few years. The old adobe houses . . . straggle about in the most bewildering fashion. . . . In the heart of the town there is a long, low range of deserted buildings formerly occupied by the military; the windows are all broken, the worm-eaten doors hang, like helpless cripples, on their hinges, and only the ghostly echo of the wind goes wandering through the empty chambers. In all the quarters of the town you may come upon houses with windows patched or broken and padlocked doors, the owners having died or wandered away, and no one (but the rats) cares to take possession of bare walls."

54

RENAISSANCE ON THE PENINSULA

And yet things were changing for the Monterey Peninsula in the early eighties, as even Lady Hardy could see: "People are awakening to a sense of the importance of Monterey, which might, and most probably will, become one of the most delightful seaside resorts in the State. . . . It has excellent facilities for bathing, a magnificent sea view, and the walks and drives about the surrounding country are beautiful in the extreme; there are wooded bosky dells, luxuriant green valleys, and undulating hills on every side . . . in fact, the only want at Monterey is accommodation for visitors . . ."

Even that want, however, was soon to be supplied, for the Hotel Del Monte—a "monster hotel of quaint Swiss architecture"—was already approaching completion in "a wood of scented pine and grand old forest trees . . . [with] a wide, magnificent sea view . . . before it . . ." The rediscovery of the Monterey Peninsula as a vacationers' playground, after so many years of neglect, was at hand.

Among the first to make the discovery were artists and writers on the lookout for a setting which might lend itself to romantic exploitation. A brace of hungry bohemians decorated the Monterey restaurant of Jules Simoneau with frescoes "done in beer and shoeblacking." Painting in Monterey during the seventies and eighties were Jules Tavernier, Leon Trouset, Jo Strong, and others. Monterey became a mecca of artistic and literary bohemians, who exploited in point and print the pictorial and romantic qualities of the town and its surrounding landscape. The few who were devoted to art for its own sake found the atmosphere more conducive to cheapness than to the creation of masterpieces; but the majority prospered and their portraits of Monterey pines and their odes to moonlight on Carmel Bay were gratuitous advertisements to the tourist trade which would later aid the Peninsula's economic renascence.

Meanwhile the Monterey merchants and their wives, after the immemorial custom of good bourgeois, observed with bated breath the long lists of distinguished guests arriving at the Del Monte. They had grown accustomed to Huntingtons, Crockers, Hobarts, Tevises, and other fashionable Californians. But soon the *Cypress* noted the coming of Thomas B. Reed, Chauncey M. Depew, Andrew Carnegie, John W. Mackay, Joseph Pulitzer, Lord Lorne, the Princess Louise, and President Benjamin Harrison, who, seeking reelection, was ready to tell them what they already devoutly believed . . . that their future depended on a good, high, protective tariff.

55

In a footnote to his earlier recollections, Stevenson commented: "But revolution in this world succeeds to revolution. All that I say in this paper is in a paulo-past sense. The Monterey of last year exists no longer. A huge hotel has sprung up in the desert by the railroad. Three sets of diners sit down successively to table. Invaluable toilettes figure along the beach and between the live oaks; and Monterey is advertised in the newspapers, and posted in waiting-rooms at railway stations, as a resort for wealth and fashion. Alas for the little town! It is not strong enough to resist the influence of the flaunting caravanserai, and the poor, quaint, penniless native gentlemen of Monterey must perish, like a lower race, before the millionaire vulgarians of the Big Bonanza."

As the 1880's brought with them progress, the council woke up to impose taxes for street maintenance in the business section, such assessments not to exceed $1 per month. It encouraged the Pacific Improvement Company to lay its water-lines from the dam on the Carmel River to Del Monte, the lines to run through Monterey. E. Michaelis was granted a franchise for a tramway, and A. C. Keating was appointed first health officer of Monterey. Electric lines and telephones followed in rapid succession.

And yet Monterey changed but slowly. Despite the increasing number of summer visitors, despite the introduction of the lumbering horsecars running at hourly intervals between Monterey and "the Grove," the building of new houses and business blocks in the tasteless style of the period, the old familes went their own way, showing only indifference or occasionally well-bred disdain at the more blatant manifestations of new wealth.

Every morning a line of women always dressed in black and with black shawls or *mantillas* over their heads made their way to the old presidio church. The men had discarded the checkered ponchos, colored shirts, and silk or fancy pants that Sherman had found objectionable, but they still had eyes as keen as ever for horseflesh, and rode with an easy grace. On great holidays whole steers were still barbecued out on the ranchos, and the whole countryside invited. In winter up to the beginning of Lent the carnival season was observed with masked balls and *cascarón* parties, at which the dancers pelted each other with eggshells, colored and filled with perfume or perfumed confetti. The young generation had learned English but spoke it with a slight accent, for the parochial schools were conducted in Spanish, and little but Spanish was spoken in the home.

In a vigorous article in the *Monterey Argus* of July, 1885, Mrs.

Nellie Van de Grift Sanchez called attention to the fact that the town was in a state of delapidation and decay, its crumbling walls, leaking roofs, and muddy streets offering a poor welcome to visiting notables. Montereños were roused to a spirit of civic pride. Whitewash brushes came out; pines and laurels were cut down and used to mask tottering walls. The famous hospitality of the old city covered any building defects; the fortieth anniversary celebration of the raising of the American flag over Monterey went off splendidly.

For many years the more progressive citizens had been clamoring loudly for incorporation of the city. At last, on June 8, 1889, the *Cypress* was able to publish the good news: "INCORPORATED! MONTEREY A CITY AT LAST! A DEATH KNELL TO SILU-RIANISM!" The *Cypress* could barely restrain its enthusiasm: "Since the landing of Padre Serra at the little beach north of the Custom house, just 111 years ago to a day, nothing of so much importance to Monterey has occurred. The 3rd of June, 1770, meant the invasion of Monterey by the representatives of the civilized world; it meant the beginning of the Christian era; the opening to the world of a new continent along the golden shores of the beautiful Pacific. . . .

"The native born, whose silvery hair now hangs in straight and stubborn locks upon his shoulders, has at last awakened from his long sleep and with catlike tread grasps his ballot and joins the phalanx of incorporationists. He seems to realize that the hand of progress is sweeping away the cobwebs of silurianism . . . "I knew this would be a city some day,' he says, 'and my only prayer has been that I might live to see it.'

"Even the old crooked streets seem to twist and strain in vain endeavors to assume a more symmetrical form—thus we find the 3rd of June, 1889, a grand day. A day made doubly historic because on that date the people decided to erect a monument in honor of the first invaders, in the shape of a live, picturesque, modern city.

"So harmoniously did they work, so interested were they in their efforts, that when the polls closed, only 24 votes out of 341 were found to declare against incorporation. Who were those lonely 24 souls will no doubt always remain a mystery. They are to be forgiven however, for perhaps they feared that it could not properly be called an election unless some opposition was manifested and they did not propose to jeopardize the legality of the election by having it all one-sided. At any rate, 317 votes were found 'For Incorporation'."

Monterey's enterprising young businessmen, encouraged by the town's incorporation in 1889, began to exert their best efforts to advertise its advantages. The public learned that "the salubrity of the climate is almost proverbial; for invalids the magnetic influence of the atmosphere grants them sleep and restful health"; and that a certain livery stable keeper had "horses for ladies and children that are gentle and kind." A local barber "besides being an up-to-date shaver, hair-cutter and hair-singer [*sic*] was an accomplished musician giving lessons on a number of stringed instruments and the brass horn." And Mr. T—— O—— in the furniture business, "besides carrying the most up-to-date designs in furniture, wall paper and encrusta decorations," was "an undertaker and embalmer . . . keeping in stock caskets of the best quality, and owning one of the costliest hearses that can be had."

Despite such signs of progress Monterey's population never, until 1900, exceeded 2,000 persons. In 1860 the Eighth Census listed 1,653 persons; the Eleventh Census (1890) found 1,662—or nine more than 30 years before. By 1900 the population had increased to 1,748. Monterey's future still held unknown developments in store.

TWENTIETH CENTURY

At the turn of the century Monterey was still, for the most part, the ancient town of half-dilapidated frame and adobe buildings and twisting, roughly defined streets in which the Spanish, Mexican, and American pioneers had resided. In 1906 Howard D. Severance became City Engineer, a position which he still held three decades later. It was a discouraging job at that time, for the town had never been properly mapped or surveyed; the streets were crooked and vague, and property lines irregular. Mr. Severance set to work to straighten out the tangle. Slowly but surely he brought order out of the chaos by moving one lot back, nipping a corner here, adding a section there. When he had them all in line, he made the first coherent map of the city, gave each lot a number instead of a name, and kept quiet about the whole thing for 20 years. At the end of that time the boundaries had become established by payment of taxes and open and notorious possession for at least 15 years.

In the first years of the twentieth century a new settlement—first known as "The Village"—was growing up to the south, facing Carmel Bay, where a little group of artists and writers—among them George Sterling, Mary Austin, James Hopper, and Fred Bechdolt,

Carmel's first postmaster, had their shacks among the pine woods, there to practice *la vie de Boheme*. The subdivision of the wooded acres sloping down to the sea drew others between 1908 and 1910— Herbert Heron, Sinclair Lewis, William Rose Benet, Alice MacGowan, Grace MacGowan Cooke, Michael Williams, and Upton Sinclair. In 1916 was incorporated Carmel-by-the-Sea.

The tourist business—which in 1946 was to hold second place among the Peninsula's money-making activities—was for long its economic mainstay: not until after World War I was the Peninsula to reclaim some of the economic prestige it had enjoyed before American occupation. Toward the end of the nineteenth century sporadic attempts had been made to exploit the natural riches of the mountainous hinterland. In the Point Sur region, tan-oaks by the thousands supplied bark for tanning leather. Over sled roads built from the wild canyons to the wilder seacoast, great loads of bark were dragged by mules, to be hoisted by cables to waiting schooners. During the year 1898, lumbermen sent out 25,000 cords, leaving 100,000 trees stripped bare to rot. Stakes for use in oyster beds and vineyards were cut, sledded, and cabled out of this wild country. In the first decade of the twentieth century, a dozen lime kilns in Bixby Canyon kept more men and more ships at work. In Stone Canyon and near Mal Paso Creek, coal mines were operated during these years. The exploitation of the county's immense deposits of diatomaceous earth was begun on a limited scale in 1905. From 1890 on, sand from the dunes along the shore was exported, and after 1900, when bottle-glass factories began to use it, it became a valuable export; in 1905 a narrow-gauge track was built to the dunes, and after 1912, as further uses for it by the construction industry were discovered, additional improvements—and eventually a sand-refining plant (see TOUR 1)—were installed. On the big ranches along the coast south of Carmel, cattle—the region's oldest source of wealth—were still pastured. The manufacture of Monterey or jack cheese—first made about 20 miles south of Monterey in 1892—was taken up by dairymen in other parts of the State when World War I cut off the supply of cheese from Europe. In the remote fastnesses of the Santa Lucias, venturesome homesteaders who had trekked in with a handful of household goods on pack animals and built homes of hand-hewn logs held by wooden pegs, kept bees and sent out tons of black sage honey. In the Carmel Valley, pioneer orchardists were growing, in the first decade of the century, the fine winter pears for which the region later would become famous. The raising of artichokes—in which Monterey County would later take first place among the five counties of the State which produce the crop—was undertaken later along the foggy coast. But most of these ventures—even those which were not eventually abandoned—were too small in scale to provide the Peninsula with a foundation for its economy. Following reclamation of the Presidio—long deserted and falling into ruins—as a United States Army post in 1902, the Government payroll helped to stabilize income. But in the main, Monterey had to rely on the profits of the tourist business until it discovered its chief economic asset—the sardine, swarming by the millions in the waters of Monterey Bay.

The "sardine capital of the world" was slow to recognize the value of the lowly fish which would spell prosperity for the whole region. Although F. E. Booth of the Sacramento River Packers' Association had established his cannery—Monterey's first—on the beach near the Custom House in 1902, it was chiefly to pack salmon. Booth's cannery in 1904 was packing four tons of sardines a day in season—but the sardine still was being used chiefly as salmon bait. In 1915, Peter Ferranti, an Italian who had worked on fishing boats in the Mediterranean, came to Monterey. Ferranti, who became Booth's boss fisherman, found only rowboats, launches, and small sailboats in use by the fishing fleet. Convinced that the lampara net used by Mediterranean fishermen would bring in fish in greater quantity than the equipment then in service, he tried it; the lampara became standard equipment for the whole fleet; it revolutionized the industry. Meanwhile the silver horde of sardines, almost inexhaustible in quantity, was discovered in 1916 to be in demand throughout the world. Within four years, nine canneries were reared along Monterey's shoreline.

Since 1920 the gleaming white sand of beaches adjacent to Monterey has been found to have an economic value transcending mere scenic attractiveness. Processed in a factory at Pacific Grove, almost a hundred carloads of the refined sand are produced monthly, for use in manufacture of bottle glass, roofing material, ceramic products, paint, electric fixtures, and soap. A related industry farther inland on the Peninsula is the mining of diatomaceous earth, a porous clay containing fossilized and minute unicellular algae, for which 300 commercial uses have been found. From huge deposits of this earth throughout the Santa Lucia Range, this industry supplies manufacturers of insulation materials, filters, paints, pigments, cement admixtures, abrasives, and petroleum clarifiers.

THE PENINSULA THROUGH FOUR CENTURIES

Whatever vicissitudes may befall its other means of livelihood, the Monterey Peninsula still has resources to fall back upon—those more genteel resources which make it the "Peninsula Playground of California." The area's reputation as a vacationer's paradise was settled in the eighties, when with a fanfare of publicity supplied by the *San Francisco Examiner* the Hotel Del Monte was flung open to socialites of the generation whose fortunes were dug, via the stock exchange, from the Comstock Lode. The grotesque suburban summer homes erected during that heyday of the Gothic Revival gave way half a century later to redwood bungalows and stuccoed villas —built on the Peninsula's pine-clad ridges and rugged shoreline by those who sought picturesque leisure and escape from a horrid modernity among its neglected landmarks and well-preserved legends.

From Monterey radiates the modern system of paved highways inviting a growing volume of tourists; further facilities for the traveler to the Peninsula are offered by bus lines, boats, and Monterey's municipal airport (completed in 1938). The wild land which rumbled with the oxcarts of the Spaniards, whose dusty trails were once trod by the mission padres, has been spanned since 1937 by the great Carmel-San Simeon Highway. Though to the passing stream of visitors it presents no view of Carmel and only a distant glimpse of the Hearst castle at San Simeon, this $10,000,000 arterial with its 32 bridges offers a thrilling panorama of the Peninsula with a glamorous past and an exciting future.

II. The Three Cities

Monterey

The mingling of unlike elements—soldiers and fisher folk, tourists and "old families"—gives contemporary MONTEREY (sea level-600 alt., 12,000 pop.), still living on its memories of a never-to-be-forgotten past and yet too hurried by today's less-romantic demands to dwell forever in history, its contradictory character. One of the most historic places in western America, the old town, crowded as it is with shrines, plaques, and mementos, might well suggest to the irreverent a carefully dusted cabinet of curios, the antiquarian's delight. But the ancient capital of Spanish-Mexican California is the modern "Sardine Capital of the World." Although its usual enterprising chamber of commerce has been quick to realize that history yields cash returns, fish canneries are still worth more than adobe *casas*. And so Monterey is torn between irreconcilable impulses—on one side, the urge to conserve and reclaim those historic and scenic attractions on which its reputation as a tourists' center must rest; on the other, to realize whatever returns may be forthcoming from a site of strategic military value to the Nation's armed forces and from a harbor whose fishing fleet and shoreside canneries are the Peninsula's economic mainstay.

Around the gently curving arc of the bay the town sprawls loosely —the somber green of wooded slopes at its back, the blue of the sea and the gray of the beach at its feet. Spreading before it, the Bay of Monterey—beautiful as the Bay of Naples—dominates the northeastern horizon; it sweeps in a majestic curve toward 19-mile-distant Santa Cruz, its water teeming with silver sardines, with the amazingly varied and prolific life of submarine gardens, its bottom hiding extinct volcanic craters and ancient canyons. The woods behind, the sea in front mark off Monterey's domain.

To realize the full charm of Monterey's environment one does best to climb one of the many streets that wander to the top of the pine-covered ridge. From here the red roofs shine against white walls; the bay gleams blue, ringed by its band of silver-gray sand, and the hills roll down to meet its waves. The light, changing from hour to hour, plays over the slopes. Along the eastern shore of the bay the soft, chaparral-covered hills swell dark against the distant mountains. The nearest ridge ends in Mount Toro, lying against the

FISHERMEN'S SHANTIES

ANANA

ARTIST ON WHARF

sky. Far in the east rises the bulk of Gavilan Mountain to save the eye from infinity; and farther north, Loma Prieta. Below, by the shore, massive tiled roofs stand out against the deep black-green of the mighty oaks surrounding gardened terraces. Round oil tanks shine with their aluminum paint, vivid under any light. From the sea in summertime the fog rolls in shrouding the slopes in dense clouds, reaching long, wispy fingers up the canyons. Over the whole landscape the pines keep their gloomy watch on the hilltop.

On the almost level shore lies the town, cut in two by the Presidio's wide green swath of tree-clad hills and turf. Beyond the bluff-edged shore line, penned between breakwater and wharf, rides the fishing-boat flotilla at anchor. To the south lies Old Monterey, a tangle of streets irregularly laid out, whose houses are scattered widely around the business center's compact cluster of squat buildings. To the north is New Monterey's checkerboard of aging frame residences, edged along the water by the docks, smokestacks, and canneries of Cannery Row.

Busiest of Old Monterey's thoroughfares is Alvarado Street, once a part of El Camino Real, running southward from the bay through the heart of town. Beyond its seaward end stretches Fisherman's Wharf with its seafood restaurants, kettles of boiling crabs, oriental girls pounding abalones, displays of squid and other strange sea creatures. Near the bay Alvarado Street smells of fish and salt water Its poolrooms are crowded; its cafes and bars are rough, dark and noisy, its rooming-houses drab; its shop windows are crammed with fishing gear and sailors' tackle. Its language is predominantly the Spanish and Italian of the fishermen and cannery workers. Farther south, where it pierces the main business section, plate-glass shop windows line the sidewalks. Alvarado Street's old adobes—only two are left—are tightly wedged among banks, real estate offices, busy restaurants, and softly lighted taverns. Along the side streets are small offices, garages, transfer companies, and lumber yards. In these blocks roughly dressed workmen rub elbows with camera-laden tourists; soberly clad businessmen, with vacationers in slacks and sport shirts. At night Alvarado Street is laced with bright tubes of neon. Though almost everywhere the past reaches into and colors the present, Old Monterey has had to make room for modernity.

At the heart of Old Monterey, a little west of Alvarado Street's southern end, is its civic center, a cluster of administrative buildings —Few Memorial City Hall, Colton Hall, Monterey Jail, and the offices of public officials—gathered in one block: Friendly Plaza.

Here in a garden rampant with color, paths and seats have been built around a fine old walnut tree between terraced beds of flaming plants. Monterey's chief beauty spot, the square is at its best at night, and especially by moonlight.

From Alvarado Street's southern end other thoroughfares lead southwest to the heights where the avenues of the town's better residential district wind over wooded slopes. Here in tree-shaded hillside settings appear the rambling hospitable homes, often built around patios, whose stuccoed facades and red-tiled roofs are the distinctive earmarks of the so-called "Spanish" style of California domestic architecture. And here too are the pleasant homes of more recent origin whose combination of Mexican and New England architectural features identifies them with the more authentic style known as "Monterey."

On both edges of town—in New Monterey beyond the Presidio to the northwest and in Oak Grove and East Monterey (Seaside) beyond El Estero to the east—live the foreign-born residents who comprise the overwhelming majority of Monterey's population: fishermen, cannery workers, and farmhands. New Monterey, where Cannery Row supports a mile of factories, is characterized by its smells: the pungent odor of horses from the Presidio stables, the aroma of fish from the canneries, the smell of the by-products from their reduction plants. Here—and in Oak Grove—the foreign languages crackle and whisper through the streets. The houses are small bungalows surrounded by clotheslines, with flower pots in front and vegetable gardens behind. On the mesa along the road to Carmel and down along the railroad tracks across from El Estero the fishermen, their lives ruled by the moon and the tides and the movements of the great schools of fish in Pacific waters, spread their nets, deep, warm brown from the tanning vats, to dry in the sun— literally miles of nets laid in long rows. The blue-shirted men talk and laugh as they mend the rents and replace the cork buoys.

THE PEOPLE

Unlike the population of Walter Colton's day, whose mingling of diverse costumes and customs inspired some rather invidious epithets from the Puritan *alcalde*—"the half-wild Indian . . . the lawless Mexican, the licentious Spaniard . . . the plodding German, the adventurous Russian"—the population of today, even more diverse, hides its difference under the anonymity of the armed forces uniforms or the workman's faded cotton shirt and blue denim pants. Even when Monterey was a Spanish-Mexican community, its foreigners who included Americans then—were numerous enough to form a *Compania Estranjera*. They are no less numerous now. Monterey has never been a Yankee town.

The medley of nationalities, each confined to its own neighborhood, includes Greeks and Italians, Chinese and Japanese, Spanish and Portuguese and Mexicans. Even more isolated are Monterey's few Negroes and Filipinos. In all the town's various foreign quarters English is the language least heard. Home of the Italians is Oak Grove, between El Estero and Del Monte; of the Japanese, the neighborhood west of El Estero; of the Chinese, downtown in Old Monterey and behind Cannery Row; of the Spanish, Mexicans, and Portuguese, New Monterey.

Descendants of Monterey's pioneers are the *paisanos* of John Steinbeck's *Tortilla Flat:* "What is a paisano? He is a mixture of Spanish, Indian, Mexican and assorted Caucasian bloods. His ancestors have lived in California for a hundred or two years. He speaks English with a paisano accent and Spanish with a paisano accent. When questioned concerning his race, he indignantly claims pure Spanish blood and rolls up his sleeves to show that the soft inside of his arms are nearly white. His color, like that of a well-browned meerschaum pipe, he ascribes to sunburn. He is a paisano, and he lives in that uphill district above the town of Monterey called Tortilla Flat . . ." Although Monterey has no real Tortilla Flat—the district is a composite of Monterey scenes blended in Steinbeck's imagination—it has its *paisanos*. It has also its Spanish and Mexicans, more recent immigrants of less mixed descent: fishermen, cannery employees, and agricultural workers, most of them. Simple, hardworking people—like John Steinbeck's naive peasant type—they are "clean of commercialism, free of the complicated system of American business . . . having nothing that can be stolen . . . or mortgaged."

Today by far the largest national minority on the Peninsula, the Italians came in large numbers—most of them from Sicily and Naples—to work in the canneries about the turn of the century. Though the Italians speak English when necessary, they prefer to speak their own language. Down by the wharf and in many of the shops Italian is spoken almost exclusively.

The spectacular festival of Santa Rosalia, patron saint of the Sicilian fisherman, comes early in September (her day is the third of that month (but is always celebrated during the light of the moon, because in the dark of the moon the men are much too busy fishing to take time out, even for such a cause. When the fishing has been good, the festival is one of thanksgiving; when it has been bad, the ceremony becomes one of supplication. After solemn High Mass, the statue of the saint is carried through the streets on a gayly decked float, from the historic old Royal Presidio Chapel to the harbor. A large following of the devout walk behind her. At the wharf the bishop, resplendent in his magenta robes, blesses the fleet. This ceremony is held under the care of the Italian Catholic Federation, the most prominent of the Italian organizations in Monterey.

The Chinese came with the Gold Rush. They drifted from the mines in the Santa Lucia Mountains to Monterey and took up their ancestral occupation, fishing. A quiet, unassuming, industrious people, they dried their catch for shipment to San Francisco. In the earlier days, "Chink-baiting" of the pigtailed coolies was the regular Saturday-night sport of cowboys in from the ranchos. The fast-shooting men from the mountains delighted to ride into town full gallop, lassoing on the wing every unsuspecting Chinaman. Monterey's original Chinatown was located at "China Point" on the shoreline between Pacific Grove and New Monterey, where the fish canneries are now. Although part of the colony still strings along a single street of oriental shops, cafes, and restaurants behind Cannery Row, where some of the Chinese are employed in the canneries, many Chinese have moved into Old Monterey as merchants and restaurateurs, creating a new Chinatown along Washington Street, which parallels Alvarado two blocks east. The colony has a cultural school attended by the younger generation, to acquaint them with the mother tongue and its classics.

Next door to Chinatown, a block east of Adams Street near the municipal baseball park, is the small Japanese quarter. The colony, which at one time was situated near Point Lobos on what is still know as Jap Bay, numbers about 500 persons. They earn their livelihood chiefly by fishing. Their specialty is the abalone, which they pursue along the coast from Monterey to the San Luis Obispo County line. Abalones are secured by divers. When the boats are tied up along Fishermen's Wharf, their rubber diver's suits are strung up to dry. They present a grotesque but fascinating picture, for the suits carry numerous patches of brilliant color, adding a festive note to their inflated scarecrow appearance. When the catch has been good there follow hours of pounding by the girls. In the twilight, when the big rooms are lighted dimly, one can see them at work, and the pattering sound drifts over the quiet bay.

Of pioneer American origin are the residents of East Monterey, known to much of the town as "Okies"—dispossessed Middle-Western farmers who came west hunting work in the fields—some of whom have found work in Cannery Row. The settlement was first known as Seaside, when many of its houses were tar-paper and packing-box shacks perched by the drifting sand. More recently the members of this community have banded together in the pioneer tradition to help one another build more substantial houses, in which they take great pride of ownership. East Monterey has even acquired a library by the same cooperative methods, founded, furnished, and built by its residents and now partly supported by the Monterey County library system.

Until fairly late in the nineteenth century a town where Spanish was as familar to the ears as English, Monterey has lost most of those features—language, customs, and architecture—which stamped it as a center of Latin culture. Officers and soldiers from the Presidio, cowboys from the ranchos, fishermen and cannery workers, marine biologists and artists—these, and not the few descendants of the Spanish and Mexican *rancheros* and *pobladores* who remain, give Monterey society today its characteristic color.

THE INDUSTRIES

The chief industry in Monterey since the turn of the century has been the large-scale commercial fishing, canning, processing, and distribution of sardines. So dependent is Monterey upon the sardine for its livelihood that the industry's seasonal fluctuations now affect the local economy with the precision of a seismograph recording earthquake tremors. Merchants solemnly claim that they observe "a falling off of trade even during the full moon periods and in rough weather when the boats do not go out."

By 1929, peak year for the industry, the huge catch of the Monterey fishermen enabled 30 canneries along Cannery Row to produce 4,000,000 cases. Following the lean years of the 1930's, the industry was revived by demand for such by-products of the sardine as oil and fish-meal, hitherto considered fit only for fertilizer. The annual market value of the sardine catch was estimated, by this time, at $7,000,000, and the value of the "fresh fish" catch—of which the rockfish, abalone, salmon, and Pacific mackerel are the most important—at $350,000 more.

From the second decade of the twentieth century on, the ever-growing world-wide demand for canned sardines has spurred the operators of Monterey's fleet of fishing boats to develop mass-production techniques, in order to supply the canneries. At first they used gasoline-powered boats only to tow the heavy "seine" boats rowed by hand from which they set their nets; then it was found that the nets could be set from the power boat itself with less effort. The distinctive "Monterey type" power boats, first used for salmon trolling, with their clipper bows and "whaleback" decks, were modified specifically for use in sardine fishing: the decks made flatter, a clear space provided for the net, and a sloping platform for sliding it over the gunwale installed. And then, in 1929, another revolutionary improvement was introduced: the purse seine, 200 to 220 fathoms long, set by machinery rather than by hand, and carried on bigger, Diesel-powered boats with greater cruising ranges, which began to supplant the former equipment.

Employing a maximum of 2,500 workers at the peak of the season, the dozen or more canneries now in business buy their sardines from hundreds of purse-seine fishermen. During 1938 the sardine industry brought $8,000,000 to Monterey. According to records, the canneries in that year handled 154,846 tons of sardines worth $1,722,298 to the fishing fleet at the market price and paid an estimated total payroll of $1,750,000 to some 2,500 cannery workers. They produced 925,253 cases of sardines, worth $2,584,094; 4,752,224 gallons of sardine oil, worth $1,330,622; and 24,685 tons of sardine meal, worth $889,660. The fish canneries carry on a variety of operations: cleaning, sorting, trimming, cutting, cooking, drying, frying, and finally canning. Each cannery has a reduction and fertilizer plant. Shipments of oil, fishmeal, and fertilizer are sent to all parts of the world. The fishing fleet and Cannery Row are basic to the economic welfare of Monterey.

Gateway to the Monterey Peninsula for 170 years, the old capital of California has been reluctant to shed the tattered glories of its past. Within recent years, however, a new spirit of progress has swept the town. After the piping of crude oil from the Coalinga field to storage tanks in Monterey, one of the tanks was struck by lightning in 1924 and the town was almost destroyed by fire; but the tanks were rebuilt at Seaside and agitation for industrial development continued over protests of old-timers who claimed that Monterey was being ruined by unscrupulous promoters. Finally in 1932, after more than 50 years of effort by businessmen, a breakwater was built to protect shipping from the turbulent waters of Monterey Bay. Monterey has been served since 1926 by its Municipal Wharf No. 2, extending 1,750 feet into the deep waters of the bay and providing berthing facilities adequate for the largest ocean liners. Here dock the coastwise schooners bringing the lumber which is today the town's chief import.

THE ARTS

It has been said that Monterey has two industries: sardine fishing and art. A country of brilliant contrasts—with its rugged coast, mountains, cypresses, its native folk of richly intermingled bloods, cultures, traditions—the Peninsula has been a mecca of painters since the early nineties. Hundreds of artists have come and continue to come from all parts of the Nation.

Chief among the bohemian painters of the earlier period was Charles Rollo Peters, famous for his studies of moonlight. A disciple of Ryder, he reduced the art of painting moonlight to such a degree of perfection that few artists have since dared to use the same subject. With Eugene Neuhaus and William Keith, he founded in 1907 the Del Monte Gallery. Peters' paintings now fetch very high prices.

With the scattering of the old carefree romantic bohemian school of painters, a new group of serious young artists appeared. Perhaps the two most important were William Ritschel and Armin Hansen. Ritschel built himself a castle by the sea and sat for hours on the cliffs above the breakers. A graduate of German academies and a tremendous technician, he paints canvases monumental in scope, done in methodical, almost photographic detail. Most of all he loves to paint huge waves breaking frantically over masses of cold, solid rocks. A strenuous worker, he is confident of his ability to portray the sea with utmost realism.

Hansen, who also paints monumental canvases of the sea, is more concerned with emotional quality than physical reality. A big man, vital and energetic, he came from Europe, where he had sailed the North Sea, to Monterey, where he lived with the fishermen and sailed with them, painting incessantly, determined to record with vigor and realism the lives of seafaring people. Always presenting earthy, primitive men under hardship and strife, his paintings convey a deep understanding of the thoughts and emotions of the fishermen. Most often his object is to portray man fighting great odds.

Paul Dougherty, who came to Monterey with a reputation in the East, is detached and subtle, a poet and a gentleman, whose canvases are masterpieces of frugal, almost cautious treatment. As are Ritschel and Hansen, he is a member of the National Academy.

While these men were painting the sea and seafarers, a school of painters sprang up who turned to the country back of Monterey for inspiration. Ever since the nineties—when painters began to appear on every hillside, along the wharves, in adobe gardens: bearded men shabbily clothed, timid art-conscious women, art students innumerable—the Monterey landscape has attracted landscapists by the hundreds. It has been described as possessing all the qualities that make for bad painting: sunlight and pleasant design and soft coloring. Its easy picturesqueness has been less a help than a hindrance to distinguished painting. Only a few have been able to throw off its insidiously lyric influence.

Of the Monterey landscapists, one of the most successful has been Burton Boundy, pupil of Robert Henri, whose paintings—modern in feeling and unstylized—catch the local scene with clarity, reducing the landscape to strong composition and simplified form. Widely appreciated by the buying public have been Percy Gray, Arthur Hill Gilbert, and William Silva, whose calm and peaceful landscapes have gone to market in Canada and England as well as in the United States. DeNeale Morgan paints the Monterey coast. August Gay's highly individual canvases use the Monterey scene intellectually. Producing strong effects with simple form, John O'Shea works rapidly for distinctive decorative effects, in both oil and watercolor. An outstanding American woman painter, Henrietta Shore produces fine decorative work. James Fitzgerald's watercolors, conservative in treatment, temper the academic approach with lively color. Suggestive of figure painting are William Hyde Irwin's solid landscapes.

The youngest generation of painters seeks refuge in Monterey from crowded, hungry cities. Influenced by years of economic uncertainty and strife, most of them are definitely concerned with the social scene—in contrast with the older painters. John Langley Howard, caricaturist and satirist, paints the social struggle with a brilliant frescolike technique. Among others whose work follows a searching, experimental vein are Bruce Ariss, Glyn Collins, Ellwood Graham, and Barbara Stevenson. Responsible for notable work, in much of which the newer influences appear, was the WPA Art Project.

Of all the arts practiced in Monterey since its discovery as an artistic mecca, architecture has been perhaps most successfully followed. In the work of the early Spanish and Mexican builders, whose simple and dignified adobe houses were ideally suited to their backgrounds, contemporary architects have found inspiration. The early homes were built of adobe—sticky clay mud moulded into bricks with a mixture of gravel and straw, tamped by hand and dried in the sun *(see POINTS OF INTEREST: No. 6)*. Because labor was scarce, the houses were very simple, usually consisting of one long narrow room divided by a single partition, with white-washed walls at least three feet thick, pierced by tiny windows, and roofs sloping, covered with handmade tile. In later years, over the one-story rectangular foundation, a second story, sometimes of frame, was often added, surrounded by a frame balcony supported on horizontal beams sunk in the adobe walls. From the eve of American occupation, when Yankee notions began to make their impression on the Spanish town, dates the evolution of that distinctive style known as "Monterey": a wedding of Spanish and New England features *(see POINTS OF INTEREST: No. 16)*.

MASTER PLAN

It is not only Monterey's architectural significance which draws visitors both professional and amateur those who come to study as well as those who come to enjoy. "Only one place in the United States rivals the Monterey Peninsula in its present possibility of being preserved and developed as a historical monument," said the Monterey History and Art Association's retiring president in his annual report for 1937. "In other places, the unique and memorable have been so covered and dwarfed by late accretions, so enlarged and marred by industrial growth, so changed by removal and modification, that as communities they have lost the essential atmosphere and spirit that might have made them unique. To a very considerable degree, the essence still remains in Monterey. Its enjoyment by the present generation and by posterity is fortunately, even yet, as much a matter of preservation as of restoration, particularly if future development can be shaped in harmony with what now exists."

To Charles Warren Stoddard, dead and buried in the old Catholic Cemetery these many years, the prospect of preserving Monterey for posterity appeared less hopeful, even before the turn of the century. "Old Monterey?" he queried. "Yes, old Monterey; yet not so very old. Old, however, inasmuch as she has been hopelessly modernized; the ancient virtue has gone out of her; she is but a monument and a memory." The Monterey Stoddard had known was the Monterey that "boasted but half a dozen thinly populated streets. One might pass through these streets . . . at almost any hour of the day, footing it all the way from the dismantled fort on the seaside to the ancient cemetery, grown to seed . . . and not meet half a score of people. Geese fed in the gutters, and hissed as I passed by; cows grazing by the wayside eyed me in grave surprise; overhead the snow-white seagulls wheeled and cried peevishly; and on the heights that shelter the ex-capital the pine-trees moaned and moaned, and often caught and held the sea-fog among their branches, when the little town was basking in the sunshine and dreaming its endless dream."

No one could better express than Stoddard the charms of that vanished civilization whose relics seemed inevitably destined to disappear after it: "When I think on that beach at Monterey—the silent streets, the walled, unweeded gardens—wistful Saturday-afternoon feeling comes over me. I hear again the incessant roar of the surf; I see the wheeling gulls, the gray sand; the brown, bleak meadows; the empty streets; the shops, tenantless sometimes—for the tenant is at dinner or at dominos: the other shops that are locked forever and the keys rusted away; whenever I think of her I am reminded of that episode in Coulton's [sic] diary, where he, as alcalde, was awakened from a deep sleep at the dead of night by a guard, a novice, and a slave to duty. With no little consternation, the alcalde hastened to unbar the door. The guard, with a respectful salute, said: 'The town, sir, is perfectly quiet'."

Perhaps it was Old Monterey's very neglect that preserved it against oblivion. For despite a century's ravages, the old town stands—"our supreme example," says Carnegie Foundation landscape engineer Emerson Knight, "of a Spanish-Mexican-Early American settlement on the Pacific Coast."

To preserve that "supreme example," Knight was commissioned by Monterey's Planning Commission to prepare a Master Plan, "not only with the primary objective of protecting its vastly important sites and buildings in authentic environment and interrelationship, but also in order to chart a wise course in meeting modern requirements of a vital growing and progressive community."

The Master Plan, completed in May, 1939, proposes a series of reconstructions and restorations, covering a period of 25 to 50 years, to preserve Old Monterey's historic integrity and beautify its environs. Among its objectives is re-establishment of the shoreline in its original aspect, as known to the early Spanish and Mexican settlers, to permit a clear view from the Custom House plaza over the bay, Along the shore a wide promenade would sweep southward from the Custom House as far as El Estero, its free view of the sea cleared by removal of Fisherman's Wharf and its sprawling structures and rehabilitation of the Booth Cannery's building to blend with the setting. Besides providing for ample space around the numerous old historic structures, the plan suggests a new generous system of parks, playgrounds, beach promenades, and a municipal bathhouse. Zoning would control future architecture around the old town, limit the height and size of future buildings, restrict gaudy public advertisements in the form of billboards or neon lights.

The Master Plan has broght to the fore Monterey's struggle of the opposites, its never-ending warfare between old and new, between those who would sacrifice the present for the past and those who would sacrifice the past for the present. An original effort in city and regional planning, the Master Plan has won the support of historians, clubwomen, artists, civic groups, and pioneers—but not of canners, fishermen and cannery workers, who see their livelihood menaced by threats of the canneries' moving to Moss Landing on the other side of the bay. Whether the plan would eventually be put into effect remained an unsettled question.

Its planner has called on Montereños to face the "problem of blending the new with the old . . . with courage and a broad approach, freed from petty interests and prejudices." "If citizens of Monterery," says Emerson Knight, "will only realize that this planning project, focalized on the concept of preserving rare historic values which they hold in trust, is not only of citywide, county and statewide significance but also is of national and even international importance, they will soon gain a clear perspective of its meaning and of its potential effect on their future lives and happiness. Great is the measure of their debt to posterity. Here is opportunity for wise treatment that will contribute to the intellectual, educational and inspirational life of an alert public of the present and future."

Monterey will not forget that debt. Proud of its age, it celebrates its birthday every year on June 3 in the old way with a *merienda*. Guitars play in the garden of the Pacific Building down by the waterfront, once the scene of bull and bear fights, now fragrant with masses of bright flowers. From the barbecue pits comes the tantalizing smell of wood smoke, frying steaks, and kettles of pungent *frijoles*. A voice is raised in the songs of Spain; the soft language of

Mexico is heard again in the streets. The spirit of the fiesta runs through the town. There is dancing in the streets in the evening; there are picnics along the beach. Boats in the harbor are gay with flags; the guns from the Presidio salute the day. The *paisanos* and their friends celebrate as they have celebrated for 170 years. At night crowds watch amateur entertainers. A cowboy from the mountains plays the harmonica, a girl from Cannery Row sings a torch song, an old *paisano* plays his guitar, and, on the edge of the crowd, a withered woman swings stiffly through the measures of the *bamba*.

And so the new Monterey honors the old.

Path of History: Points of Interest

To direct tourists to its historically important landmarks, the City of Monterey adopted in April, 1938, the "Path of History" developed by Colonel Roger S. Fitch, United States Army, with the aid of data compiled by Mrs. Laura Bride Powers. Marked by a red and orange dotted line painted on the pavements which follows a route 2.8 miles long, describing a loop around the city beginning and ending at the site of the old plaza, the "Path of History" passes or nears most of Monterey's historic sites and buildings. Most of these have been indicated by metal markers by the Monterey History and Art Association with the cooperation of the City of Monterey. With the aid of the tourist map published by and available from the Monterey Chamber of Commerce, the visitor may find with ease points of interest situated both on and off the outlined route.

1. Monterey's Chamber of Commerce, 585 Munras St., stands on the SITE OF THE PLAZA, a triangular area of about a city block, bounded by Munras, Pearl, and Tyler Sts. From 1806 until 1898 the *pueblo's* first *carcel* (jail) stood here; from 1840 to the 1880's, the *cuartel* (quarters or barracks).

The jail, which figures prominently in the folktales of Monterey Indians, was a sturdy structure made of great blocks of adobe and roofed with heavy red tile. Strong rawhide thongs fastened its handhewn pine beams and joists. At one time it was floorless, and the earth so wet a stick would sink some distance into it. The interior was so dark objects could not be seen for more than a yard. Frequently it was so crowded that some inmates had to stand while others slept. Outside in the plaza, Indians were whipped daily for minor offenses.

The erection of the *cuartel* for Mexican troops was ordered by Governor Alvarado in 1840. Contractor for the approximately $10,000 adobe-and- redwood barracks was Don José Abrego. Americans later used the building as their capitol, then as a schoolhouse, a library, and a meetinghouse for the Methodist Episcopal Church.

After most of the plaza's public buildings were destroyed, Simoneau's Restaurant stood here (a service station occupies its site). Simoneau's was a favorite meeting place for artists, who sometimes paid their bills with wall decorations done in shoeblacking and beer. A descendant of the famous old restaurateur, Fred Felix, recently disproved the story that he was an ignorant tamale peddler, as many magazine articles had pictured him. Simoneau had many philosophical discussions with Robert Louis Stevenson during the latter's visit

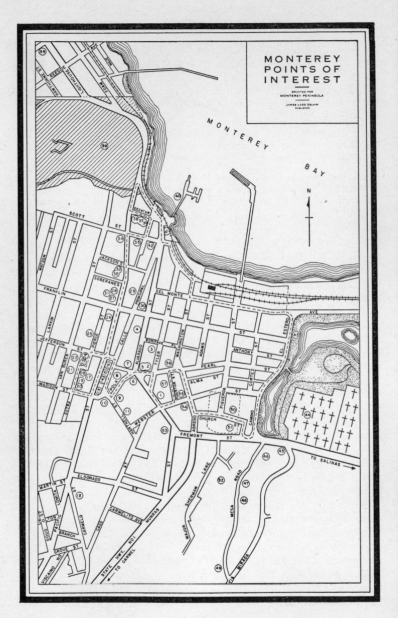

in 1879; later Stevenson not only corresponded frequently, but every time he published a book he sent a volume to Simoneau with an inscription.

2. Once occupied by General José Castro *(see No. 46)* when he was military commandant of the Department of the North, the much-reconstructed CASTRO HEADQUARTERS *(private)*, NW. cor. Pearl and Tyler Sts., originally a one-story adobe, is a barnlike structure devoid of ornamentation, whose worn whitewash reveals in many places its adobe-brick and chalk-rock facade. At the rear, enclosed by a half-ruined rock and adobe wall, is the old BULL AND BEAR PIT (visible from Tyler Street), one of the few left in California, to which natives and settlers came from great distances to watch a hungry, tortured bear fight a specially trained bull. The two animals were tied at opposite ends of a rope so that neither could escape during the fight. The struggle usually was long and hard and the bear won most often because of his ability to attach himself to the bull's tongue, a difficult and impressive tactical feat. Betting was heavy, but was concerned with the length of time it would take the bear to seize and eat the bull's tongue, rather than with the identity of the victor.

3. Around the one-story adobe home of Don José Mariano Estrada, Casa Estrada, the modern, three-story MISSION INN, 456 Tyler St., has been constructed. Built about 1828 on this spot, the *casa* probably was first converted into a hotel about 1849. The first-floor interior reveals the old beams, heavy and handhewn, that were set into the adobe where additional strength was needed. Of Santa Barbara architectural style, the present building has central balconies on the two upper floors and smaller ornamental balconies jutting out from the windows. The windows, with their small panes of glass, are in the best early Spanish tradition. The weathered white (verging on cream) of the walls is well contrasted with the rich, deep brown of the woodwork. Window boxes and bright flowers add a living touch to the building.

Don José Estrada, *alferez* (ensign) of the Monterey military company from 1806 to 1818, during most of which time he was *habilitado* (paymaster), won a promotion to the rank of brevet lieutenant in 1818 for his services against the pirate Bouchard and another to lieutenant for his aid in supressing the Indian revolt in 1824. Retired from military service in 1829, he held the position of *sub comisario* at Monterey in 1832-33 and of *juez de campo* (judge) in 1835. His son, José Ramón, who became *alcalde* of Monterey in 1836 at the age of 25 during the turbulent reign of Governor Mariano Chico, was deprived of the wand of office and placed under arrest *(see No. 57)*. It is said Don José did not mind the arrest but was highly incensed when Governor Chico insulted his aged father, an offense of no little import in old Monterey.

After the American conquest the Estrada adobe was enlarged until it had become, by the 1880's, a three-story structure, which for a time claimed to be one of the Pacific Coast's leading hotels. It was known at various times as the Pancho House, the St. Charles Hotel, and the Everett House. Acquired in 1902 by C. D. Casper, who remodeled it and added a music hall, it was further enlarged with the addition of a wing by his heirs and finally given its present name.

4. Once a rambling one-story adobe with a rear full-length veranda overlooking an elaborate garden facing Main Street, the CASA SANCHEZ, 414 Alvarado St., was long ago converted to commercial use, serving successively as police station, candy shop and tearoom, barber shop and beauty parlor. (It is still known locally as "My Attic" in remembrance of its tearoom days, when tables were placed on its upper floor). Of the original structure, built about 1828 or 1829, all that remains is the southern part—which boasts the only old balcony on Alvarado Street—the rest having been added later. Whether it originally was built or later was purchased by the man whose name it bears, Gil Sánchez, is unknown. Having arrived from Mexico in 1820, Sánchez served as *regidor* in 1836 and in 1852 helped found Santa Clara College. When the northern section of the house was wrecked in 1890, his daughter, Ygnacia María Sánchez, remodeled it and made it her home until her death in 1917.

5. What was said to be Monterey's FIRST UNITED STATES POST OFFICE, 497 Alvarado St., occupied the two-story adobe business building—now white-painted and green-shuttered, its second story board-covered—which Dr. D. Callaghan built in 1846. Here were his office and drugstore. After the American conquest he offered the building to the Government.

6. The COOPER HOUSE *(upper floor private; lower-floor museum open irregular hours; donation expected)*, 508 Munras St. (also known as the Munras Adobe), is a long, two-story, cream-colored adobe building whose railed wooded balcony overhangs the sidewalk. The doors are heavy, the windows flanked by solid shutters that can be locked from the inside. The house and its high-walled garden extend a half-block. This was the home of Captain John Rogers Cooper, half-brother of Thomas O. Larkin. Cooper, shrewd,

OLD CUSTOMS HOUSE

FISHERMAN

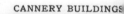

CANNERY BUILDINGS

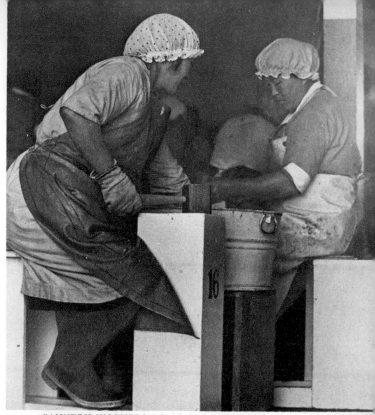

CANNERY WORKERS POUNDING ABALONE

FISHERMAN   FISHERMAN

CALIFORNIA'S FIRST THEATER—EXTERIOR

CALIFORNIA'S FIRST THEATER—VIEW FROM STAGE

fiery Yankee skipper, known as Juan de la Manca (John of the Arm) because of a shrunken arm, was one of the first Americans to settle in Monterey and adopt Catholicism and Mexican citizenship (he took the name of Juan Bautista). The house was built in 1829 for his bride, Doña Encarnación Vallejo, sister of General Mariano Vallejo, and is still the property of their descendants. The lower-floor museum houses relics of early California and rare early photographs.

A native of Alderney Island in the English Channel, Cooper settled in Massachusetts as a boy. As master of the *Rover,* he came to the Pacific Coast in 1823. He made voyages to China and other countries until 1826, when he entered the hide-and-tallow trade in Monterey. Naturalized in 1830, he served as *regidor* in 1834-35. He took up a seafaring life again from 1839 to 1844, commanding the Government schooner *California* on its voyages to Mexico. Appointed harbormaster of Monterey in 1851, he held the position for many years, living meanwhile with his family on his Rancho El Sur down the coast *(see TOUR 3).*

During the Solís revolt, when the foreigners supported the rebels, the plotters met in this house. It is legend that Cooper rolled out a barrel of rum, plied the insurgents into a state of stupidity, and thus saved the town from pillage. When trapper Jedediah Smith, believed the first American to cross the Sierra Nevada, arrived in Monterey with his eight starving companions, the captain stood bond for his supplies and quick departure from California.

Because of trade restrictions, smuggling was popular and profitable, and was one of Cooper's many activities. The English brig *Star of the West* foundered on the Point Lobos rocks in 1846 and about half the cargo—put up in waterproof wrapping for mule-train transportation—was salvaged. Cooper rushed to the scene of the wreck with men and creaking ox-drawn *carretas,* collected the floating spoils, hurried the "damaged goods" through the customs duty free, and made a small fortune. Protests of John Parrott, United States Consul at Mazatlan, owner of the cargo, went unheeded.

The high adobe, tile-topped garden wall of the Cooper House is one of Monterey's finest and best preserved. The adobe bricks with which it is covered were made in basins about 20 feet in diameter and 2 feet deep dug into the earth near the site of construction. In these basins loam, sand, adobe clay, and straw (or tile chips and other binding materials) were mixed with water until they were of a thick, soupy consistency, then taken out, put into molds, and dried in the sun. After the bricks were laid on the chalk-rock foundation, branches or twigs were placed on top and cemented with adobe. Professor G. W. Hendy of the University of California, after examination of the adobe brick composition of this wall, has discovered the existence of early California flowers, field crops, weeds, and even plant diseases from the fossils contained in the adobe bricks.

7. Once a flourishing saloon and gambling house, the LA PORTE BUILDING (sometimes called the Casa Alvarado), 490-98 Alvarado St., housed in a small second-story addition to the original one-story adobe, the office of Juan Bautista Alvarado, governor of California from 1836 to 1842. In the rear of the tavern, which was managed by Mauricio Gonzales, a high adobe wall enclosed an arena with crude seats, tiered circus-fashion, where Mexican acrobats staged gymnastic feats.

Assessed to Alvarado in 1854, the building was purchased in 1874 by the La Porte brothers, who added a frame upper story. It was completely reconstructed in 1936.

8. Don José Amesti—wealthy Spanish-Basque *juez* (judge), *ranchero,* and onetime *alcalde* of Monterey—built the two-story CASA AMESTI *(private)*, 516 Polk St., in 1825, shortly after his marriage to Prudenciana Vallejo, sister of Mariano Vallejo. This adobe, with its front and rear balconies and walled rear garden, is a fine example of Spanish Colonial architecture. Trim and white, it maintains much of its original exterior appearance. The interior has been modernized. The double doors of heavy weathered wood are modern additions, as are the iron bars protecting the windows.

Amesti gave the house to his daughter Carmen in 1848, when she married Don Santiago (born James) McKinley, a former Scots sailor who had been left ashore by a whaler in San Francisco in 1824. McKinley, who had become a Mexican citizen, owned and operated a schooner plying the California coast. Later he joined a successful shipping firm. He was arrested in 1847 for participation in the revolt against Governor Manuel Micheltorena, but was released. He died in the adobe in 1876.

For a time the old Amesti-McKinley home was operated as a roominghouse by a Frenchwoman. As was the custom, it was built flush with the street; but its occupant was determined to have a garden in front of her place. Each year, therefore, she planted a few flowers between the unpaved street and the house; and each year when the street was repaired the workmen allowed her flowers to remain. Polk Street acquired such a peculiar bulge in front of the

Casa Amesti that the city fathers finally were forced to forbid the Frenchwoman from stealing any more of the roadway. It still retains its bulge.

9. Used in 1851-52 as a courtroom for the first Federal Court held in Monterey under American rule, say some historians, the CASA DE LA TORRE, 599 Polk St., probably served also as the residence of Mexican judge José Joaquín de la Torre, who held court here in 1839. A good example of Spanish-Colonial architecture, it was begun in 1836 and is said to have been 3 years and 18 days in construction. Its three rooms were ranged around a patio, partly roofed, which served as kitchen and dining room. The building is now occupied by a gift- and book-shop which conducts a small art gallery specializing in the works of lesser-known young artists.

The pale green, three-foot-thick walls are well preserved; the adobe bricks, baked in the sun for months, still show the hundred-year-old footprints of coyotes and squirrels. The whole building is hand-fashioned in all its parts; the narrow, heavy doors are hand-covered. Window sills the depth of the walls form indoor shelves; originally used as seats and storage space, they now display books and other articles. Many of the small windowpanes of handmade glass are those originally brought around the Horn from New England in sailing vessels.

10. Built in the late 1830's by an English sailor turned doctor and druggist, the STOKES HOUSE (*private*), 500 Hartnell St., today one of the few adobes to retain its original architectural simplicity, was then one of the more pretentious homes in the Mexican capital. Still surrounded by its trim garden, the house is a two-story, whitewashed, shingle-roofed adobe with a veranda in front, loggia in rear, and balconies set on slender wooden posts, enclosed at each end, across both front and rear. It was the home of Dr. James Stokes, who arrived in Monterey about 1834, married María Josefa Soto, and became consulting physician to Governor Figueroa. In the *sala* (ballroom) which he built onto the east end of the house were held many of the town's social functions, notably its *cascaró bailes* (cascaron balls). It was rumored that Stokes plotted to make California an English protectorate, but he welcomed the American conquest, and raised the United States flag over the *pueblo* of San Jose in 1846.

The building was purchased in 1856 by Honoré Escolle, native of Marseilles, who converted one room into a store. As business prospered, Escolle opened a bakery in the fashionable Washington Hotel and another store in the Cooper Adobe. The bakery was not a success, so Escolle, practical Frenchman, moved the huge oven to the backyard of his home and converted it into a kiln for pottery. He sent to France for a skilled pottery worker and with his aid operated the first kiln in the State. Escolle died and the property passed to other hands in 1895, but the oven, well preserved, still stands in the old back yard.

From the outside, the walls, covered with mud plaster and white-wash, thick and smooth in texture, appear mottled, due to cracks which are now dust-filled. The walls of the ground floor, laid on stone foundations, with inch-wide mud mortar joints, are three feet thick; those of the second floor, but two feet, the offset occurring on the inside so that the rooms above—bedrooms—have more floor space than those below. On the inside the narrow doors are equipped with massive wooden bolts in iron brackets. The living room still houses many of the original furnishings.

11. Boxlike, two-storied, its three-foot adobe walls resurfaced with clapboards, the so-called FREMONT'S HEADQUARTERS (*private*), 359 Hartnell St., may have served Major John C. Frémont of the hard-riding California Battalion for an office in 1846-47, as legend relates, although Fremont stated that he slept on a hill at the end of town during his sojourn. The building also is said to have served earlier some of the military purposes of Frémont's opponent, General José Castro. He is supposed to have given away later a part of the property, retaining under Spanish custom, however, a right-of-way over the land so long as any member of his family lived. Assessed to Dr. James Stokes in the assessment records of 1851, the building later passed through the hands of various owners, including one-time Mayor Robert F. Johnson.

12. Most Montereños lived in houses like the one-story CASA DE SOTO (*private; best viewed from Cass St., S. of El Dorado*), 816 El Dorado St., probably built in 1820 by Joaquin de Soto. Standing atop a knoll, it looks through treetops toward Monterey Bay. The Casa de Soto is unrestored and unoccupied, half hidden by tall weeds, and flanked on two sides by cypresses. The little rectangular house is gray and patched, its adobe bricks unprotected in many places, its small windows boarded over. Its roof, originally thatched, is covered with age-blackened tile, made almost exclusively by Indians. (It is said that an expert Indian worker could turn out as many as 125 tiles a day. Contrary to popular belief, the tile was not molded on the thighs of Indian women, but on forms made by the Indians from appropriately sized tree trunks). The casa's adobe

bricks, $1\frac{1}{2}$ feet square and 3 feet thick, are cemented together with mud and plastered (inside and outside the house) with a mixture of mud, broken tile, and twigs. At the gateway in the rickety fence stand two old tanks, on one of which is scrawled "100 VA JOSE MARIA SOTO." Near the doorstep is an old fireplace, where cooking was done outside the home, as was the custom of all Montereños in early days.

13. Knit together into one barnlike adobe-and-frame structure, the two weathered, white, green-shuttered, two-story CASAS GUTIERREZ, 590 Calle Principal, were built by Lieutenant-Colonel Nicolás Gutiérrez, twice Governor of California, who had his headquarters here in 1836. They have been so extensively remodeled that they bear little resemblance to the original houses. The upper story of the western half of the building is made of wood. It was bought by the Monterey Foundation for the preservation of historic buildings, landmarks and sites, established in 1945.

In 1835, popular Governor José Figueroa, believing death imminent, sent for Gutiérrez, military head of the department, to take his office. Before Gutiérrez could arrive from San Gabriel, Figueroa appointed José Castro political head of the department. After Figueroa's death the political and military commands were divided between the two until Mexico conferred upon Gutiérrez full powers, pending the appointment of the new governor. The appointee, Governor Mariano Chico, had a brief, scandalous career, and upon his forced retirement 7 months later, Gutiérrez again became governor.

Gutiérrez, a Mexican of Spanish birth—a foreigner to the impetuous Californians—was disliked, and under the leadership of young Juan Bautista Alvarado and his friend, José Castro, open revolt broke out. The rebels secured the only old cannon, and when the single shot of the revolution crashed near the governor's headquarters in the Plaza, he promptly surrendered. Following capitulation of the Presidio on November 5, 1836, Gutiérrez and his associates were deported to Lower California.

14. A handwrought iron weather vane on the steeply sloping roof of the HOUSE OF THE FOUR WINDS (*private*), Calle Principal near Madison St., so stimulated the imagination of the Indians that they gave the house its name. This one-story adobe, small and attractive, was built by Thomas Larkin in 1835 and used by him as a store. For a while it served as headquarters for Henry Halleck, Secretary of State. During the early days of American occupation the house was a hall of records. Local Mexican officials had been lax

with public records, and the Americans were little better. Many records were lost or destroyed, and titles to land grants mysteriously mislaid, causing great confusion in later attempts to settle land claims.

The House of the Four Winds now is headquarters for the Monterey Women's Civic Club.

15. The small, one-story SHERMAN'S QUARTERS *(private)*, 464 Calle Principal (inside the walls of the Larkin House property), was built by Thomas Larkin in 1834. Lieutenants William Tecumseh Sherman and H. W. Halleck lived here from 1847 to 1849 while they served under Colonel Richard B. Mason, military governor of California. The spiked cannon in front of the house, part of their equipment, long was used as a hitching post.

The structure has changed little through the years. Its chipped whitewashed walls reveal the adobe bricks beneath. (The use of lime—mixed with tallow and cactus-plant juice—for whitewash was thought by early Montereños to be a means of preventing the spread of communicable disease.) The door of the little building is one of the finest examples of its type in Monterey, and illustrates the fine sense of proportion of its builders.

A skeleton once found in a well in the yard of the house gave rise to a wild rumor that the place was used by the Spaniards as a burial place for murdered political prisoners.

16. When the LARKIN HOUSE *(private)*, 464 Calle Principal, was built in 1835 by Thomas O. Larkin, it created so great a sensation in Monterey that a new style of domestic architecture, named for the town, was evolved—a style which would be rediscovered, a century later, and copied by home builders all over the Nation. Previously the Mexican and Spanish adobes of Monterey had been long, severely rectangular, one story in height, with roofs of thatch or tile sloping two ways. Larkin, whose tastes in architecture had been formed in his native New England, built a two-story home of adobe, square with a four-way sloping roof and a balcony and veranda that were typical of Cape Cod architecture. The combination of the Spanish and New England styles so impressed his neighbors that Montereños who could afford it began building two-story homes with balconies and verandas. The four-way roof they could not copy and it is said they held excited meetings to evolve a solution to this problem. Since the balconies and verandas, necessarily, were built of wood, the demand for timber gave rise to a lumber industry in this area.

The Larkin House, owned today by Larkin's granddaughter, presents much the same appearance as it did when it was built. It is a two-story adobe, now coated with brown plaster, with a shingled roof and balcony covered with climbing roses rising above a veranda. The southern section of its garden wall is of the original adobe; the gates are modern. The windows, with small panes of glass, 8 by 10 inches, containing many flaws, are set flush with the adobe walls.

Thomas Oliver Larkin came to California from Boston about 1832 to join his half-brother, Captain John Cooper. He intended to manufacture flour, but remained instead to open California's first retail and wholesale store. His hard work, tact, popularity, and intelligence made him the most influential American in Alta California. He built Monterey's first wharf, established the first non-military hospital, brought first American woman to live in Monterey, and became the father of the first Yankee child born in the capital. Having acquired a large amount of property through his thriving mercantile trade, he became the first United States Consul in California, 1843-1846. Because of this official position, his home, which served as a store and office as well as a residence, naturally became the headquarters for Americans. Apparently his countrymen recognized his shrewd business ability, for there are many letters among his papers asking his advice or giving him power-of-attorney in business deals. In 1846 Larkin was captured by the Mexican forces just before the battle of Natividad and was held as hostage for some weeks; but he was kindly treated, for his influence and popularity were well known throughout the State. The house remained Larkin's home until 1849, when he exchanged it for the San Francisco property of Jacob P. Leese, another prominent merchant, who had been his partner for a while.

17. Monterey's civic center, FRIENDLY PLAZA, facing Pacific St. between Jefferson and Madison Sts., is a one-acre terraced plot of lawn, shrubs, and flowers, edged by stone walls and intersected by brick paths. Its heart is a round brick-paved court surrounding a venerable black walnut tree, under whose spreading leaves benches are placed. The plan for the park, one of three submitted at the request of the Park and Playground Commission, was drawn up by a group of Monterey artists and accepted by the City Council October 7, 1930. In imitation of early Spanish gardens, native California shrubs and flowers have been planted in preference to exotic flora.

18. COLTON HALL *(open weekdays 9-5)*, Friendly Plaza, is an imposing building of severe appearance whose two-story stone

facade seems prim and disapproving beside the native adobes. Built by the Reverend Walter Colton in 1847-49, this bit of New England undoubtedly afforded him some satisfaction during those frequent times when he became homesick. Colton came to California in 1846 as chaplain of the *Congress*. For three years after his appointment, July 28, 1846, he served as Monterey's first American *alcalde,* his position having been confirmed by popular vote on September 15, a fact which satisfied his sense of democracy. Colton never thoroughly approved of the gayety and lightness of the Californians, nor of their drinking and gambling, their indifference to the church, and their laziness in things commercial. His responsibilities as *alcalde* weighed so heavily upon his conscience, however, that he tried at all times to be unbiased in his decisions. He started the first newspaper in California and presided at the first jury trial in the State *(see THE PENINSULA THROUGH FOUR CENTURIES).*

Colton saw the need of a building to house a school and assembly hall. With Yankee shrewdness he looked for means to raise the necessary funds. In his journal, under the date of March 8, 1849, he wrote: "The town hall, on which I have been at work for more than a year, is at last finished. It is built of white stone quarried from a neighboring hill, and which easily takes the shape you desire. The lower apartments are for schools; the hall over them—seventy feet by thirty—is for public assemblies. The front is ornamented with a portico, which you enter from the hall. It is not an edifice that would attract any attention among public buildings in the United States, but in California it is without a rival. It has been erected out of the slender proceeds of town lots and labor of convicts, taxes on liquor shops, and fines on gamblers. The scheme was regarded with incredulity by many; but the building is finished, and the citizens have assembled in it, and christened it after my name, which will go down to posterity with the odor of gamblers, convicts, and tipplers."

Completed in the spring of 1849, the building served as meeting place for the Constitutional Convention held from September 1 to October 15 of that year. Among the 48 delegates were such men of note as John A. Sutter, H. W. Halleck, Thomas O. Larkin, Stephen C. Foster, Abel Stearns, Mariano G. Vallejo, José A. Carrillo, and Robert Semple. The constitution was signed by the delegates on October 13, 1849 *(see THE PENINSULA THROUGH FOUR CENTURIES).*

For more than two decades thereafter the building was used as a school and as the seat of Monterey County. Tradition states that school was dismissed when there was a prisoner to execute because the porch of Colton Hall made a handy scaffold.

Except for the addition of two elaborate stairways, the partitioning of the second floor into rooms, and the plastering of the building inside and out, Colton Hall remains unchanged. Owned by the City of Monterey, it houses the Police Department and Municipal Court.

19. The one-story MONTEREY JAIL, Friendly Plaza N. of the City Hall, its native-rock walls broken by deep-set barred windows, was erected in 1854 to replace the adobe jail built by *Alcalde* Colton in 1847. Notable prisoners here were Tiburcio Vásquez, young American-hating bandit *(see No. 21)*, and Anastacio García, participant in the locally famous Roach-Belcher vendetta *(see Nos. 44 and 56)*. Wanted for killing two Montereños, Garcia opened fire upon a posse that had come to arrest him and killed three of its members, one of whom was José de la Torre, member of an influential Monterey family. When the furor had quieted, García came from his hiding place in the hills, was captured and jailed. During the night a group of friends forced the the jail and asked García to leave with them. García was delighted, but his pleasure was brief: before he had realized the import of the visit his "friends" had hanged him from the jail rafters. It was assumed that he knew too much. The sheriff's record of the event says simply: "Anastacio García, went to God on a rope."

20. The modern, L-shaped FEW MEMORIAL CITY HALL, S. end of Friendly Plaza, was designed by Ryland Raiguel and built in 1934, with funds left by Agatha Few, as a memorial to her husband, Charles R. Few, a prominent Monterey citizen. A one- and two-story building, it houses the Council Chamber in its two-story northern wing. A colonnade runs its length, leading to a patio paved with red bricks and terraced with patches of brilliant flowers.

The City Hall incorporates in the foot of its "L" the one-story BROWN-UNDERWOOD ADOBE, the older portion of which was constructed in 1843 by *Alcalde* Santiago (James) Stokes. The *alcalde* sold the property in the same year to José María Sánchez, conducting the latter through the building while he pounded walls, opened and closed doors, and performed similar ceremonies indicating ownership.

The adobe changed hands three times more—once belonging to Charles Underwood—before it was purchased by the City in 1934 and remodeled with money bequeathed for that purpose by a wealthy citizen. Trim and white, its full-length veranda faces the broad green lawn of Friendly Plaza.

21. The stuccoed CASA VASQUEZ *(private)*, 546 Dutra St., is only half an adobe, for its upper story is entirely of wood. Its yard, extending in front of and along the east side of the house, is overgrown with trees and shrubs—a small wilderness of flowers, greenery, and weeds. The sidewalk in front of the property is separated from the yard by a fence; from the street, by a shoulder-high wall of cement made to resemble adobe. Originally a one-story house protected by a portico facing east, it was the typical unpretentious home of Dolores Vásquez, sister of Tiburcio Vásquez, notorious bandit of the 1870's and godson of the county's first sheriff.

Fate put the Vásquez home directly in back of the jail—and the bandit knew both places well. Through all the years of his forced travels he had many friends in Monterey and more than once spent the night at home while the sheriff was searching for him in other parts of the county.

An intesely emotional person, young Vásquez hated the Americans bitterly—for he had been raised in the era of political change, being constantly torn with the suspicion and hatred aroused by the inevitability of the conquest. His escapades were often amusing, for he possessed the courtesy and sly humor of the Mexican combined with a good sense of drama. Like most bandits of his day he was a Robin Hood to his countrymen and a menace to Americans. Ironically, his downfall was occasioned by his honesty. He had been arrested and taken to San Jose for trial on the charge of murder. He denied all accusations, and was near acquittal—for no one could furnish positive identification of him. Then a young clerk named McPhail appeared at the trial. He had been stopped by Vásquez' gang at the scene of the murder, and Váquez had refused to take his watch from him. McPhail saw the bandit in the prison yard, said "Hello, Vásquez!"—and the latter, taken off guard, smiled and answered, "Hello, young fellow. A fine watch you had . . . I have often regretted that I did not take it." He was hanged on March 19, 1875.

22. The facade of its century-old adobe walls sheathed with cream-colored clapboards, the CASA ALVARADO *(private)*, SW. cor. Dutra and Jefferson Sts., has acquired a full-length front veranda of red brick since its erection in 1836. The windows, which once looked out on a garden large as a city block, retain the shutters of other days. Residence of Don Juan Bautista Alvarado during his

term as governor (1836-1842), the house was the scene of prolonged festivities when in 1839 this Monterey-born *politico* and direct descendant of *conquistador* Hernando Cortés brought home his bride, Martina Castro of San Pablo. Stormy politics had kept him so busy that he had been obliged to marry Martina by proxy in Santa Clara.

Alvarado's troubles were the result of defections among his accomplices, José Castro and Isaac Graham's contingent of Americans, who had aided his successful revolt against Governor Gutiérrez in 1836. Castro he managed to defeat in an election, and the most active of the Grahamites he deported to Mexico. The international incident these deportations precipitated had not blown over before the governor's position was beset by the rival claim of Carlos Carrillo. This opponent was silenced in 1838 when the Mexican government finally confirmed Alvarado's election, and he ruled without resistance until displaced by Manuel Micheltorena in 1842.

Domestic difficulties also harrassed Alvarado. His cook, one *"Señor* Professor" Raoul, an excitable Frenchman whom he prized as the best chef in all California, was given to fits of temperament and tantrums which frightened the servants and were a strain on the governor's patience. Awakened one morning by wild sounds from the garden, Alvarado rushed out to find the gibbering Raoul pointing an unsteady finger at the flagpole denoting the governor's residence: a polished human skull, gleaming in the sun, was tied atop the pole. Ignoring the apologies of his employer, the *"Señor* Professor" packed his belongings and fled. Alvarado ascribed the presence of the skull to grave-robbing Mexican political enemies. Such sacrilege, he stated, was a crime "too monstrous for a native Californian."

At the conclusion of his term of office in 1842, Alvarado sold his house to Portuguese trader Manuel Dutra de Vargas, (the ex-governor's secretary in later years), who acquired the place, "consisting of a three-room house and tule roof, for the sum of 300 silver dollars." Dutra in 1851 operated a general store in one end of the premises. From about 1862 until 1874 the house was occupied by County Clerk W. M. R. Parker, who performed many marriage ceremonies there. Since 1934 the old adobe has been the home of Manuel Dutra's grandson and his family. The interior contains a fireplace designed and built by Walter Colton before local politics caused him to desert a mason's trowel for an *alcalde's* gavel. When in 1925 the roof was repaired, workers found old wooden pegs and rawhide thongs so well preserved that they again were used. The clapboards covering the front wall had become necessary at an earlier date: tourists had weakened the structure by digging out such relics as baby's shoes and bits of pottery, mixed as binder material into the adobe bricks by the original builders.

23. Lumber for the GORDON HOUSE *(private)*, 527 Pierce St., was milled in Australia, shipped to England, and reshipped around the Horn to Monterey. A plain frame house, it was built in 1849-50 by Philip Roach, last *alcalde* and first mayor of Monterey. It was one of the first all-wooden houses to be built in California, and although its owner did not trust California adobe as a building material, its design follows the simple line and pattern of the adobes.

Roach sold the house in 1850 to William Johnson, *síndico* (recorder) to the *ayuntamiento* (city council). Not until 1871 did it come into the hands of Samuel Gordon, its occupant for three decades. It has changed hands six times since.

24. In 1858 the land occupied by the one-story DE LA TORRE ADOBE *(private)*, 502 Pierce St., was valued at $7.50, and the house itself at $150. Francisco Pinto had built the adobe about 1852, on land granted him two years earlier by *Alcalde* Philip Roach. The property was sold, mortgaged, and resold—once for $7.50 back taxes!—homesteaded by José de la Torre, deeded twice as a gift, and sold several times again before it came into the possession of its present resident, local artist Myron Oliver. Its original three rooms have been augmented by the addition of several frame leantos. Otherwise unchanged, the charming, white-painted, red-roofed building is partially hidden by flowers and shrubs.

25. Long, sweeping branches of a tall cypress shade the CASA JESUS SOTO *(private)*, 460 Pierce St. This one-story building with its small deep-set windows, a fine example of early Monterey architecture, is believed to have been built in 1842 by Francisco Soberanes. Remodeled by its present owner in 1931, it retains its original lines, illustrating the feeling for simplicity and beauty possessed by the early builders.

Later the adobe was acquired by Jesus Soto, and later still by Tony Dutra. Dutra, who found it would cost much to modernize and repair it, allowed it to stand vacant, to be occupied occasionally by drifters and thieves. In time it became known as "haunted" and as "The Bandit House."

26. The CASA SERRANO *(restaurant)*, 412 Pacific St., is a good example of the story-and-a-half type of adobe. Its upper floor is a loft reached by an outside stair at the north end of the building.

Its builder, Florencio Serrano, arrived in Monterey with the Híjar colonists in 1834, became a teacher, a clerk, a secretary of the *ayuntamiento*, secretary to the prefect, and finally *alcalde*, succeeding Walter Colton to the last office in 1848.

27. The PRESBYTERIAN CHURCH, NW. cor Franklin and Pacific Sts., has the date of 1849 on its capstone. David Jacks, who arrived in Monterey in 1850, started a Sunday School here. The children used to rush from their catechism at the Catholic Royal Presidio Chapel to Jacks' Scottish Presbyterian Sunday School every week because he gave each of them a nickel for attending. The church property with its manse is at present valued in excess of $50,000; the membership consists of approximately 120 persons.

28. The ST. JAMES EPISCOPAL CHURCH, near NW. cor. Franklin and Pacific Sts., was organized in 1854 with Bishop William Kip conducting services at Colton Hall. There were 60 present. The lack of an Episcopalian house of worship in Monterey led to the building of the present structure in 1876 by Reverend J. S. McGowan, who previously had held services in a dance hall of the Washington Hotel. Records refer to "several prominent people from British ships who worshipped at St. James, among them Princess Louise of England." When news came of Queen Victoria's death in 1901, the church was draped in royal purple; a memorial service was held, the crew of several ships being present. The bishop and deacons of the diocese have contemplated the sale of the church building in recent years, since the majority of the communicants now attend St.-Mary's-by-the-Sea in Pacific Grove.

29. The first convent school in California stood on the SITE OF ST. CATHERINE'S ACADEMY, 327 Calle Principal (designated by a marker), housed in a two-story adobe building erected as a hotel in 1850 by Don Manuel Jimeno, Secretary of State under Governors Alvarado and Micheltorena, 1839-45.

St. Catherine's Academy was opened, through the efforts of Bishop Joseph Alemany, by three nuns: Mary Goenare, Mary Francis Stafford, and Mary Aloysia O'Neal, who came to California by way of Panama, arriving in December, 1850. On January 1, they opened their school in the Hartnell residence under the spiritual care of St. Catherine of Sienna with eight pupils. Before long the school had outgrown its quarters and the church purchased Jimeno's hotel. Here they had room for the 150 pupils who came from all over California to study reading, writing, grammar, mathematics, French, English, Spanish, music, art, and needlework. Here, too, Concepción

Argüello took the veil, becoming the first novice of the Dominican Order in California. Superior training offered at the convent was generally recognized; it ranked as a leading educational institution. The fee was $400 for tuition, room, and board.

When the convent was moved to Benicia in 1854, the lower floor of the building was converted into a chapel; the upper, into a banquet hall. Later virtually abandoned, the building became a tenement and shelter for wandering Indians. Charles Warren Stoddard wrote in 1885: "I saw the old convent windowless, its halls half filled with hay. The roof had fallen in . . . it was a pitiful sight." In 1888 Father Angelo Casanova ordered the adobe structure wrecked.

30. So grotesquely rebuilt that it bears slight resemblance to its former self, the CASA RODRIQUES-OSIO, 380 Alvarado St., houses a restaurant and clothing shop on its ground floor, an office and residence in its second story. Of the original two-story adobe with an overhanging balcony, little, if anything, was salvaged from ruin. According to the usually accepted legend, it was built in 1819 by Don Jacinto Roríguez, successively lieutenant and *alferez* in the army, *celador* of the Customs House (1843-46), and delegate to the first Constitutional Convention (1849), and later acquired by Don Antonio María Osio, twice customs administrator (1828-30 and 1838-42). Since Rodríguez was but four years old in 1819, however, it is more probable that the house was built by Osio himself in 1838, and later acquired by Rodríguez, as another version of its origin relates. During the Constitutional Convention, it is said that Rodríguez practiced his speeches on the shore, delivering himself with such enthusiasm and grandiloquence that the boys would hide in the brush to listen. The house was a center of gayety for the delegates, who enjoyed themselves at parties and dances night and day. The last night of the convention was celebrated here so successfully that some of the delegates could not tear themselves away. The constitution was therefore brought to them to be signed with guests at the party as witnesses.

31. Built sometime in the 1860's by Monterey County's first American judge, Josiah Merrit, the MERRIT HOUSE *(private)*, Pacific St. between Franklin and Soberanes Sts., is a well-preserved two-story adobe with a balcony, standing in a formal garden. Like many another of Monterey's adobe relics, its construction has been erroneously ascribed to a man already long dead when it was built —Don Ignacio Vallejo, father of 13 children (of whom the most famous was Mariano Guadalupe), deceased at the age of 83 in 1831.

Merrit, who married a judge's daughter, Juana Castro, soon after his arrival at Monterey in January, 1850, helped organize Monterey County, of which he served as county judge until 1854.

32. A small blue wooden gate in a tall cypress hedge opens onto a fine old garden before the restored CASA SOBERANES *(private)*, 314 Pacific St., known as "The House of the Blue Gate." The two-story hillside adobe was erected by Don José Estrada, ranking officer of the presidio during the Mexican regime, and later sold by him to Don Feliciano Soberanes, son-in-law of Don Ignacio Vallejo. The house became headquarters for the Vallejo clan on its frequent visits to Monterey, and has been called the Vallejo Adobe.

33. Martin Doud built the old frame HENRY HOUSE *(private)*, 302 Pacific St., about 1880, lived there for several years with his family, and moved elsewhere. In the early nineties Charles D. Henry, who had come to Monterey from Iowa with his wife and two daughers, made his home here. And it was in this old house, on February 10, 1899, that his daughter Lou married the young engineer recently graduated from Stanford University, Herbert C. Hoover, destined to become President of the United States 29 years later. Soon after the marriage the Henrys moved from the house to a new home they erected in the Doud Tract in the southern end of the city.

34. California's FIRST THEATER *(open 10-12, 1-5; free)*, SW. cor. Pacific and Scott Sts ., is a long, one-story adobe-and-wood building, painted white except for its tree-shaded, ivy-covered western end, which is broken by a huge brick fireplace. Built in 1846-47 by English sailor Jack Swan as a seamen's saloon and boarding-house, it was in the fall of 1847 the scene of what was probably the first minstrel show on the Pacific Coast, given by three Montereyans and four Army volunteers. Shortly afterward several members of Colonel J. D. Stevenson's disbanded regiment persuaded Swan—whose profitable saloon was emptied by *Alcalde* Colton's prohibition laws—to convert part of his "House that Jack Built" into a theater. A stage was built in one end of the dining hall and separated from the rest of the room by a wooden partition which served as a curtain. This "curtain" was lifted from the bottom like the lid of a box and hooked to the ceiling. Candles and whale-oil lamps were used for footlights. Posters made by hand with blacking-pot and brush announced the first performance: *Putnam: or the Lion Son of '76*. Seats sold for $5 each and the house was packed.

Eventually new houses put the first theater out of business. By

1874 it again was a boarding house. Finally it was abandoned and allowed to fall into ruin until 1909, when it was purchased by a group of historically minded persons and deeded to the State for a museum. In 1937 it was reopened with a performance of *Tatters: Pet of Squatters Gulch*. The Denny-Watrous players—"Troupers of the Gold Coast"—comprising local talent from all walks of life, now stage regular performances in the First Theater that are extremely popular.

The interior of the theater is extremely plain. The wooden benches, which accommodate about 150 persons, are built progressively taller toward the rear of the room because the floor is level. The building's northern end becomes a barroom on play nights. Here too are relics of early theater life, including old programs, some Indian relics, and examples of primitive art.

35. Of extremely simple architecture, the well-preserved, two-story CASA DE ORO (House of Gold), 200 Olivier St., today a State Monument, is built partly of chalk-rock and partly of adobe. It was erected prior to 1846 on orders from General Manuel Castro, probably as a barracks for his men. Lieutenant William T. Sherman quartered some of his troops here during the American occupation in 1846-47.

The name "Casa de Oro" is accounted for by several stories. It is said that in 1851 the premises were occupied by a store where miners deposited their gold for safekeeping; that it was a saloon where customers paid for their drinks in gold dust; that it was a clearing house for gold brought from the mines; that it was once known locally as the "mint" and began to solicit funds for carrying on the war. Francisco García, an employee of the Custom House, placed all of his gold at the disposal of the government, and for his generous act was declared exempt from taxation forever. After 1855 the property was purchased by David Jacks, whose heirs deeded it in 1939 to the State.

36. An old-fashioned frame house is CASA VERDE *(private)*, Olivier and Decatur Sts., where Charles Warren Stoddard lived and wrote many of his California stories and poems. The author is buried in the old Catholic cemetery near El Estero *(see No. 44)*.

37. A Virginian, Gallant Duncan Dickinson, who brought his wife and six children overland with the tragic Donner Party in 1846, lived with his family in the FIRST BRICK HOUSE IN CALIFORNIA *(restaurant)*, 351 Decatur St. On a 90-yard strip of land which cost him $29 in 1848 Dickinson had the boxlike, gable-roofed little

CALIFORNIA'S FIRST THEATER—BAR ROOM

OLD PACIFIC BUILDING

OLD PACIFIC BUILDING, VERANDA

LTON HALL

ROYAL PRESIDIO CHAPEL

CHAPEL DOORWAY

CASA DE SOTO

ADOBE WA

building built as the wing of his home—but he left for the gold fields in 1849 and never returned to complete the house. Actual construction on the building was done by Dickinson's son-in-law, A. G. Lawrie, a brickmason who moulded and fired the bricks as well as laid them.

Originally the house held six rooms—three on each floor, the lower three dirt-floored. Of red brick, unpainted, it stands in a tiny yard overrrun with flowers, shrubs, and trees, enclosed by a green wire fence. Its front door and the door in the small balcony above are painted a bright blue.

38. Built in 1855, the gleaming white-painted two-story adobe OLD WHALING STATION *(private)*, 391 Decatur St., was originally a boarding house for the Portuguese whalers of the "Old Company," organized in the same year. Now trim and well kept, it has a balcony facing the street which was added during restoration in 1903. The extensive garden is bordered by a tile-topped adobe wall extending for nearly half a block, high enough to hide all but the tops of the trees. The company's signboard and many of its harpoons are preserved by the building's owner.

In a chapter on whale fishing, "which for the last 25 years has constituted one of the most important of our local industries," *The Handbook of Monterey and Vicinity* (1875) stated: "It was for the purpose of catching the Humpbacks, known to be numerous in this bay, that the Monterey Whaling Company was organized in 1854. In the fall of that year, Capt. J. P. Davenport, an old and experienced whaler, got together a company of 12 men. . . . They had two boats, and met with pretty good success, as the whales were tame and easily caught in the old fashioned manner with harpoons and lances . . . The price of oil falling to 25 cents per gallon, the company was disbanded. . . .

"The whales however were not allowed to rest, for in 1855 the company of Portuguese known as the 'Old Company' was organized with 17 men and 2 boats. Although at first they used no guns, they succeeded in taking about 800 barrels of Humpback oil annually for about three years . . . In . . . 1858 . . . Capt. Davenport again started in with two boats well manned and equipped with bomb and harpoon guns. Both companies whaled in the bay . . . getting from 600 to 1,000 barrels annually per company . . . In 1861 the Carmel Company was organized . . . [and] in the spring of 1862 they moved to the present station on Carmel Bay."

Explaining the "means of capturing these marine monsters," *The*

Handbook of Monterey and Vicinity described the whalers proceeding at the first streak of dawn in their boats, six men to a boat, to the whaling ground off Point Pinos where they lay on their oars, waiting. "Suddenly some one sees the wished for column of mist foam, and cries out, 'There she blows—' Then . . . the boat is headed for the whale and the guns made ready to fire. When within a short distance of the animal the oars are 'peaked,' and the boat is propelled by paddles so as not to disturb the wary whale. Having arrived within shooting distance, which is about 40 yards, the harpoon, connected with a long line, is fired . . . Down goes the whale, the line with a turn around the 'loggerhead' of the boat being allowed to run out for several hundred yards, when it held fast. The whale generally makes a direct course for the open ocean, dragging the boat . . . Soon however it becomes weary and comes to the surface to breathe; now . . . the boat approaches as near as possible and a bomb lance is fired. In case this enters a vital part the animal dies instantly, but oftener . . . the same maneuvering as before is repeated until 2 or 3 bombs have been shot before the animal is killed. It is then towed to the two works, where the blubber is removed, cut into small pieces and boiled out."

During the year when the "Old Company" began operations, the whaling fleet operating between the California coast and the Sandwich (Hawaiian) Islands numbered 500 vessels, and it later grew to 640. The Monterey whalers, who produced as much as 1,500 barrels of whale oil in one year, hunted chiefly two species—the humpback and the California gray, each of which usually yielded from 25 to 40 barrels—the former being caught between mid-August and December; the latter, between December and April. It was not uncommon in those days to see on the streets of Monterey the tattooed South Sea Islanders in native dress who were used aboard the whaling vessels as harpooners—men greatly admired for their independence of spirit by the local Indians, who invented legends about them. The industry was short-lived, however; the two Monterey companies— "New" and "Old"—were merged into one, numbering 23 men, at the close of 1873. Four years later the entire Pacific Coast fleet had declined to 40 vessels.

39. The PRESIDIO OF MONTEREY, foot of Pacific St., occupies a 360-acre military reservation extending back from the Bay shore into pine-clad hills lying between the old and new residential sections of Monterey. Removed in 1902 from its original location on the site of the old Spanish presidio *(see No. 50)* about a mile south-

ward, the post in its modern form represents nearly 40 years of improvement upon Spanish, Mexican, and early American fortifications. With the Presidio of San Francisco, founded in 1776, it is one of two Army posts to retain original Spanish names; and the Presidio of Monterey is the older of the two.

Since August 15, 1940, this 170-year-old post has been United States Army headquarters for the Fort Ord Area embracing the Presidio, Fort Ord (Clayton), eight miles north of Monterey, and Camp Ord, five miles east of Fort Ord. It was headquarters for Lieutenant General John L. DeWitt, commander of the Fourth Army (troops of the Third and Ninth Corps Areas and Ninth Coast Artillery District). Here are stationed the Eleventh United States Cavalry, and the Second Battalion of the Seventy-sixth Field Artillery, normally comprising a total of about 60 officers and some 1,200 enlisted men. The Eleventh Cavalry, which served with distinction in the 1915 punitive expedition against Pancho Villa in Mexico, is the only equestrian troop in the Army; until recent motorization the Seventy-sixth was one of the Nation's few field artillery units with horse-drawn ordnance. The Presidio of Monterey, as headquarters of the 21,500-acre Ford Ord Area (which began preparing in the fall of 1940 to receive some 35,000 men, drafted under the Selective Service Act) is the largest military reservation in the United States. An additional 7,000 acres were leased for its use early in 1941.

The historic significance of the Presidio's present site antedates by more than three centuries its present military importance. Near the southeastern corner of the reservation landed, in 1602, Sebastián Vizcaíno and his crew and, 168 years later, Padre Junípero Serra. Although the founders of Monterey chose another location for their presidio, the present site once more achieved prominence in 1818 when an improvised battery there vainly attempted to repel the attack of Hippolyte de Bouchard's crew of pirates, disguised as Argentine insurgents, who chased the defenders of Monterey inland and sacked the town. The earthworks thrown up for this occasion continued in later years to be known as El Castillo (The Fort); they were replaced by more reliable fortifications following American occupation.

Soon after Commodore John D. Sloat, on July 7, 1846, captured Monterey, construction was begun on a battery of barracks about 20 yards south of El Castillo, on a hill overlooking the Bay of Monterey. First named Fort Mervine in honor of its original commander, the post subsequently was known as Fort Stockton, and finally, until incorporated in the Presidio, as Fort Halleck. Fort Mervine, like the old Spanish presidio, had long been abandoned and almost forgotten when in 1902 the Army selected its site for the construction of barracks to house troops returning from service in the Spanish-American War.

The reservation's subsequent development has made the restored Presidio of Monterey one of the most modern and attractive of the Nation's major Army posts. On its heights, commanding fine views of the Bay, winding roads lead to a combination parade ground and stadium with concrete bleachers and parking space, a motion picture theater, a recreation hall, a swimming pool, tennis courts, and an excellent polo field. Here too are the administration building, hospital, supply depots, officers' homes and club, enlisted men's barracks, and other buildings. Its historic sites and monuments form links between the Presidio's aspect of modernity and its rich heritage.

The VIZCAINO-SERRA LANDING PLACE, near the Main Gate, is marked by a granite Celtic cross in the center of which an effigy of Serra stands clasping a palm above a replica of Mission San Carlos Borromeo. The monument, erected in 1896 or 1897, was the gift of J. D. Murray. (A portion of the oak tree which once stood here, and beneath which Father Serra first celebrated mass on the Peninsula in 1770, is at the Royal Presidio Chapel in Monterey.) The nearby SERRA MONUMENT, on a hill north of the Main Gate, consists of a life-size statue of Serra standing in a boat. Erected in 1901, the monument was the gift of Jane L. Stanford, wife of former Governor and United States Senator Leland Stanford.

The SITE OF EL CASTILLO, north of the Serra Monument, is indicated by a marker. From the *castillo* was fired the only shot in the Castro-Alvarado revolt against Governor Gutiérrez in 1836. Its dugout calaboose, used by the Mexicans for confinement of outlaws, continued to serve American authorities for some years after 1846 as a jail for the sobering-up of inebriate Montereños.

On a hill east of Main Gate is the SITE OF FORT MERVINE. Of the United States troops who occupied the fort following capture of Monterey in 1846, General W. T. Sherman wrote in his memoirs: "The company of artillery was . . . on the hill under command of Lieutenant Ord, engaged in building a fort whereupon to mount the guns we had brought in the *Lexington,* also in constructing quarters out of hewn pine logs for the men." Building of the earthworks and blockhouse, here described, was completed about 1847 by Company F, Third Artillery, and some of Colonel J. D. Stevenson's regiment of New York Volunteers under Lieutenants Ord, Sherman, and Halleck. First named for Captain William Mervine, a member of Commodore Sloat's command, who initiated its construction, the fort was dismantled in 1852. During the Civil War two log huts built here were occupied by two companies of infantry, but these primitive barracks were removed after the war when the troops were withdrawn, and Fort Mervine as never rebuilt.

The nearby COMMODORE SLOAT MONUMENT, north of Fort Mervine's site, is a memorial to the commander of United States Naval forces which on July 7, 1846, initiated the conquest of California by running up the American flag over the Custom House in Monterey. The 11-foot bronze statue, representing the commander standing beside a capstan on the quarter-deck of his flagship, the *Savannah*, was erected on its 13-foot stone pedestal by the Grand Lodge of Masons of California on July 7, 1896.

40. Jutting out into the bay from the curving sandy shore in front of the old Custom House is FISHERMAN'S WHARF. The pier is roughly in the shape of a lopsided H, its eastern arm a little shorter than its western one. The restaurants, landings, supply shops, and warehouses that line its sides are weathered to a soft grey. Spoken Portuguese, Italian, and Japanese blur into a medley of foreign sounds. There is always excitement, a waving of arms, a shuffling of booted feet.

Brightly painted little motorboats dart around heavy purse seiners, and brass-trimmed pleasure boats ride at anchor, sandwiched in between prosaic fishing craft and excursion launches for deep-sea fishing. Brawny-armed Italian fishermen row their heavy dories, standing, just as they did in their native land; and once each year they bring the lovely figure of their patron Santa Rosalia from its niche in San Carlos Church to bless the fleet.

When the fish are running, the fishermen work long hours. The wharf is a confusion of men shouting and the smell of fish is strong in the air. Largest boats in the harbor are the Diesel-powered purse seiners, carrying a crew averaging 12 men per boat, which bring in sardines for the local canneries. The crew of each boat participates in the earnings on the basis of a share of the catch. Nets used—the purse seines—made of linen, are more than a mile in length and cost thousands of dollars. The smaller boats used by the market fishermen, usually gasoline-powered, vary in length from 25 to 40 feet, the larger ones operated by two or three men; the smaller, by a single fisherman. They bring in albacore, a white-fleshed tuna used almost exclusively for canning which commands a high price on the market, and shark, the liver of which now is in extensive demand because of its high vitamin content. During the albacore season, which begins the latter part of August, boats come from San Francisco and as far south as San Pedro to participate in the catch. When fish are not running, the bay near the wharf is a jumble of brightly painted boats and bobbing masts and most of the fishermen spend their time repairing boats and nets.

In some of the warehouses oriental girls pound abalone steaks to make them tender and ready for shipment. The late Pop Ernest, whose restaurant, now operated by his son, stands at the end of the pier, is credited with spreading the popularity of the abalone as an addition to the modern menu. His fame spread over the State and the demand for his abalone steaks was almost larger than the supply. Pop helped to pass the State laws limiting catches, closing the season during the breeding period, and forbidding the exportation of this shellfish beyond the boundaries of California.

The first wharf at this site was built in 1845 by Thomas O. Larkin; the second, by David Jacks and Company. The original pier, costing about $8,000, was constructed of stones quarried by military deserters, Indians, and civil prisoners. A Mexican citizen, Esteban de la Torre, furnished 1,500 cartloads of stone at $1 a load, and an early English settler, W. R. Garner, sold Larkin the piles for $4 each.

In 1870, when the growth of commerce necessitated enlargement of the municipal pier, the City of Monterey raised funds for the purpose by leasing it to individuals. A lease granted in 1916 allowed the F. E. Booth Company to build a fish cannery beside the wharf. (Notice has been given the Booth Company that the lease will not be renewed when it expires in 1941.)

41. Oldest public building on the Pacific Coast is the OLD CUSTOM HOUSE *(State Landmark; museum open 10-5 daily)*, Calle Principal at Decatur St., a long, one-story, tile-roofed, rock and adobe building flanked by two-story wings with balconies, facing east toward Monterey Bay. On sunny afternoons oldtimers swap tales in Italian and Mexican on the benches that line the long cement-paved veranda along the building's eastern, northern, and southern sides. The veranda overlooks a level, clean-swept garden of shrubs, trees, and paths partially enclosed by a stone wall.

It is generally believed that construction of the building's oldest part—a small, almost square structure, now the north wing—was undertaken in 1814, when Captain Don José Darío Argüello became *ad interim* governor following the death of Governor Don José Joaquín de Arillaga. Only a few years earlier, Boston trading ships had begun to call at the port, trading manufactured goods for hides and tallow. To collect duties—often as high as one-fourth the value of the cargo—and prevent smuggling, the Spanish government had stationed customs inspectors at Monterey and San Diego. But so infrequent were the arrivals of merchant ships during Spanish rule that the early history of the Custom House was uneventful, its serenity undisturbed except by the brief excitement attending the sacking of the town by the pirate Bouchard, who landed his forces on the beach in front of the building—therafter named La Playa de los Insurgentes (The Beach of the Insurgents).

Following establishment of the Mexican Empire in 1822, however, Spanish trade restrictions were lifted and California ports opened to foreign ships. Since the province was required to pay its governmental expenses out of customs duties under the new regime, the Custom House at Monterey—now declared chief port of entry—assumed a new importance.

The Custom House was probably enlarged in 1822 by addition of a wing extending southward from the original structure, com pleted in 1823. Whether this addition, when completed, was the 80-foot-long wing, built of stone and tile-roofed, with a veranda along its eastern side, which later composed the building's central portion, is unknown. In substantiation of the contention that it was not, an inventory drawn up by José María Herrera in 1827 has been cited. It merely lists "a new building near the new boat landing and consisting of two rooms, a large one that is being used as a storage room and for the convenience of the new corporal of the custom house guard and the other for the guard corps. It is constructed with a peaked roof of adobe and roofed with sheet metal and tile." Here the Boston merchants had their goods appraised—Yankee manufactured articles and Chinese silks—and paid their customs duties. Besides a tonnage charge, they paid a tax of 25 per cent on goods sold, after deducting 12.5 per cent. (The import tariff on goods brought by Mexican vessels was only 10 per cent.) Despite the high tariffs, the annual number of vessels calling at California ports increased from 9 in 1821 to 47 in 1825.

The arrivals of foreign ships were often celebrated in the big room of the Custom House by great balls, so well attended that the guests overflowed into the colonnade, where oriental lanterns were strung up. The story is told of one ball, greeted with excitement more intense than usual because everyone anticipated dancing the newly imported waltz. At the last moment came a message from Padre Vicente Sarría at Mission San Carlos Borromeo, threatening excommunication to any one who should be so evil as to perform this highly improper dance. Amid the general grumbling, Teresa de la Guerra, young bride of W. E. P. Hartnell, approached Governor José Argüello to ask: "Do you hold, Governor Argüello, that this waltzing is really sinful?" The governor, resplendent in a beautiful coat adorned with 24 gold filigree buttons, bowed over her hand as he replied: "The only sin I am conscious of is not being able to beg you for the honor of the dance, Señora Hartnell. Did I but know how to waltz, and were there music, and did I feel like waltzing, I should most certainly waltz!"

The government officials unfortunately found the customs revenue too attractive. By 1826 so many new duties had been imposed that they totalled 42.5 per cent of the cargo value. Trade fell off sharply. The traders resorted to smuggling. Meanwhile, since Monterey controlled the purse strings, it began to incur the jealousy of the southern Californians. The control of the customs became a major political issue. During the period of rising sectionalism and factionalism in the 1830's, changes in the personnel of the Monterey Custom House were frequent and drastic as one governor after another—and all his appointees along with him—was ousted from office.

The growing political turmoil of the period culminated, in 1836, in a rebellion against Governor Nicholás Gutiérrez, engineered by Juan Bautista Alvarado, customs appraiser, and Angel Ramirez, customs director, who picked a quarrel with Gutiérrez over the posting of Custom House guards. Joined by José Castro, they led an army—chiefly composed of deserting sailors, American trappers, and other foreigners—which captured the presidio November 5, 1836, and deposed the governor *(see THE PENINSULA THROUGH FOUR CENTURIES)*.

Having won the governorship, Alvarado appointed William Edward Petty Hartnell collector of revenues for the year 1836-37 and, after him, Antonio María Osio, who retained the office until 1842. Between 1836 and 1840, an average annual revenue of 70,000 *pesos* was collected from an average of 27 vessels which visited the coast each year. Osio, with the aid of deputy treasurer José Abrego, increased the revenues by improvements in management and accounting. The unsuccessful attempt of Mariano Guadalupe Valleje to remove the customs post to San Francisco in 1841, however, disrupted everything (it also embroiled Vallejo and Alvarado in a controversy which led to removal of both from office). And when the new governor, Manuel Micheltorena, took office, Osio lost his job.

Enterprising Thomas O. Larkin contracted with the Mexican government in 1841 to rebuild the Custom House. In his estimate he gave the total cost as 2,300 *pesos*, which was to be paid one-half in coin in advance and one-half in merchandise from the first three ships required to pay duty. In the course of reconstruction, which continued through 1842, it is probable that the central portion was extended, a second story added to the north wing, and a portico built facing the sea. In later years additional construction was undertaken: Larkin's account book shows, under the date of December 23, 1844, a contract for $1,800 for building the south end and, under the date of March, 1846, another for building a smaller room. According to some authorities, Larkin's additions marked the building's final completion; according to others, a replica of the north wing was built at the south end and the central wing partitioned following the American occupation in 1846.

Trade went on as usual. Though required by law to call first at Monterey to clear their cargo, most skippers found some reason to visit another port first. The customs guards usually could be bribed not to notice that goods were being smuggled ashore duty free. Customs receipts fell perhaps 25 per cent below what they should have been.

The feud between northern and southern Californians over disposal of the revenues burst out again toward the end of 1844. When Pío Pico became governor in February, 1845, he appointed Juan Bautista Alvarado administrator of the customs. The returns for 1845 amounted to 145,000 *pesos* paid by 60 vessels. They promised to be even better in 1846: more than 30 vessels had arrived by the end of June. The governor, however, was quarreling with General José Castro over revenues. The arrival of American warships, one by one, in California ports seems not to have disturbed him until it was too late.

At ten o'clock Tuesday morning, July 7, 1846, 250 American marines and seamen landed on the beach from Commodore John D. Sloat's flagship, the *Savannah*. Since the Custom House was the only public building in good condition, they lined up in a square at its north end, hoisted the American flag over it while a 21-gun salute was fired, and listened to the reading in English and in Spanish of Sloat's proclamation. The Custom House was then garrisoned.

The first newspaper in the State, *The Californian,* issued on cigar-wrapping paper, was printed on August 15, 1846, on an archiac, discarded press set up in the Custom House. The north end of the building was occupied by Lieutenant William T. Sherman in the following year. For three months during that year the south end was used as a hospital.

Although the building began serving in its former function again in 1847, during which year $25,000 was collected from 67 vessels, it soon declined in importance because all other California ports were opened.

When gold was discovered, the branch custom house at San Francisco became the main port of entry. The Monterey Custom House was maintained, although it soon collected less in duties than was required to pay its officials, until orders came from Washington in 1868 to close it. Until the early 1890's it housed Captain William G. Lambert, appointed custodian, and his family, who took up housekeeping in the south wing, stabling the family cow in the big room. Finally the building was abandoned to fall into ruin.

At the turn of the century, the old landmark, abandoned and dilapidated, a rendezvous for the homeless, was rescued from complete decay by the Native Sons of the Golden West, who leased it from the Federal Government for $1 per year, transferred their lease to the State the following year, and secured passage of a bill by the State Legislature appropriating funds for its restoration. The appropriation of more money in 1917 made possible continuance of the work. On July 7, 1929, after presentation of a petition from Monterey assemblyman Ray Deyoe, Governor C. C. Young opened the landmark to the public. And on January 1 of the following year it was taken over by the Division of State Parks of the Department of Natural Resources, which undertook further restoration work.

The large central room now houses a museum containing jewelry, clothing, laces, china, firearms, and saddles used by early Montereños. It has early Monterey newspapers, score of rare photographs of the old town, and a photostatic copy of the signature page of the first State Constitution. Of particular note are timbers and fixtures from the *Natalie,* wrecked on the beach in 1833, which had carried Napoleon from Elba back to France in 1815, when it was the sloop-of-war *Inconstant.* On the second floor of the north wing is a Bohemian Club exhibit of manuscripts by George Sterling and Charles Warren Stoddard.

MONTEREY

42. James (Santiago) McKinley- in 1835 erected the two-story PACIFIC BUILDING, 200-22 Calle Principal, one of the largest adobes in Monterey, as a hotel and saloon, chiefly for seafaring men. A long, two-story structure with overhanging balconies in front and rear, it had behind it a bull-and-bear-fight arena—now the site of the adobe-walled MEMORY GARDEN where the City of Monterey annually celebrates its birthday with a fiesta. Around the lime-stone and chalk-rock walls enclosing the sunken pit congregated the Montereños who witnessed the last fight, staged here in the 1870's.

From a seamen's tavern of more or less ill fame, the building was converted about 1855—when McKinley sold it to David Jacks—into the residence of the Presbyterian minister (and in later years, according to one tale, into a Presbyterian church, when David Jacks led a rump faction out of the established congregation following a disagreement with some of the elders). Subsequently headquarters for the Salvation Army, the building became more and more dilapidated until owners, the heirs of David Jacks, finally were persuaded about 1923 to undertake its restoration. Its first floor was converted into an Army recreation center for Fort Ord soldiers in 1940.

Still owners of the Pacific Building are David Jacks' heirs, three sisters now resident in San Francisco, whose telephone directory lists them as "Jacks L M & V." To Monterey, where memories of David Jacks' prodigious land-acquiring exploits are not forgotten, they are known as "L., M., and V." In the tradition of David Jacks, they make occasional business visits—in a limousine of almost legendary length—to attend to the vast properties they inherited.

43. A splendid example of the one-story adobe with overhanging portico and handhewn shingles, the former FRENCH CONSULATE *(open)*, cor. Franklin St. and El Estero, now owned by the City of Monterey and used as Girl Scouts headquarters, was removed in 1931 from its original location at Fremont and Abrego Streets to its present site. During removal it was taken apart and reassembled, brick by brick, with such care that its authenticity was not impaired; missing parts were restored with bricks made from adobe on the site.

Erected about 1840, the adobe was the home and office, between 1845 and 1847, of Louis Gasquet, French consul, whose arrival on the *Primavera* in March, 1845, stirred up apprehension over supposed French designs on California. Installed here with a cellar elaborately stocked with rare vintages, Gasquet looked out after French interests, watching with alarm the growing control of the

Americans and repeatedly but vainly urging his home office to intervene. The Americans, uneasy at his presence, spread stories that he was plotting with James A. Forbes, British vice-consul, against the United States. When the American flag was raised over the Custom House in 1846, Gasquet resented the imposition of martial law, protesting the posting of a sentry near his house. The quarrel which followed led to his arrest and exile to San Juan Bautista. Gasquet's successor, J. A. Moerenhaut, fared as badly at the hands of Sloat, Stockton, and Frémont, all of whom refused to recognize the consular credentials because the French flag was not displayed over the consulate, though the name and coat-of-arms were in evidence.

44. The bodies of many of Monterey's great—and of some of its less respected—citizens lie in the CATHOLIC CEMETERY *(open)*, Fremont St. opposite Via Mirada, established here in 1832 by the fathers of nearby Royal Presidio Chapel. Oak-studded, grassy, and early surrounded by the quiet waters of El Estero, this is the third burial ground to be established in Monterey. The site of the first, adjoining the Presidio Chapel, had been chosen by Father Serra; the second, outside the north wall of the old presidio, was known as the Campo Santo de Monterey (burial ground of Monterey).

The present cemetery was surrounded by a wall, traces of which remain. Here lie Latin and Nordic side by side—Vallejos, Soberanes, Leeses, Merrits, McKinleys, and Abregos. The old tombstones are weatherworn, their names almost obliterated. The grave of Charles Warren Stoddard, American literary celebrity of the late nineteenth century, is shaded by a clump of oak trees.

Two graves—marked "Isaac Wall, Nov. 5, 1885" and "Thomas Williamson, murdered in Monterey County, Nov. 5, 1855"—recall Monterey's bitterest, bloodiest, and most destructive feud, the Roach-Belcher vendetta, in which at least 10 men met violent deaths. The feud grew out of the desire to possess the great landholdings of Concha Sánchez, whose husband, José María, was drowned in the Pájaro River on Christmas Eve, 1852. When the trunk containing the legal papers and deeds of her valuable ranch disappeared, Concha married an American lawyer, Thomas Gordon, to protect her interests. Gordon was drowned when the steamer *Jenny Lind* exploded before it reached San Francisco. In the meanwhile William Roach, sheriff of Monterey County, with Louis Belcher as bondsman, was made administrator of the estate. Avarice soon ended their friendship; and as the rift grew, factions began to gather about the two men. Concha hurriedly married another lawyer, one Dr. Sanford; but he met Roach's brother-in-law in Monterey, the two exchanged shots, and again Concha was a widow. Sanford's brother-in-law, Thomas Atwood, blew out his brains in the Washington Hotel. On November 5, 1855, Isaac Wall and Thomas Williamson left Monterey for San Luis Obispo, and rumor had it that their pack train contained papers of the estate. Their bodies were found beside a temporary camp on the Salinas River, both bearing fatal knife wounds. Suspicion pointed to Anastacio García, who was said to have been hired by William Roach. Three more men were murdered when the posse from Monterey tried to arrest García. The Washington Hotel became the scene of the next episode in the feud—Louis Belcher, while at the crowded bar, was shot down by an unseen assailant. He accused García.

Comparative quiet reigned for a time. Concha, ever hopeful, married another young lawyer, George Crane, a Virginian from the Stevenson Regiment. García was captured, finally, and "went to God on a rope." Roach, having grown older and a bit tired of all the fighting, retired to his ranch, from which he sallied only on occasional trips to the town saloon. Sometimes, when company and alcohol made him boastful, he talked too much of his part in the colorful days. One night he did not get home. His bullet-riddled body was found at the bottom of a well. The feud had claimed its last victim and with its finish, Concha Ortega de Sánchez de Gordon de Stanford de Crane was freed both of the strife that surrounded the ownership of the property, and of the property. Her final days, blind, were spent in a little house in San Juan, in the care of a devoted daughter.

The Catholic Cemetery figures also in the tale told by the priest, Father Mestres, who came to Monterey in 1893, of the funeral procession which had to be staged twice. It formed the first time—a procession of mourners who displayed their grief with terrifying howls and screams—to escort the body of a dead Portuguese fisherman in his pine box, carried in a deep-bottomed open wagon, to the cemetery. Unfortunately the box top was not nailed down. When the wagon reached Fremont Street, it was halted by a flood of recent rains, five feet deep. The driver told mourners that he did not think he could cross. But the women in the procession insisted that the corpse must not be halted on its way to heaven. Unwilling to argue, the driver drove on. As the wagon pulled into the water, gradually it sank deeper until it was entirely covered and all that remained above water was the driver perched high and dry on the seat. In the middle of the street, while the water swished about him, the horse stopped. Unhurried—and unwilling to urge on the animal, of whom he was very fond—the driver cut himself a chew of tobacco. Crying and moaning, the women ran along the edge of the street, pleading that it would do the dead fisherman no good to start his journey heavenward all wet. At length the driver, convinced, pulled out his whip and gently prodded the horse. With a rude jolt the creature jumped ahead, pulling the wagon furiously out of the water. But the back gate came loose, the water swished through the wagon bed, and the corpse in its unnailed coffin went sailing down the stream. Followed by screaming women, it went down Fremont Street, down the gully leading oceanward, into Washerwoman's Gulch, and into Monterey Bay. Monterey was thrown into an uproar. Boats were launched. All day the search went on. But not until nightfall was the corpse found, far out near Point Pinos. Loaded into a boat, it was brought back home. And next day the funeral was staged all over again, the whole town following the hearse to see that nothing interrupted again its journey to the cemetery.

45. Marshy WASHERWOMAN'S GULCH, Fremont St., E. end of El Estero, was once the gossip center of Monterey. Here Indian women washed and pounded the linens of the fastidious Californians and discussed the current news. Wrote Walter Colton on January 13, 1847: "So much for the wash-tub mail. You may think lightly of it as of the soap-bubbles that break over its rim; but if you are wise you will heed its intelligence. It . . . has announced . . . revolution, plots, and counterplots . . . Who, in other lands, would dream of going to an old woman, washing her clothes in a mountain stream, for the first tidings of events in which the destinies of nations tremble?" and again, on January 25: "All that has reached us through this singular mail is confirmed this morning . . ."

When the padres first came to Monterey this spot was their vegetable garden, the *huerta vieja* (old garden). As Monterey's population grew and its laundry increased, the washerwomen appropriated the place, attracted by a generous supply of fresh water. According to legend, it was here that María Bonifacio learned of her lover's marriage; and here young Vásquez came to learn the news when it was dangerous for him to appear in Monterey because of the price on his head.

46. Overlooking Monterey from what is known as the Mesa Tract, the modern adobe and stucco CASA CASTRO, first house on E. side of Mesa Rd. (best seen from Via Mirada), conspicuous with

its white walls and red tile roof in its ample, wall-enclosed garden, incorporates the small adobe Casa Castro built in 1845 by Manuel Diaz on land owned by his father-in-law, General José Castro. As late as 1915, four years before the novelist and short story writer, Gouverneur Morris, began building his mansion (which he never lived in) around the old adobe house, cattle roamed the mesa as they had ever since it became a cattle range in the days of early Spanish settlement. The Casa Castro, as it appeared when Morris bought the property, was a shingle-roofed, mud-colored, four-room adobe dwelling, with a lean-to of unpainted boards, standing unprotected by trees or a garden wall.

This was the home of José Castro, soldier and patriot, and his wife, beautiful green-eyed Modesta, who, typical of the more well-to-do Hispano-Californians—educated, hospitable, courtly—divided their time between this home and their adobe on the plaza at San Juan Bautista. Castro's career began when he was a young man in Monterey, a contemporary and friend of Juan Bautista Alvarado and Mariano Vallejo. Starting as a member of the *disputación* (assembly), he was active in both political and miltary affairs until he had achieved military command of the Department of the North and ultimately the position of temporary governor. It was he who put up the last strong stand against the American conquest. There is an old story that when he finally surrendered to the Americans he gave up his sword without complaint, but he removed his spurs and pitched them onto the house roof. "He who wants may have my sword; but who wants my spurs must climb for them."

47. A select school for girls—the first in Monterey—was conducted in the two-story CASA BUELNA *(private; best seen from Via Mirada)*, second house on the E. side of Mesa Rd., by its builder, Antonio Buelna, Mexican soldier turned schoolteacher, during the years 1818-21. Buelna was a close friend of Don Manuel de Boronda, a neighbor and fellow teacher. A son, Antonio, became Monterey's *alcalde* in 1831. The Casa Buelna has been modernized and restored.

48. When the charming CASA BONIFACIO *(private)*, third house E. side of Mesa Rd., was built in 1923, some of the adobe bricks and tile removed from the demolished original Casa Bonifacio (439 Alvarado Street) were incorporated in it. The original adobe was built in 1835 by José Rafael Gonzales, customs administrator, 1833-36, *alcalde* of Monterey in 1836, and *commandante de cela-*

dores at the Custom House, 1837-46; the present dwelling was built by the California artist, Percy Gray.

Clinging to a broad arbor to the right of the adobe wall and gate is an ancient red Castilian rose vine known widely as the "Sherman Rose." According to legend—lately disproved—Lieutenant William T. Sherman, while stationed at Monterey, met and fell in love with Señorita María Ygnacia Bonifacio, who lived in the original home on Alvarado Street. Before he could marry her, however, he received orders to return to the East. The day of his departure he and Señorita María Ygnacia planted the Castilian rose in the garden and the lieutenant promised to return "when the roses bloom." María Ygnacia waited, year after year, and the rose bloomed again and again. At last, when she had grown quite old, Sherman returned to Monterey —and brought his wife with him. Doña María died unmarried, still faithful to her youthful lover.

Although this tale was believed by every Monterey tourist for many years, recent research has proved that the romantic story was fabricated by one Daniel O'Connel, a man of great imagination and great thirst, who invented it as an aid in wheedling money for his alcoholic refreshments. The real Señorita María Ygnacia, daughter of an Italian or Austrian immigrant, Giovanni Bonifacio, who was employed by W. E. P. Hartnell as a stevedore from 1822 to 1834, lived in the house from 1860 until her death in 1916, having inherited it from her mother. It has been discovered, however, that she was never more than slightly acquainted with Sherman, if at all. So firmly believed was the legend that when the First National Bank of Monterey proposed to erect a bank on the property, it offered "to give the historic adobe thereon to any civic body which will promptly remove and preserve same, elsewhere in the City of Monterey."

49. The reconstructed two-story BARETTO ADOBE *(private)*, Mesa Rd. and Via Mirada, of uncertain age, is faced with a veranda and balcony. The exterior woodwork of doors, windows, and balcony is a severe dark brown against the whitewashed adobe walls. Potted geraniums hang from the balcony rail. Originally the *casa* was owned by the politically prominent Dutra family.

Houses of this type usually were built crosswise to the points of the compass, so that the sun would shine into each room at some time of day. The patio faced south to catch the winter sun; the veranda, north, for the cooling summer winds. On the ground floor were the living room, dining room, *sala* (ballroom), kitchen and storerooms, and the veranda from which stairs led to the balcony.

CASA AMESTI—DOORWAY

HOUSE OF THE FOUR WINDS

CASA AMESTI

CASTRO'S HEADQUARTE[

STOKES HOUSE

CASA DE ORO

CASA BORONDA

Bedrooms on the second floor were entered from the balcony, but in later days the outside stairways were removed.

50. Until Mexico declared its independence of Spain, most of Monterey was confined within the adobe walls which once outlined the SITE OF THE OLD SPANISH PRESIDIO, bounded by Webster and Fremont Sts. between Camino El Estero and Abrego St. Here on June 30, 1770, the officers and friars of Portola's founding expedition "were assembled on the beach" as Hubert Howe Bancroft tells the story, "where an enranada, or shelter of branches, had been erected and a cross made ready near the old oak. Water was blest, the bells were hung, and the fiesta begun by loud and oft repeated peals . . . The church ceremonies ended, Portola proceeded to take formal possession in the name of Carlos III by hoisting and saluting the royal flag of Spain and going through the usual form of pulling grass, throwing stones and recording all the prescribed acts. Finally the officers and friars ate together under the shade of trees near the shore, while the soldiers and others enjoyed their feast a little apart." Thus were founded the Mission and Presidio of Monterey.

On a site "a gun-shot from the beach and three times as far from the port," the men built the "royal fortress," which was merely a log stockade surrounding a handful of log and adobe huts, defended only by two small cannon. Having accomplished the foundation of Monterey, Gaspar de Portolá sailed for New Spain aboard the *San Antonio*, leaving 24 men—of whom 19 were soldiers, commanded by Lieutenant Don Pedro Fages—to hold the northernmost Spanish settlement in the Western Hemisphere. The little garrison was faced with an uncertain future. When in 1772 the failure of the supply ships to arrive left them with no food but a few vegetables and a little milk, Fages took 13 soldiers southward to the site of San Luis Obispo and killed enough bears to supply the Montereños with meat until supplies arrived. The presidio was still a poor and lonely place the year afterward when Padre Francisco Palóu described it as having an adobe chapel and a room for a visiting friar, an adobe house for the *commandante,* and a jail, with soldiers' quarters and other rooms built of wood. The whole was enclosed in a wooden palisade with a cannon mounted in each of the ravelins at the four corners. The earliest huts, crude affairs of wood plastered with mud and roofed with rush, were very unsatisfactory during the rainy season. The soldiers hated the life on the lonely northern frontier, where they had little pay, not much to eat, and no wives to comfort them.

When Captain George Vancouver made his first visit in 1783, he commented sourly that the guns were mounted on a "sorry kind of barbet battery, consisting chiefly of a few logs of wood irregularly placed, behind which those cannon, about 11 in number, are opposed to the anchorage of any enemy vessels, but with very little protection in the front and on their rear and flanks which were entirely open and exposed." By this time a stone and adobe wall—4 feet thick and 15 feet high—had replaced the log stockade. When Vancouver returned nine years later, the presidio authorities had made some attempt to repair the damage done by fire in 1789 by rearing more substantial structures of adobe and stone. Although the square was still only partly enclosed, a blockhouse stood at each corner. Only the *commandante's* house had flooring inside, the others being dirt-floored. At the turn of the century, when Commander Mariano Carrillo made his report, the enclosure was described as measuring 110 yards on each side. On the north side, inside the main entrance which faced the Royal Presidio Chapel, stood the guardhouse and warehouses; on the west, the houses of the governor, *commandante,* and the other officers; on the east, soldiers' houses and a blacksmith shop; on the south, soldiers' houses. The walls were built of stone and adobe, the houses roofed with tile. Already, however, the structures were reported to be in bad condition, their walls cracked and apt to collapse, so flimsy were the foundations.

At the beginning of the nineteenth century the presidio's military force of 110 included 7 artillerymen, 20 Catalonian volunteers, 50 privates, 9 officers, 2 or 3 mechanics, and a phlebotomist (bloodletter). The pay was small, food and clothes insufficient. Even officers' wives had to take in sewing and washing to supplement the family income. The common soldiers had to buy their own food, clothes, arms, and horses. Discipline was lax and depredations were common.

The presidio had so declined in importance by 1818, when Hipolyte Bouchard's pirates captured and sacked Monterey, that no attempt was made to defend the town from behind its walls. The defenders chose instead to make their futile stand behind the earthwork fortifications of El Castillo *(see No. 39)* on the hill above the port. And when the flag of Spain was hauled down and the flag of Mexico hoisted in 1822, it was over the Custom House—not over the presidio—that the new flag floated.

51. In use for a century and a half, the ROYAL PRESIDIO CHAPEL OF SAN CARLOS BORROMEO DE MONTEREY *(open 9-5: adm. 25c; guide),* 550 Church St., California's only

extant presidio chapel, has welcomed the faithful since its completion in 1795. Founded as Mission San Carlos by Padre Junipero Serra in 1770, but converted the following year into the Royal Presidio Chapel when Serra moved the mission to Carmel *(see CARMEL MISSION)*, the first church building was completed and dedicated in 1775—the handiwork of soldiers and sailors, untutored Indians, and convicts from Branciforte (Santa Cruz). Fire so badly damaged it in 1789 that Governor Pedro Fages laid the foundation for the present building of stone and adobe. Among the various additions made from time to time were the wing, added sometime between 1835 and 1840; a transept and altar, in 1858; and numerous improvements made by Father Casanova between 1868 and 1893 One of California's best examples of Mexican architecture, the church in all its ornateness is the handiwork of patient Mexican Indian laborers, some of them imported from Mexico, whose naive renderings of Mexican decorative motifs are rare examples of primitive art. Of special note is the bas-relief of Our Lady of Guadalupe, carved in chalk rock at the very top of the facade.

Left of the main entrance stands a statue of *Our Lady of Lourdes,* guarding a spring, and kneeling before her is Bernadette, the little peasant girl who became a saint. Once whalebone formed the walk, but is was removed because the ladies caught their high heels on the sharp edges. The olive trees in the garden were planted by the padres. The tree stump in the rear is reputed to be that of the oak tree under which Vizcaíno said mass in 1602 and Father Serra in 1770.

Most of the church's relics are in the parish house next door, from which they are brought out for use only on special occasions. (Following completion of a new church on the other side of the parish house, they will be returned to the chapel, which will become a museum.)

The Stations of the Cross are the originals; the statues of *St. John,* the *Sorrowful Mother,* and the *Spanish Madonna* were brought by Serra himself. As old as the church is the statue of *Our Lady of Sorrows* in the sacristy. The fine silver altar service includes candlesticks, a six-foot crucifix, cruets, and an incense burner. Of rare interest is a Portuguese crown, brought to Monterey by the whalers when most of their profession were from Portugal. Some of the vestments used in the early days have been preserved, though badly faded now, as have many of the records in Father Serra's handwriting. Members of 21 of the old families are buried within the church. Francisco Pacheco lies by the altar railing.

A comparative newcomer to San Carlos Church is the statue of *Santa Rosalia*. She is the patron of the fishermen of Palermo, who brought her to Monterey with them to guard the fishing fleet. Her festival comes in September (the exact date depends upon the moon and the catch); then the sailors carry her down to bless the boats all freshly painted in her honor.

52. The CASA BORONDA *(private; best seen from State I)*, Boronda Lane, is the oldest residence in Monterey and one of the oldest in the State. Manuel Boronda was invalided out of the army in 1817 and given a piece of land on which to build. He built this long, low, three-room house with adobe bricks and thatched the roof with tules—the marsh reeds so common in California—tied on with rawhide thongs. Because the hill slops gently, the house follows that line—the northern section being 15 inches lower than the southern. The original floor was of solid-packed dirt, swept clean and kept smooth by the tramping of many feet.

Today the exterior is little changed, but the interior has been improved by eight successive generations of Borondas. Steps in the center of the house offset the slope of the building. A few ancient things still remain, among them a beautifully wrought stone jar, smooth as porcelain, hollowed out by Indian hands more than a hundred years ago, and a picture of the Blessed Virgin brought from Spain by a pioneer member of the family.

It is told that before tile had replaced the tule roof there was constant fear of the structure being deroofed by high winds. When the gales howled down the canyon, whistling and singing about the old adobe, the Borondas would prostate themselves on the floor and chorus a prayer that the leather thongs might hold.

It was in this house that Manuel Boronda opened the first boys' school in Monterey. Paper was scarce and expensive, and it was doled out sheet by sheet. Each student was required to use his paper thoroughly—front, back, and margin—before he was allowed another sheet. When George Allen, a young Quaker, married a Boronda girl, he carried on the teaching tradition.

Here, too, in 1836, occurred a tense moment in the Castro-Alvarado revolt. Alvarado met Isaac Graham at the Boronda home in an attempt to enlist the Americans in his cause. While conferring, the young rebel saw through a window a body of eight soldiers coming up the hill, evidently in search of him. He made his escape on Graham's horse amid a shower of bullets.

The Casa Boronda is part of the setting for a novel, *Cathedral in the Sun*, by Anne B. Fisher, written after seven years of research on the Boronda family.

53. On the street that since has been named for him, Don Esteban Munras, agent of the Spanish government, built in 1822 the CASA MUNRAS *(private)*, 656 Munras St. It was in this year that he married Catalina Manzanelli, daughter of a Genoese merchant and Casilda Ponce de León, descendant of the famous discoverer of Florida. Not only was Don Esteban's home pretentious for its time —it boasted the first fireplace in a California home—but it was the first house to be built outside the walls of the presidio. Descendants of the original owner still occupy the house. Completely modernized, it retains little of the character of the original.

54. Largest adobe in Monterey is the two-story, 25-room CASA PACHECO *(private)*, 602 Abrego St., built about 1840 by Don Francisco Pacheco, wealthy landowner and ex-soldier. Don Francisco's daughter married the socially prominent Don Mariano Malarin, and the *casa* for many years was their summer home.

Originally the house, of the Santa Barbara type of architecture, was entered from Webster Street by way of a large recessed veranda above which ran a gallery of the same size. Its present gallery, facing Abrego Street, does not extend the full width of the building, but is framed on either side by the adobe walls; deeper than the usual Spanish balcony, it is reached by wide stairways that rise on either side from the ground-floor exterior. The gallery's heavy supports are in harmony with the building's massive walls.

Casa Pacheco has been restored several times. During its last restoration in 1929, undertaken by the present owner with the object of restoring the old house as nearly as possible to its former size and appearance, the roof was lowered four feet to its original height. It has been many things: a roominghouse, a dance hall, a private hospital operated by its present owner, Dr. Martin McAuley. Once it was a house for women of easy virtue frequented by *vaqueros* (cowboys) from the surrounding ranchos. They came in their working clothes and sometimes, lacking money, they paid for their pleasures with their heavy, beaten-silver spurs.

55. Don José Abrego built the older part of the CASA ABREGO *(private)*, 592 Abrego St., in 1834—the year he arrived with other colonists led by Don José María Híjar. The vessel that brought them

to Monterey—the *Natalie,* in which Napoleon had escaped from Elba—was sold to smugglers the following year. One night while the crew celebrated ashore the ship's anchor chain broke, and she drifted onto the rocks and was wrecked. Don José used some of the timbers salvaged from the *Natalie* when he enlarged his house. Originally he used the *casa* only as a place of business, but in 1846, when he married Josefa Estrada, half-sister of Governor Alvarado, he made it his residence.

The Casa Abrego has been restored. It is a one-story building, trim, white, and red-roofed, with a veranda of the type sometimes described as "a fence around a platform." (The ornate imported doors opening into the adobe from the veranda were not part of the original building.) It is joined on the north by a high, gleaming-white wall that shelters one of the most beautiful patio gardens in Monterey. The *casa's* south wall is buttressed, a practice not common with early Monterey builders.

Abrego was one of the few really energetic native Spaniards in Monterey, amassed a comfortable fortune by his mercantile business. One of the first three pianos brought to the Pacific Coast and the first full-length mirror were his prized possessions. He placed the following inscription in the piano: "In 1841, Captain Stephen Smith arrived with his vessel in Monterey, and I engaged him to bring me a piano on his next trip . . . In March 1843 he returned to this city in a brigantine; he had three pianos on board. I bought this one of his for $600. . . ."

A charming tale is told about the full-length mirror. Julia Abrego, his lovely daughter who was married at 16, had never seen her full reflection. Don José installed the new mirror at the foot of the stairs. That evening as his daughter descended the stairs in evening dress she caught sight of herself in the mirror, and without realizing what she saw, turned to her husband and asked, "Who is that lovely girl?"

During the latter part of the Mexican era the Casa Abrego was a center of social life in Monterey. Here was staged elaborate *casarón bailes* in which dancers pelted each other with the *cascarones*—eggshells filled with perfume and attached to long sticks (sometimes, say old Montereños, lead or other solid substances burst from the *cascarones*).

Don José also was active in political affairs. During the Alvarado-Castro revolt he was prominent in the campaign at Monterey. It was he who found the only cannonball in the capital—the one shot that forced the surrender of Governor Gutiérrez. When Commodore Ap

Catsby Jones "captured" Monterey *(see THE PENINSULA THROUGH FOUR CENTURIES)*, Governor Alvarado retired to his ranch at Alisal and left José Abrego, as civil representative of the State, to handle the formalities.

56. On the SITE OF THE WASHINGTON HOTEL, NW. cor. Pearl and Houston Sts., designated by a marker, stood until its demolition in 1914 the three-and-one-half-story adobe building which preceded to Hotel Del Monte as the Peninsula's chief hostelry. Originally the adobe residence of Don Eugenio Montenegro, having been erected in 1832, it was already a hotel at the time of the American occupation. Thereafter it was enlarged to accommodate increasing demands until it was over 200 feet in length, with a two-story annex extending 100 feet at a right angle. Its owner in 1849, Don Alberto Trescony, leased it for $1,200 a month to a former private in Colonel Jonathan D. Stevenson's regiment, who put up more than a hundred guests—among them many of the delegates to the Constitutional Convention—for $200 a month each, without board. Gambling and gaiety flourished so noisily that the sounds of dissipation are said to have disturbed the pious at San Carlos Church, blocks away. At least they drew the wrath of *Alcalde* Colton, who frequently raided the hotel and fined the gamblers. It was here, on June 15, 1856, that one of the bloodier episodes of the Belcher-Roach vendetta, which rocked the county for years, took place: the shooting of Louis Belcher, as he stood at the bar, by an assassin who escaped unrecognized after firing a single shot from behind a pillar by the stairs. As long as social life flourished in Monterey, the hotel remained its center. But it began a rapid decline when the county seat was removed to Salinas; and when the Hotel Del Monte was opened, it was no longer in any position to compete.

57. In the fall of 1879, Robert Louis Stevenson lived in the larger of two wooden and adobe buildings that today are joined and known as the STEVENSON HOUSE *(craft shops)*, 536 Houston St. While living here he found time to work on *The Amateur Immigrant* and *Vendetta of the West* and to report for Monterey's newspaper, the *Californian*—at a salary of $2 a week. He wrote to a friend: "I will send you herewith a Monterey paper where works of R. L. S. appear, not only that, but all my life on studying the advertisements will become clear. I lodge with Dr. Heintz; take my meals with Simoneau; have been only two days ago shaved by the tonsorial artist Michaels; drink daily at the Bohemia saloon; get my daily paper from Hadsell's . . . in short, there is scarce a person advertised in

that paper but I know him, and I may add scarce a person in Monterey but is there advertised." Stevenson lived only three months in Monterey, but he grew to love the sleepy little village. "Monterey is a place where there is no summer or winter," he wrote. "And pines and sand and distant hills and a bay all filled with real water from the Pacific..."

The buildings forming the Stevenson House are two stories high, without the traditional front balconies, but joined in the rear by a short balcony reached by an outside stairway. They were built by Rafael González, long-suffering father of the tempestuous Ana Castanares, center of Monterey's most notorious early-day scandal.

When Governor Mariano Chico came to Monterey without his wife he brought with him his beautiful "niece," Doña Cruz, to whom he was unduly attentive. Even the liberal Californians could not accept this situation gracefully. Doña Cruz, shunned by the more respectable women of the community, formed a friendship with the wife of José María Herrera, Doña Ildefonsa, a woman of flexible moral standards. At this point Doña Ana Castanares became involved: her husband, José María Castanares, became the lover of Doña Ildefonsa. Delighted Montereños lost little time in informing Doña Ana. Her tongue was not noted for its gentleness, and soon Herrera, incensed by the gossip about his wife, traced it to Doña Ana and sued her for slander. The case dragged on for some time— to the increasing delight of Montereños. At last Herrera dropped his suit, but not to be left unavenged, prosecuted the lovers on the grounds of adultery. It was a lengthy and exciting trial. Castanares was imprisoned and Doña Ildefonsa was put in custody of a highly respectable citizen.

At this point a troupe of players visited Monterey. On the night of their scheduled performance Montereños were startled to see Chico appear in the governor's reserved section with Doña Cruz on one arm and the by-now notorious Doña Ildefonsa on the other. Respectable matrons fled from the hall.

A breach of gubernatorial etiquette had occurred, and *Alcalde* Ramon Estrada was not one to allow such an insult to the town or to his office. He hastened to the jail, freed Castarnares, and together they returned to the theater. The remaining members of the audience were tense with expectation. Castanares alone seemed self-assured. He smiled gayly toward the Governor's place and blew a kiss to Doña Ildefonsa. Chico immediately went into one of his famous rages. By turn he stormed, stamped, and yelled—turned red, then purple—and finally stalked from the room. The show did not go on.

On the following morning Chico, dressed in full regalia and accompanied by his special troop, rode through the streets to *Alcalde* Estrada's home, stopped before the house, and amid the concentrated attention of much of the town demanded Estrada's wand of office. Estrada smilingly handed over the insignia, then retired to his walled garden. Chico retreated with complete loss of face. This situation in great measure hastened his departure for Mexico.

After the collapse of the slander suit against Doña Ana, she sued her husband for divorce, which the court considered favorably, allowing her to return to her father's house and receive $200 annually from Castarnares. A few months later she returned to him and the divorce was annulled.

58. Center of operations of Monterey's sardine-canning and sardine-reduction industry—whose annual output is unequalled elsewhere in the world—is CANNERY ROW, Ocean View Ave. between the Presidio and Pacific Grove, a long sweep of paved street lined by sardine canneries and small restaurants specializing in food popular with the cannery workers: Japanese, Mexicans, Chinese, Portuguese, Spaniards, Italians, and Native-born Americans. Humming with activity at the peak of the season, the canneries call their workers by whistle blasts, whose distinctive tones, different for each cannery, are known to the whole neighborhood. Drab and businesslike by day, Cannery Row is gay and brightly lit at night. The restaurants, frequented by soldiers and cannery workers, their neon signs blazing such names as "La Ida's," "Clair's," "The Lone Star," are noisy with music and feminine laughter. Neon arrows point up alleys toward other business establishments. For "other" description, see *Cannery Row* by John Steinbeck.

Pioneer plant is the Booth Cannery, which began operations locally shortly after 1900 and was almost alone in the field until 1915. Some 30 plants were in operation during the First World War; of these, more than a dozen remain today, employing in season—late August to February—from 200 to 2,500 workers.

Before the opening of each season, representatives of the Monterey Boat Owners' Association meet with the canners to determine the price per ton to be paid for the season's catch. The major profit to the canner lies in the manufacture of by-products: oil, meal, and fertilizer; but his activities are regulated by the State Fish and Game Commission, and he is compelled to pack the equivalent of

$13\frac{1}{2}$ one-pound cans of sardines as food (for human consumption) out of each ton of fish purchased.

Each cannery dock is equipped with machinery for hoisting sardines from the boats and with a mechanical blower. The fish are pumped through the revolving blower by a salt-water pump to the scaler (where they are weighed), thence over endless-chain elevators into large tanks of water and into the cutting shed. The severing of the fish heads (waste parts), formerly done by hand, is now done by machine. The sardines come out of a tank upon a narrow platform, are picked up by hand, and pass through the cutting machine. Next they are brought to the packing tables, where girls place them in cans. The fish are now ready to be cooked.

If the fish are to be fried or broiled the cans are left open; if they are to be steam-cooked, sauce is added and the cans are capped. Two capping machines are used: one taps the lids into place, the other seals them air-tight. The capped cans containing uncooked fish pass to a metal trough, from which they are placed on steel trays on iron trucks. When loaded, these are moved into a retort. Filled to capacity, the retort is securely closed, steam is applied, and the fish are cooked under high pressure until soft. When removed from the retorts the cans are cleaned in hot-water tanks, and after cooling are sent to the warehouse. Later they are put through the lacquer machine and labeled.

Sardines are rendered into oil or fish meal under terrific pressure. The oil is very valuable; canners store it in metal tanks while awaiting a favorable market. The meal is packed in 100-pound jute sacks and shipped to the East and Middle West, where it is purchased in large quantities by cattlemen, hog-raisers, and dairymen for feeding purposes. It is also highly rated by chicken-raisers because of its high nitrogen content, and is used for human consumption in Africa and China. The fertilizer made from waste sardines is packed in sacks and shipped in open cars to avoid spontaneous combustion. A high-grade fertilizer, which benefits the land without overheating the soil, it is used extensively by truck farmers and commercial flower-growers.

59. The two-story MILTON LITTLE RANCH HOUSE (*private*), since replaced by a modern structure, 289 Lighthouse Ave., was built in 1851 as headquarters of a 640-acre ranch within whose former boundaries are New Monterey and Pacific Grove. It was made of galvanized iron sheets cut and grooved in New York and of timber from Australia. Little had ordered materials for six houses.

The lumber arrived without mishap, but when the iron was being un-loaded at the wharf in Monterey a sailor jumped to the deck of the tender and overbalanced the load, spilling material sufficient for two houses into the bay. (Of four such houses built by Little the only one extant is the Kimball Hotel, 235 Alvarado Street.) Little came to California from New York in 1844 and for a while engaged in the mercantile business as a partner of Thomas Larkin. In 1848 he married Mary Eager. Mrs. Little kept gold for many miners, stored in a large trunk in bags tagged with their owner's names. She feared constantly that ships would pile up on the rocks of the bay and kept a light burning nightly in a window of her house. The night she died the family failed to light the lamp and a schooner was wrecked.

Pacific Grove

The Peninsula's "City of Homes" and onetime citadel of Methodist morality, PACIFIC GROVE (40 alt., 7,500 pop.) is a quiet community of tree-shaded cottages, immaculate public buildings, and a few large commercial and industrial establishments, occupying the sandy slope between Point Pinos and New Monterey. The checkerboard pattern of its streets extends northward to the Bay of Monterey at Lovers' and Cabrillo Points and westward to Asilomar *(see TOUR 1)*; the pine-clad heights of its southern boundary offer striking contrast to the wide white dunes on the west and to the dark rugged shoreline on the north which hurls back the long surge of the Pacific.

"It has long been established a medical fact," observes a brochure of the Pacific Grove Chamber of Commerce, "that a residence in a country wooded with pines is peculiarly beneficial for all those suffering with bronchial or throat infections." And to the testimony of a Methodist minister in 1873, who with his family had found it healthful to sleep in hammocks under the local trees, was due the decision of Bishop Jesse Truesdale Peck of the Methodist Episcopal Church to found a summer encampment here in 1875. In this endeavor the Bishop was aided by Scottish-Presbyterian David Jacks, from whom about 100 acres, including the site of Pacific Grove, were purchased and laid out in lots. During the year cottages and tents sufficient to accommodate some 400 persons were set up at a cost of about $20,000, and on August 9 was inaugurated the first camp meeting, which lasted three weeks. Summer religious sessions were held annually thereafter, and in later years the "Pacific Grove Retreat," as the resort popularly was known until its incorporation as a town in 1889, was a haven for conventions of the Chatauqua Society, the State Sabbath School, the Women's Christian Temperance Union, the Y.W.C.A. and Y.M.C.A.

With a climate "the most equable in the known world, and with a location so healthy that doctors scarcely make a living," a *Handbook of Monterey* issued in 1875 predicted that "it bid fair to become an unrivalled summer resort." And so it did, but not before Robert Louis Stevenson in 1879 was able to observe the community in its pastoral simplicity: "One day—I shall never forget it—I had taken a trail that was new to me," he relates in *Across the Plains*.

124

PACIFIC GROVE

"After a while the woods began to open, the sea to sound nearer at hand. I came upon a road, and, to my surprise, a stile. A step or two farther, and, without leaving the woods, I found myself among trim houses. I walked through street after street, parallel and at right angles, paved with sward and dotted with trees, but still undeniable streets, and each with its name posted at the corner, as in a real town. Facing down the main thoroughfare—"Central Avenue," as it was ticketed—I saw an open-air temple, with benches and sounding-board, as though for an orchestra. The houses were all tightly shuttered; there was no smoke, no sound but of the waves, no moving thing. I have never been in any place that seemed so dreamlike . . . Indeed, it was not so much like a deserted town as like a scene upon the stage by daylight, and with no one on the boards. The barking of a dog led me at last to the only house still occupied, where a Scotch pastor and his wife pass the winter alone in this empty theatre. The place was 'The Pacific Camp Grounds, the Christian Seaside Resort.' Thither, in the warm season, crowds come to enjoy a life of teetotalism, religion, and flirtation, which I am willing to think blameless and agreeable."

The "life of teetotalism, religion, and flirtation" did not long remain a Methodist monopoly, however, and an influx of settlers attracted more by the retreat's natural beauty than by its salubrious moral climate compelled the invocation of a code of "blue laws" which made the community an outpost of Puritanism for almost half a century. Not finally codified and revised until 1938, these municipal ordinances which are no longer enforced included the following provisions: "It shall be unlawful for any minor under the age of 18 years to be on any of the public streets of the city of Pacific Grove between the hours of eight o'clock p.m., and daylight of the following morning from November 1 to May 30 of each year and between the hours of 9 p.m., and daylight of the following morning from June to October 31 of each year unless by direction of the parent, guardian, or other person having the lawful consent of said minor." This "curfew law" passed in 1893 was mild compared to some provisions of another ordinance enacted in 1920: "It is hereby declared to be unlawful for any person while dancing to assume or maintain any position which tends in any way to corrupt the good morals of any person attending said dance hall"; and furthermore, "Dances known as the tango, turkey trot, bunny hug, or shimmie are hereby prohibited and declared to be unlawful." As late as 1933 the town's forces of enlightenment were obliged to repeal a provision of an ordinance passed the previous year which declared: "It shall be unlawful for every person wearing a bathing suit or portion thereof, except children under ten years of age, to appear in or upon any beach or in any place open to the public . . . unless attired in a bathing suit or other clothing of opaque material, which shall be worn in such a manner as to preclude form, from above the nipples of the breast to below the crotch formed by the legs of the body . . . All such bathing suits shall be provided with double crotches or with skirts of ample size to cover the buttocks."

To Pacific Grove's pioneer settlers the progress of modern conveniences was considered a work of the Devil as dangerous as temptations of the flesh. The "stile" through which Stevenson entered the retreat in 1879 was until the nineties a gate which was locked each night at 9 o'clock, and the community was enclosed until after 1890 by a fence to prevent both the intrusion of interlopers and the sale of lots to the ungodly. The locked gate, however, was too much even for a personage presumably as law-abiding as Judge Cyrus Alexander of Salinas who, caught out after 9 o'clock without his key, broke down the gate. It was never locked again. From the present junction of Lighthouse and Fountain Avenues a dirt road offered communication with Monterey; over this road until 1882 passenger service was furnished by a four-horse stage. A horse-car system inaugurated in 1891 by Don Juan Malarin was superseded in 1903 by a trolley line which ran for 20 years before its "Toonerville" mode of operation forced it into bankruptcy: the obliging motorman-conductor, who never refused a passenger a ride for lack of the fare, would stop anywhere en route to let people off, would "back up" to pick up persons, or even wait for passengers who had business to transact along the way. Such service was too good to last, and during the late 1920's the abandoned tracks were torn up to make way for the modern bus line established in 1930. To pioneer improvements of this highway, however, the early-day residents of Pacific Grove were militantly opposed; and it was Charles R. Tuttle, the town's first druggist, who was chosen by irate citizens to stand trial in a test case which resulted in abandonment of attempts by Monterey to compel the taxpayers of the Methodist community to pay for upkeep of the road. The citizenry of Pacific Grove accepted with no better grace the advent of motor vehicles on their streets; an ordinance passed in 1905 states that "it shall be unlawful for any person to ride or drive any automobile, locomobile, motor bicycle, or other wheeled vehicle propelled by steam, electric, or gas power in any of the streets of the city of Pacific Grove at a rate faster than 10 miles per hour."

Such a state of affairs, however, was being dissipated gradually by the ridicule heaped upon it by editors of the *Monterey New Era* ("Fog in Monterey today," observed one of these in the nineties. "Last night the Pacific Grove gate must have accidentally been left open") and by the arrival of new settlers with modern ideas. A retail establishment founded in 1891 has grown today into the largest department store on the Peninsula, comprising 50 departments. Though the establishment of factories still is severely restricted, the American Can Factory, founded on the boundary line between Pacific Grove and New Monterey, is one of the major industrial plants on the Peninsula. Transported by truck from Monterey's Municipal Wharf, huge sheets of tin are converted by the $1,000,000 factory into oval cans used by the sardine canneries at Monterey. Other industries located in Pacific Grove are two boatbuilding yards, the larger established in 1915 and equipped for construction and repair of all types of fishing and pleasure craft. A planing mill and lumber yard and a steam laundry, both built before enactment of restraining ordinances, comprise the remainder of the city's industries. A sand plant *(see TOUR I),* though considered a Pacific Grove industry, is outside the city limits. Three banks offer adequate financial facilities both for the municipality's normal population and its large overflow of summer visitors.

Administered since 1927 by a city-manager form of government, Pacific Grove boasts the largest percentage of American-born residents of any California city, the largest percentage of registered and active voters, and more churches than any city of comparable size in the Nation. Descendants of its revivalist pioneers still maintain a dominant influence in municipal affairs, but social conventions have become less severe within the last decade, and devotion to education, science, and popular festivities gradually is introducing the nonsectarian and gayer forms of culture which long have prevailed elsewhere on the Peninsula. Gone are the days when persons could be fined $25 or spend 25 days in jail for playing a ball game in the streets: Pacific Grove now has a Municipal Baseball Park, which was built by relief workers in 1933 in a pine-sheltered amphitheater formed by the Del Monte Properties' old abandoned quarries near the city's southern limits. A municipal beach and swimming pool *(see POINTS OF INTEREST: No. 5),* golf links, six public parks, and other modern recreational facilities add to Pacific Grove's attractions of climate and natural scenery. Modern schools, a library and museum containing valuable collections, and a laboratory for the study of marine fauna and flora *(see POINTS OF INTEREST: No. 1)* are sources of social and cultural enlightenment.

Though its public-spirited and progressive citizens include among their plans for the future a 250-foot memorial observation tower and museum to honor Juan Rodríguez Cabrillo, discoverer of Point Pinos, the Spanairds whose civilization is so intimately associated with Carmel and Monterey remain as historically remote from Pacific Grove as the Indian relics which repose in the city's public and private museums—or those puritanical taboos which its people have outlived.

RKIN HOUSE

CASA ALVARADO

SPANISH STYLE TODAY

OTTAGE AT PEBBLE BEACH

OLD WHALING STATION

CALIFORNIA'S FIRST BRICK HOUSE

STEVENSON'S HOU

Points of Interest

1. The HOPKINS MARINE LABORATORIES *(open week-days 9-5)* of Stanford University's Division of Marine Biology and Oceanography occupy $7\frac{1}{2}$ acres on China (Cabrillo) Point; also under its control are the adjacent coastal waters, whose marine life is studied (from glass-bottomed boats) by the university students. Courses include Natural History of Marine Animals, Marine Biology, General Microbiology, Comparative Physiology, and Marine Invertebrates.

First of the station's two units, the three-story, concrete Alexander Agassiz Laboratory—erected in 1917 and named in honor of one of the Nation's leading oceanographers—houses an aquarium, a small museum, several laboratories, and a library. The Jacques Loeb Laboratory, a two-story concrete structure erected in 1928, bears the name of a noted experimental biologist who investigated marine fauna in the vicinity of Pacific Grove from 1902 to 1910. Devoted to research in experimental biology, its laboratories are supplied with fresh and salt water; to avoid vibration in the laboratory the sea-water pumps are located on the extreme western side of Cabrillo Point.

The Hopkins Marine Life Refuge, a two-mile stretch of municipal beach water extending a thousand feet into the bay, was established in 1931. (Persons not connected with the Marine Station or the university are prohibited by a local ordinance from catching or collecting any marine life in this protected area.) The cool climate, the clarity of the sea water, and other natural advantages make possible extensive hydrobiological surveys of the Bay of Monterey, which offers an astonishing variety of marine fauna and flora; excellent material is here available for research in cellular biology, experimental morphology, embryology, and taxonomy (the latter is concerned with invertebrates, a species still requiring investigation). Pioneer research by Dr. Loeb at the original laboratory resulted in the discovery that unfertilized eggs of sea urchins would produce embryos when subjected to a chemical formula and returned to normal sea water—an experiment in parthenogenesis which startled the scientific world.

Endowed by railroad tycoon Timothy Hopkins, supported by David Starr Jordan, Charles Henry Gilbert, and Oliver Peebels Jenkins, the laboratory was founded in 1892; then known as the

129

Hopkins Seaside Laboratory, it consisted of a small frame building near Lovers' Point. Growth of the institution occasioned its removal to the present site in 1916. Since 1941, the station has been operating under an endowment income, provided by a "Trust in Perpetuity," established by Timothy Hopkins with the Wells Fargo Bank & Union Trust Company in San Francisco, under which 60 per cent of all income is allocated to the Hopkins Marine Laboratories for maintenance and improvement.

2. The living room of her home houses MRS. C. S. FACKENTHAL'S COLLECTION OF INDIAN RELICS *(open to specialists only)*, 750 Laurel Ave., the Peninsula's most significant non-public collection of aboriginal remains and anthropological specimens—the latter consisting of five skulls and several Indian skeletons. One of the skulls was found by workmen excavating near the Murray Hacienda in New Monterey during building of the Southern Pacific line into Pacific Grove. Another, that of a woman, was discovered near Point Lobos; two others, on Fan Shell Beach, where one of the skeletons also was found. Teeth in two of the skulls are intact. A second skeleton, unearthed by the late Reverend Fackenthal, was donated to Princeton University.

Mrs. Fackenthal's hobby since 1890 has been the collection of Indian arrowheads, of which she possesses 3,000; one of these was made by Ishi, last man of the extinct Southern Yanax tribe of Shasta County, whose language is lost to living tribes and ethnologists. Also in her collection are shells of 300 species of marine and land crustacea, every variety found on this coast.

3. Zoological specimens of the Peninsula and the Bay of Monterey are chief exhibits at the PACIFIC GROVE MUSEUM *(open 10-4 daily except Mon.)*, Forest Ave. at Grove St., whose coral-tinted stuccoed building is surrounded by neat lawns, pink concrete walks, and flowering shrubs. Beyond the vestibule, with its beamed ceiling, tiled floor and doors of Philippine mahogany, are two relief maps under glass: one represents Monterey County; the other, the floor of the Bay of Monterey. They were completed in 1936 by Dr. Harold Heath, former Professor of Zoology at Stanford University. The collections of butterflies of California *(main floor)* and marine algae of Monterey Bay *(mezzanine)* are reputed to be the most complete in the Nation. Other exhibits include the marine life of Monterey Bay and birds, minerals, fossils, pine cones, and insects of Monterey County. A feature of the collection on the mezzanine floor is a very rare specimen of the now extinct Carolina parakeet,

only species of parrot native to the United States, which once was found between Florida and Virginia. On the main floor are specimens of 1,000-year-old Hopi Indian pottery and large collections of American currency and coins.

The museum's present building, erected in 1932, was the gift of Mrs. Lucie B. Chase, Pacific Grove resident. When founded in 1882 by schoolteacher and chatauquan Mary E. B. Norton, who was its first curator, the museum consisted of a series of shacks. Many of the specimens collected during half a century were found to have been ruined by exposure when the exhibits were removed to their new home.

4. One of California's best small libraries, the rectangular mission-style PACIFIC GROVE PUBLIC LIBRARY *(open weekdays 10-9, Sun. 2:30-5)*, Central Ave. at Fountain St., for which Andrew Carnegie contributed $10,000, stands amid lawns, trees, and shrubbery. Its roof of red tile extends over a recessed frontal portico approached by wide concrete steps, the cornerstone of which is inscribed: "Founded with Masonic Ceremonies November 9, 1907." The annex at its northern end was built in 1938.

A partition of arches divides lengthwise the well-lighted main interior room, which is finished throughout in white pine. Beyond an arched entrance at its south end is the children's room, furnished with a large fireplace. Among the library's 16,000 books is the Alvin Seale collection of more than 1,200 volumes pertaining to the South Seas, considered to be the most comprehensive collection of its kind in the West. Included are a complete set of Darwin's *Voyage of the Challenger;* sets of works by explorers Hakluyt, Vancouver, and Cook; a Ptolemy; and numerous ancient maps and atlases. Many of these books are extremely rare; some of them are in richly tooled bindings; some contain the handwritten logs of clipper ships and windjammers.

5. A crescent of gleaming white sand, the MUNICIPAL BEACH *(fishing boats and tackle 25c per hr., $2 per half day, $3 per day)*, Ocean View Ave., extends northward from the foot of Forest Ave. toward the tip of Lovers' Point. Directly within the main entrance lies an open-air swimming pool, from which stairs lead down to the beach, crowded with bathers on sunny days. Well patronized are the glass-bottomed rowboats *(available May 1-Sept. 15; adults 50c, children 25c)*, from which may be observed varieties of starfish, shellfish, jellyfish, and marine vegetation in the best submarine gardens on the Pacific Coast.

Above the beach and extending its full length lies a parklike strip of landscaped lawn shaded by cypress trees. This was once a flourishing dahlia garden, and brought early fame to Pacific Grove. The approach to Lovers' Point is marked by a large boulder which bears a granite plaque, a memorial to Dr. Julia Platt, noted biologist and local resident, who inaugurated various civic improvements.

Over the castellated crags and huge boulders piled at the end of Lovers' Point (Point Anlon), the breakers at high tide roll in from Monterey Bay to dash with flying spume the headland named by legend and designed by nature as a trysting place for sentimental youths.

6. A fine of $500, six months' imprisonment, or both, is the penalty for disturbing the BUTTERFLY TREES, occupying $3\frac{1}{4}$ acres near the western end of Lighthouse Ave. Since 1870 this grove of pines has been an annual haven for many thousands of Monarch butterflies (L., *Danaus menippe*). Each fall they arrive, to cling in swarms, their brown, black-bordered wings folded and motionless, to the brown bark of the pines and to hanging clusters of Spanish moss. According to John Adams Comstock's *Butterflies of California*, this insect belongs to a genus adapted to a tropical climate and is the only North American species addicted to migration.

7. Completed in 1855 and rebuilt in 1907, POINT PINOS LIGHTHOUSE *(open Tues., and Thurs. 2-4)*, foot of Lighthouse Ave., casts a 29,000-candlepower alternating beam, visible in clear weather from a distance of 15 miles, across four-fifths of the horizon. Its light, 189 feet above high tide, is intensified by powerful catadioptric lenses. The diaphragm of its foghorn is operated by compressed air. The white tower stands on ground believed to have been occupied at one time by Indians, whose arrowheads have been found on the point. Quarters for two keepers and their families are located in the base of the tower. Its first keeper was Charles Layton, later slain in a fight by Anastacio García. Burning in succession lard, whale oil, kerosene, and finally electricity, this old beacon—tended twice by women—has stood guard for clippers, whalers, side-wheelers, and modern craft entering or passing the Bay of Monterey.

8. A long crescent of white sand backed by dunes, MOSS BEACH, facing Spanish Bay south of Point Pinos, is so named for the vast expanse of sea moss which appears when the submarine gardens are uncovered to view at low tide. Here Monterey crab fishermen come to hunt crabs in the crevices of the rocks when the tide is out, exploring the cracks with their fingers and picking up the crabs

with their hands. Chinese gather seaweed, let it dry in the sun, and ship it to San Francisco (where it is used both as a food-stuff by their countrymen and as a source for agar-agar). Off-shore appear heards of seal the year round. The beach attracts fishermen, both for its surf fishing and its shellfish—abalone, crabs, and mussels (the latter should not be gathered during the seasons of the year when they are poisonous). Although the surf bathing is good, high breakers make it dangerous in fall and winter. At the northern end of the beach is a marker commemorating Sebastián Vizcaíno's discovery in 1602 of the Peninsula, this section of which he named "Point of Pines."

Carmel-By-The-Sea

The suburban Montmartre, that pretty town besieged by tourists, and real estate promoters, CARMEL-BY-THE-SEA (220 alt., over 3,000 pop.), has managed for nearly 45 years to remain a haven of the seven arts, in spite of their participator's ways of life and fame, and the locality's lures of balmy climate and natural beauty, which constitute a subtle threat to their retreat. Situated on a cove of Carmel Bay, its white curve of beach sheltered on the south by rugged Mission Point, Carmel-by-the-Sea is an exotic combination of seaside resort and woodland glen. Exclusive of neighboring subdivisions the town proper occupies an area roughly a mile square. Its older section lies inland on hillsides clad with oak and pine, on the lower slopes of a spur of the Santa Lucia Mountains known as the Black Hills. The gridiron formation of its modern streets extends northwestward to the shoreline from the mouth of the Carmel River. Hidden under the fragrant pines, most of the village is invisible from any one point, except at night, when the lights shine through the trees. The business section, small, compact, is distinctive for the rugged individualism of its architecture: since each property owner has built with supreme unconcern for the tastes of his neighbors, business buildings of almost every conceivable architectural style have their frontage along Ocean Avenue. Nor is this rampant individualism confined to the business district. Tucked in corners of the hills are small cottages of every type—some of them conglomerates of many types.

For many, Carmel's cultural assets are overshadowed by the beauty of its beach. Carmel Bay swings in a graceful arc from Pescadero Point to Point Lobos. The beach, anchored at either end by crags, is a fine wide stretch of glistening white sand, reaching from the dunes, flower-grown, to the hard-packed flats at tideline. At high tide the sea sweeps against the crags, sending up showers of foam. At low tide the black rocks lie lonely in their salty pools on the level sand. The water is clear and deep in color, intense in its blueness, almost purple, shading to jade green.

Carmel is not old as a town, although Misíon San Carlos Borromeo del Río Carmelo (Mission St. Charles Borromeo of the Carmel River), from which its name, popularly shortened to Carmel, is derived, had already begun to fall into ruins a century ago. During the 1880's cattle ranches held by the descendants of the Spanish *rancheros* covered the townsite. But visitors to Monterey walked or rode over the hills and often lingered here on its southern slope. Long before anyone thought of building a town, Arnold Genthe and David Starr Jordan knew and loved the region: Jordan had publicized it as early as 1870. The president-to-be of Stanford University —who became the pioneer purchaser of building lots 40 years later when J. F. Devendorff and Frank Powers began sub-dividing their large holdings and putting them up for sale at tempting prices—was not quite, however, of that select company of notables—squatters until this time—whose shacks among the pines constituted in 1904 "The Village," dedicated to Art and Life and Work. George Sterling was one of the first and certainly the most famous; to him, to Mary Austin, who wrote in her "wickiup" (tree-house), to James (Jimmy) Hopper and the other young artists and authors who were its pioneer settlers Carmel owes the impulse for its determined struggle against paved streets, gas and electricity, hotels and jails.

Recalling these days more than two decades later, Mary Austin wrote: ". . . when I first came to this land, a virgin thicket of buckthorn sage and sea-blue lilac spread between well-spaced, long-leaved pines. The dunes glistened white with violet shadows, and in warm hollows, between live oaks, the wine of light had mellowed undisturbed a thousand years . . . We achieved, all of us who flocked there within the ensuing two or three years, especially after the fire of 1906 had made San Francisco uninhabitable to the creative worker, a settled habit of morning work . . . But by the early afternoon one and another of the painter and writer folk could be seen sauntering by piney trails . . . there would be tea beside driftwood fires, or mussel roasts by moonlight—or the lot of us would pound abalone for chowder . . . And talk—ambrosial, unquotable talk . . . There was beauty and strangeness; beauty of Greek quality, but not too Greek, 'green fires, and billows tremulous with light,' but not wanting the indispensable touch of grief; strangeness of bearded men from Tassajara with bear meat and wild-honey to sell; great teams from the Sur, going by on the high road with the sound of bells; and shadowy recesses within the wood, white with the droppings of night-haunting birds. But I think that the memorable and now vanished charm of Carmel lay, perhaps, most in the reality of the simplicity attained, a simplicity factually adjusted to the quest of blood and fuel and housing as it can never be in any 'quarter' of city life."

It was a pleasant life for the villagers. They lit their nocturnal excursions with candles or old buggy lamps, worked hard during the day and played on the beach with dinners of mussels, abalone, and jugs of "dago red." It was a long walk over the hills in those days and often walking was the only way to reach Carmel, for Sam Powers, driver of the stage from Monterey, frequently made his passengers walk to save the sweating team. Ocean Avenue was a dusty trail spotted with "milk shrines"—stands on which each resident left the bottles to be returned, with the money for refills jingling against the empty glass. The spirit of the *haciendados* still prevailed on the great ranches roundabout, where the Coopers, the Graggs, the Sargents, the Murphys entertained with barbecues. The town bulletin board carried news of their doings, of world events, successes, meetings—all the information usually contained in a local newspaper. Lone officer of the law was Gus Englund, tax collector, traffic officer, chief of police, bailiff of the court, and janitor of the council, who rode his big horse around the trails on a continual quest of helpfulness.

The population grew. "The year of the earthquake and fire brought us, for brief intervals," wrote Mary Austin, "Will Irwin, Jesse Lynch Williams, Henry Milner Rideout, Ray Stannard Baker and Lincoln Steffens . . . Harry Leon Wilson made his home there . . . and for a time Mike Williams, incomparable talker, Irish and fey, and destined, though none of us suspected it, to become the editor of the most intellectual Catholic weekly in America today . . . Professor folk from the Universities of California and Leland Stanford made their summer homes in the village . . ." Others came, either as visitors or temporary residents: William Rose Benet, Sinclair Lewis, Upton Sinclair. An ardent Fletcherite was Sinclair, and while the others ate mussels at the Point Lobos parties, he sternly limited himself to tomatoes.

But inevitably the world moved in on the group of serious artists; the leisure class came to Carmel, the dilettantes and the charlatans who used art as an excuse for leading a life they fondly believed to be "bohemian." With the newcomers came rising prices, came stores, came city government. In 1916 Carmel was incorporated. Unimpressed, its founders—and kindred spirits who shared their views—stood pat. Perry Newberry ran for office on a ticket that frankly declared:

"Believing that what 9,999 towns of 10,000 want is just what Carmel shouldn't have, I am a candidate for trustee on the platform, DON'T BOOST. I am making a spirited campaign to win by asking those who disagree with me to vote against me.

"Don't vote for Perry Newberry
   If you hope to see Carmel become a city.
   If you want its growth boosted.
   If you desire its commercial success.
   If street lamps on its corners mean happiness to you.
   If concrete street pavements represent your civic ambitions.
   If you think that a glass factory is of greater value than a sand
      dune, or a millionaire than an artist, or a mansion than a lit-
      tle brown cottage.
   If you truly want Carmel to become a boosting, hustling, wide-
      awake lively metropolis.
DON'T VOTE FOR PERRY NEWBERRY."

The recalcitrant Carmelites fought the installation of gas and electricity on their wooded slopes. Long and violent were their struggles to preserve the region's natural beauties. They fought for zoning laws to save the beach from hot-dog stands and seaside concessions. They bonded the town to buy the sand dunes along the shore.

Carmel in 1946 represents a compromise between its artistic population and the liberal element among its ordinary citizens. Though it accepts certain modern conveniences, even hotels and banks, it owns no public utility, and will not tolerate house numbers or mail delivery. Its business thoroughfare, like the streets which provide doubtful access to dwellings located according to individual tastes, is divided by a central parkway in which a tall line of pine trees grow. Neon signs are not permitted, and the small painted store signs do not project obtrusively over the sidewalks. In curious contrast to this striving for naturalness are the little shops which might have been devised in Hollywood for a Walt Disney epic.

Controlled by a commission form of city government consisting of a five-member council under chairmanship of its mayor, Carmel has been noted for the personnel of its civic administration, who have been either literary personalities or professional people sympathetic to the town's artist population. Commercial interests, by and large, have proved more congenial to the artists than the idlers, charlatans, and dilettantes who flocked to the colony in the 1920's; nevertheless many a battle royal with the boosters of predepression prosperity had to be won before relative security from the horrors of "Main Street" was assured. "All in all," observed a local brochure in 1931, "Carmel has used more energy in its attempt to remain unpretentious than most small towns use in striving to become business centers." Again, in 1934, a local magazine (Carmel has been a hothouse for "arty" and ephemeral publications) wailed that "the quaint little village had put aside natural quaintness, and grown into a fashionable watering place, with paved streets, civic pride, mayors out of which metropolitan newspaper headlines are fabricated, and a galaxy of somewhat famous, almost famous, and would-be-famous people including several amateur communists."

For all its growing worldliness, Carmel has retained a certain small-town intimacy. So common are visiting celebrities that they are all but ignored. The two weekly newspapers print offerings from resident contributors which range from poetry to gossip. One devotes a weekly column to news and anecdotes about the dogs of the village. The canine population is large and beloved. Dogs are known by family names; thus "Bonnie Smith" is as much of an individual as any two-legged inhabitant, and as newsworthy. And when "Biff Clark" on one memorable occasion (according to local report) came up the street with a note tied to his collar, the whole town was excited. Biff was corraled by an anxious mob and the note read. It was a request to a neighbor to feed Biff the two days his master expected to be out of town.

Despite the passing of that "old Carmel" which Mary Austin in 1927 mourned with nostalgia born on her walks about the Peninsula with George Sterling, Carmel has preserved and strengthened in its art collections, schools, clubs, and theaters the heritage created by such residents as photographers Arnold Genthe and Edward Weston; artists Maynard Dixon, Jo Mora, Elizabeth Strong, and William Ritschel; authors George Sterling, Mary Austin, Don Blanding, Martin Flavin, Lincoln Steffens, Jesse Lynch Williams, Albert Rhys Williams, Harry Leon Wilson, and Robinson Jeffers. Of these only a celebrated minority have established permanent residence; but however transitory their sojourns here, these Carmelites each have contributed something to the curious admixture of reality and legend which gives the town its international reputation.

Though founded mainly by writers, Carmel in the days when its streets were meandering dirt roads and hazardous trails leading to obscure cottages was primarily an artists' colony. Center of this ardent group of young painters was the Carmel Club of Arts and Crafts, where instructors William Chase, C. P. Townsley, Matteo Sadoni, Paul Kirkland Mays, and Cornelius Botke taught and where such visiting masters as George Bellows and Jonas Lie were imitated and admired. Since its organization in 1934 the Carmel Art

Association has been for Peninsula artists what the old Arts and Crafts Club was to their predecessors. Among the town's private collections, perhaps the one most indigenous to the Peninsula is that of Louis Slevin. This first postmaster, first express agent, and first treasurer of Carmel has collected examples of everything pertaining to the region—photographs of vanished places and dead celebrities, Indian petroglyphs from caves near Tassajara Springs, beetles and lizards—in his years of tramping about the Peninsula in company with Professor George Davidson, California oceanographer, and other kindred spirits. Another Carmel pioneer, whose scientific interests led to establishment of research institutions on the Peninsula *(see PACIFIC GROVE POINTS OF INTEREST: No. 1)* was David Starr Jordan, authority on marine fauna of the nearby coastal waters.

Music and the drama in Carmel were developed in close conjunction with other arts to which the colony has been devoted. Amateur performances after 1912 were followed by concerts of national significance in later years; and after its establishment in 1923 the Arts and Crafts Theater presented such plays as Lord Dunsany's *The Queen's Enemies,* Charles Caldwell Dobie's *Doubling in Brass,* and *The Thrice Promised Bride,* by Chen Chin Hsiung. From 1924 until its destruction by fire in 1935 the Theater of the Golden Bough offered a wide variety of plays, opening with Maurice Browne's and Ellen von Volkenburg's performance of the play, *The Mother of Gregory.* Constructed for experimental drama, the Golden Bough had a projecting semi-circular platform connected to the main stage by a flight of wide shallow steps; its indirect lighting and small balconies whose arched entrances harmonized with the curve of the ceiling made it one of the Nation's most beautiful "little theaters." *(See POINTS OF INTEREST, No. 8.)*

To commemorate the founding of Mission San Carlos, the Serra Pageant has been a unique artistic achievement. The first "Serra Pageant," which was written by Perry Newberry, was performed on July 4, 1911. In the intervening years it has been occasionally revived. Other pageants, notably one by George Marion, have also been produced.

The Carmel Bach Festival, held annually in July, has been a musical feature of national significance since its inauguration in 1933 by a corps of Carmel artists, writers, and musicians under the direction of conductor Ernst Bacon and the Denny-Watrous Concert Management. Presented in the Sunset School Auditorium and at the mission, the festival program has included such works as Sebastian Bach's *Christmas Oratorio, Peasant Cantata,* the cantata *Phoebe and Pan,* and *Concerto in D Minor* for harpsichord and orchestra. Highlight of each series is the concluding *Mass in B Minor,* sung in the mission by the full chorus accompanied by the full orchestra. The festival consists of five concerts, two organ recitals, and a series of lectures on related musical subjects. The group is made up of 60 musicians and a chorus of 50 singers; amateurs and professionals of national reputation, they are under the direction of Gastone Usigli.

Despite its reluctant conversion to modernity, Carmel remains a place where the remote past is linked with the present, where legend and implausability go hand in hand with the hardest facts and the latest inventions. Old residents continue to look wistfully backward at their lost paradise of dirt roads, their abalone feasts on moonlit beaches, their "milk shrines"—all the bohemian gaiety and ardent toil and delectable conversation devoted to the better things of life. Of these primitive delights the last is still possible in Carmel, and doubtless will be as long as an engulfing commercialism can be held at bay. So also will persist the legend of the "Lost Mine of the Padres," believed to exist somewhere near the old mission; so will recur the mystery of the whereabouts of Serra's bones, of the white horse and ghostly rider once seen by a caretaker at the Mission gate.

Carmel is still the place of tree-obstructed streets, rustic little gardens, wild groves of pine, and odd studios where pursuit of perfection in the arts is accepted as a legitimate occupation. And interlopers who came to scoff or to exploit the town's quixotic and unconventional natives have been seduced to a way of life which outsiders are likely to regard with amazement.

Points of Interest

1. Inspired by medieval religious art, the SERRA SHRINE in Carmel Woods consists of a statue of Serra carved in oak by Jo Mora which stands on a high stone pedestal beneath a tiled gable supported by oak timbers. The head of the effigy is painted in life colors; its robes in Franciscan gray. Flanking the shrine are oaken benches bearing the inscription:

To the Immortal Memory of Padre Junípero Serra,
Servant of Christ, Adventurer, Artist, and Engineer,

Placed by the Del Monte Properties Company
July 22, 1922
Designed and Executed by Jo Mora, Sc.

On the day of dedication an ancient *carreta*, adorned with pine boughs and red-and-yellow bunting and drawn by a team of horses, driven by a Spanish-Californian in gala attire, bore a replica of the Serra statue from Carmel Mission to the shrine, which Father Mestres unveiled before an assemblage of Peninsula citizens and dignitaries.

2. A square block of land filled with native flowers, fountains, and ancient live oaks, DEVENDORFF PARK, Ocean Ave. across from the Post Office, commemorates J. F. Devendorff, who with Frank Powers acquired and subdivided the land on which Carmel stands.

3. Carmel's World War monument, the SOLDIERS' MEMORIAL FOUNTAIN, Ocean Ave. facing San Carlos Ave., stands on the site once occupied by a water trough faced with redwood bark, used as a manger in Christmas-time Nativity Plays. Its cornerstone was laid November 11, 1921, by Colonel John N. Jenkins of the Presidio of Monterey.

4. Showplace for the handiwork of Peninsula artists, the CARMEL ART GALLERIES AND SALES ROOMS *(open 2-5; free)*, Dolores and Sixth Sts., rambling the width of two city lots, are maintained by the Carmel Art Association. Set back from the street under large oak trees, the building is constructed of wood and white adobe bricks, with hand-fashioned doors painted bright Indian red. To this group, organized in 1934, belong artists who make the Peninsula their part- or whole-time residence. It succeeded the Carmel Club of Arts and Crafts, established in 1905, which had literary,

141

music, bird-study, and even boys'-club sections, as well as its arts and crafts groups. Its summer school, opened in 1912, was first taught by William Chase. The present association, whose president is National Academician Paul Dougherty, is supported by a membership of 150 and an annual appropriation from the City of Carmel.

The galleries, to which a new fireproof wing was added in 1938, contain storage facilities for more than 500 paintings. The exhibitions, changed monthly, show oils, watercolors, prints, drawings, and decorative work, accepted for hanging with the approval of a board of judges.

5. Many metropolitan cities would be proud to own the art collection in the RALPH CHANDLER HARRISON MEMORIAL LIBRARY *(open daily 11-9, Sunday 2-6)*, Ocean Ave. and Lincoln St., which is housed in a building revealing the Basque motifs characteristic of its architect, Bernard Ralph Maybeck of Berkeley. Completed in 1928, the library is the gift of Ella Reid Harrison in memory of her husband, who served as California Supreme Court Justice from 1890 to 1903. Besides valuable books on oriental art and culture, the library contains the Harrison Collection of etchings, with notable additions in other media by Carmel artists. Among the etchings are eight by Sir Francis Seymour Haden, Albrecht Dürer's *The Death's Head,* Rembrandt's *The Triumph of Mordecai,* and an anonymous *Dante.* The watercolors of California wild flowers by Louise Hutchinson share the room devoted to the Harrison ensemble with such oil paintings as the *Old Whaler's Cabin—Point Lobos* by Charles Rolo Peters, *A Landscape* by William Keith, and William P. Silva's *The Mission Orchard in Spring*.

The present library is the successor to the library maintained in a one-room shingled building on the same site until 1927 by the Carmel Free Library Association, which Frank Powers and a committee of 10 organized in 1903.

6. The LINCOLN STEFFENS HOME, Ocean and San Antonio Aves., was the residence of the veteran "muckraker," journalist, and philosopher; of his writing wife, Ella Winter; and of their son, Peter, born after Steffens had reached the age of 60. A series of low, rambling buildings joined together, the home, "Tuckaway" (originally owned by California artists Cornelius and Jesse Botke), is set back in spacious grounds of lawn and shrubbery in view of the sea. Here Steffens wrote his autobiography—his best-known book—during the last years before his death in 1936. It remains the property of his widow, now Mrs. Donald Ogden Stewart.

7. An inspiring example of the use of native materials, perpetuating in its adobe, stone, and redwood construction the Peninsula's oldest architectural tradition, the new CARMEL HIGH SCHOOL, Ocean Ave. and State 1, is as up-to-date in its uncompromisingly modern design as the day in September, 1940, when it was completed. On a high plateau on the eastern edge of town stand its five buildings, all connected by open copper-roofed arcades, their redwood-shake roofs overhanging adobe-brick and glass facades on stone foundations. The interiors represent the most progressive features of modern school design; bilateral lighting from immense room-length windows on two sides, planning of each room by sound experts to create perfect acoustics, distinctive color schemes for each of the five buildings. The library is equipped with a huge red-brick fireplace, with desk lamps on each table. All of local origin are the stone, adobe, and redwood used in the building. The manufacture of the adobe bricks, all adobe construction, and the landscaping were done by the Work Projects Administration.

8. First open-air community theater in California, the FOREST THEATER, Mountain View Ave., celebrated its thirtieth anniversary in 1940 with a Shakespeare festival. Founded in 1910 by Herbert Heron, poet, playwright, producer, and businessman, it opened with a performance of Constance Lindsay Skinner's Biblical drama, *David*. As remembered many years later by a member of the cast, Mrs. Nellie Montague, this inaugural performance was the occasion for "Carmel's first after-the-show cast supper around a beach bonfire whose sparks, to our intoxicated gaze, linked the moon; and where our elders, in a spontaneous burst, parodied their recent performances. The fire died, and we trouped home in the soft dark, chanting George Sterling's latest contribution to his never-ended Abalone Song:

> "Some live on hope,
> And some on dope,
> And some on alimony.
> But this old mut
> Would rather cut
> A slab of abalone."

Since 1910 more than a hundred plays ranging from *Macbeth* to *The Mikado,* by playwrights as diverse as Euripides and A. A. Milne, have been presented. Presented to the City of Carmel by the Forest Theater Society in 1937, the theater was rebuilt by the Work Projects Administration and reopened three years later with the first of a scheduled series of Shakespearian festivals. Its performances are usually given on week-ends during the summer months. The casts are drawn from local citizens and summer visitors.

On a slope surrounded by tall pines, spectators sit on redwood benches overlooking a concrete stage 50 feet wide and 55 feet deep. With a permanent capacity of 600, the theater covers an entire city block. By necessity the staging of plays is somewhat unorthodox, since a minimum of scenery is used; often a change of scene is managed by changing the lighting or shifting the action to another part of the stage, or to the forestage, a dirt path extending in front of and along each side of the permanent stage; frequently the actors enter from the surrounding woods. When spectacular effects are indicated, the stage may even be extended to include the whole amphitheater.

9. Suggestive of his dramatic poetry is Robinson Jeffers' TOR HOUSE *(private)*, on a wild five-acre tract a hundred feet above the granite rocks and crashing surf of Carmel Point. The author of *Tamar, Roan Stallion,* and other works inspired by the Monterey Peninsula, built with his own hands, from boulders carried up the bluff, this home in which he and his wife and twin sons have lived since 1927. From windows of its redwood living room are visible the expanse of Carmel Bay, Point Lobos, and in the distance the Santa Lucia Mountains. The walls of the room are lined with books, many in Gaelic which attest to Jeffers' affinity for the homeland of his Irish ancestors.

After the five years' labor spent in building this house, the poet began construction in the same fashion of his nearby "Hawk Tower," surmounted by a turreted platform which provides spectacular view of the surrounding landscape. From his sons' room on the ground floor an outside stairway and a secret inner one lead to Una Jeffers' room on the second floor; the tiny room above is sometimes used as Jeffers' studio. His wife's room in the tower contains a carved unicorn; among other objects he collects are organs and figures of the Madonna. In the dining room of Tor House is a head of Jeffers executed by sculptor Jo Davidson, and here also stands a spinning wheel brought from Ireland by Una Jeffers' grandmother. Desiring seclusion, the Jeffers have no telephone or radio.

At the rear of the house is a garden overgrown with wild flowers, eucalyptus, and Monterey cypress; house and tower are surrounded by a low stone wall which encloses a court in which sweet alyssum grows in wild profusion. From the highway the Jeffers home is approached by a path of crushed seashells.

III. Shore and Valley

Del Monte

Without a rival in the world, they say, its magnificance unequalled even by the fashionable spas of the French and Italian Rivieras, the Del Monte resort engirdles the neck of the Monterey Peninsula with an array of luxurious facilities which invites the elite of inter-national society. From Hotel Del Monte, amid spacious and parklike grounds overlooking the Bay of Monterey, to Pebble Beach on Carmel Bay lie the great golf courses and the miles of bridle paths which constitute favorite outdoor playgrounds of the wealthy, the titled, and the famous of several continents. Twenty thousand acres of shore and forest and mountain on the Peninsula and environs are devoted to polo fields, racetrack, trapshooting grounds, tennis courts, beaches, and swimming pools; in the adjacent waters deep-sea fishing, and boating are enjoyed; in the interior are facilities for stream-fishing, a game preserve, and a guest ranch with stables of fine horses. Social center of this vacationer's paradise par excellence has been for 60 years that Hotel Del Monte which has survived two disastrous fires, a decade of neglect, and the ridicule of those who doubted the wisdom of its original builders.

The energy and vision which the "Big Four"—Charles Crocker, Leland Stanford, Mark Hopkins, and Collis P. Huntington—devoted to the construction of the Central Pacific Railroad (now the Southern Pacific) in the 1860's was in 1878 applied to the conversion of the Monterey Peninsula into a resort intended to bring wealth and fashion to the Pacific Coast via the new transcontinental passenger line. In 1879, the year following its incorporation, the Big Four's Pacific Improvement Company purchased from David Jacks 7,000 acres including the site of Hotel Del Monte. This land formerly comprising the Pescadero, Puenta Pinos, and Lagunita Ranchos of María Baretto, was acquired by Jacks for 12c an acre and by the Pacific Improvement Company for $5 an acre; the Del Monte properties, including the Seventeen Mile Drive and Pebble Beach, are now worth several thousand dollars an acre. Other large tracts, subsequently bought and sold, enabled the corporation to launch its great modern real estate developments.

To apathetic Peninsulans, discouraged by the devastating drought and depression of the seventies, the opening of the luxurious Hotel Del Monte in June, 1880, was "Crocker's Folly" and foredoomed to failure. Its success, however, was immediate and spectacular; and back to their homes in the East and abroad went enchanted visitors bearing tales of the wonderful hostelry amid scenery and climate soon to be renowned the world over. They told of the 126 acres of landscaped gardens, of the racetrack and the swimming pools, of the fascinating maze where venturesome mid-Victorians could play hide-and-seek with themselves among gravel walks four feet wide and cypress hedges seven feet high. And most marvelous of all was 340-foot-long Hotel Del Monte itself with its thousands of gaslights, almost as many mirrors, hot and cold water even on the top floors, and the amazing convenience of telephonic communication with the stables. Winter or summer throughout the eighties the private Del Monte station saw as many as 500 trunks and pieces of luggage arrive on a single train. Handsome carriages and sleek horses shipped as freight by wealthy visitors came to add the social graces of the tally-ho to the Seventeen-Mile Drive's natural charm.

Swept by a disastrous fire in 1887, Hotel Del Monte like a rococo phoenix promptly rose again more splendid than before. Its miles of thick red carpets and its ponderous Victorian furniture announced to visiting presidents and potentates that the best tradition of California luxury was still preserved. The legend of Del Monte's charm and comfort continued to spread far and wide. So flourished the resort with its long verandas and general aspect of a Swiss chalet throughout the "Gay Nineties" and until the turn of the century. Then suddenly the advent of the automobile, though undependable and still a luxury, began to destroy the exclusiveness based on the horse-and-carriage trade which constituted the Hotel Del Monte's chief asset and attraction. The great renaissance of sports, led by the newly imported game of golf, brought about a decline in popularity of those grand features of the resort which had depended on the patronage of the elite: its racetrack and its polo fields no longer resounded to cheering crowds and thundering hooves. Gradually in the wake of a dying era Del Monte acquired the rundown atmosphere of neglect and decay. A pathetic attempt at revival was the opening in 1907 of an art gallery devoted exclusively to works of California artists and the inauguration of biweekly dances. The dances were staid and old-fashioned affairs; no smoking was permitted in the dining room and there was no grill to lend informality. The management's grim determination to hold the fort against evil times was inflexible.

Such was the condition of the famous resort when in 1915 the

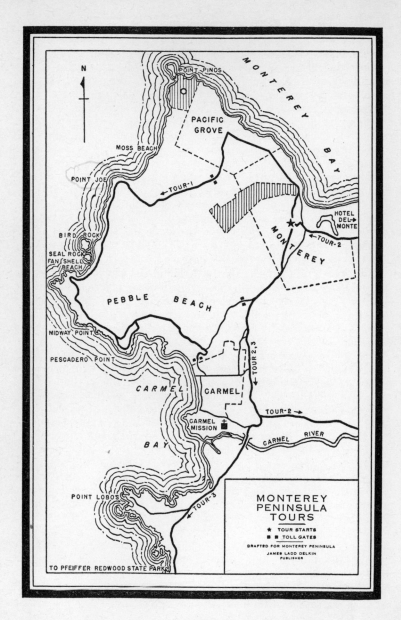

148

DEL MONTE

Pacific Improvement Company's new manager, Samuel F. B. Morse, arrived on the scene with a record for efficiency and intimate social connections with the Crocker family. This descendant of the American inventor of the telegraph and ex-captain of the Yale 1906 football team, at 25 the superintendent of a huge irrigation project in the San Joaquin Valley, had the imagination and exuberance necessary to save Del Monte from oblivion. His first step was to place Carl S. Stanley in charge of the hotel, with the aid of whose expert management he had the resort on its feet again within a year. Simultaneously Del Monte Lodge was built at Pebble Beach (see TOUR 1), the unfiinshed Seventeen-Mile Drive was completed, and Del Monte Forest amid hills in the heart of the Peninsula was laid out with over 100 miles of bridle paths. Four years later, in February, 1919, Morse and a group of wealthy San Franciscans incorporated in Del Monte Properties the liquidated assets of the old Pacific Improvement Company.

This record of progress was interrupted at 3:30 in the morning of September 27, 1924, by a fire which broke out mysteriously in the cupola above Hotel Del Monte's main entrance and rapidly engulfed the wooden central structure. Fortunately for some 700 sleeping guests an orchestra was detaining a few belated dancers in the ballroom, and these spread the alarm which averted any loss of life. Even so, as flames spread to the hotel's rambling old wings, persons who feared the cries of "fire!" might be a hoax to rouse them out in scanty attire were reluctant to flee for their lives. First to be carried to safely was 80-year-old Mrs. Henry Quinby, for nearly 50 years a guest of the hotel. When all the fire-fighting equipment on the Peninsula failed to halt the blaze, dynamite was used to destroy the famous semicircular corridors between the two wings and save those extremities from total destruction. The hotel's art collection, the Shreve jewelry exhibit, and Olympic Club trophies were saved. Damage was estimated at $1,250,000; loss to guests in personal property was $250,000. Though the hotel refused to close, many socialite guests clad in pajamas and bathrobes boarded a special train for San Francisco.

Such dramatic destruction of the main structure of Hotel Del Monte merely saved Del Monte Properties the eventual cost of consigning its outmoded architecture to a wrecking crew. The losses were covered by a $1,000,000 insurance policy, and as soon as the debris was cleared construction was begun on the modern buildings which again make Del Monte Hotel one of the show places of the world. Art treasures and trophies saved from the former structure by employees and guests were installed in the new establishment. The Monterey Peninsula Country Club, constructed in 1925, became a recreational center for residents of expensive villas built at Pebble Beach and of the more modest homes on the southern edge of Del Monte Forest. (Along with protective building restrictions, residents on Del Monte Properties' subdivisions receive recreational privileges in the resort's golf courses—of which the Pebble Beach links are the best known —swimming pools, and hunting preserves).

To socialite guests of Hotel Del Monte, however, its methods of operation and its financial problems are obscured by a plethora of comforts and conveniences calculated to dazzle and charm even those accustomed to the dazzling and charming. "It is a fire-proof building containing 400 rooms designed to handle big conventions as well as seasonal guests," *Fortune* magazine stated matter-of-factly in 1940. "It is of the so-called Mediterranean style of architecture—elaborate with its huge fire-places, a 200-foot dining room without one reassuring pillar, and carved and painted ceilings that remind you of the old Library of Congress, without the cupids." Small private dining rooms, cottages for those desiring seclusion, a stockbroker's office (member of the New York Stock Exchange)—these are only a few of the facilities to fit every taste and every degree of wealth.

Near the hotel, amid grounds richly planted with flowers and shrubs from many lands—cork oaks, Grecian laurels, genuine cedars of Lebanon, maidenhair and tulip trees, taxodium (akin to sequoia), and English holly—the Roman Plunge with its loggia, warmed sea water, and plot of white sand is most convenient for outdoor sport and recreation. The Del Monte Golf Course lies adjacent to the hotel on the west; north of the Roman Plunge lie the tennis courts and a lake on which float swans and other aquatic birds. St. John's Chapel, built on the grounds in 1891, holds regular services for Del Monte's guests and has been the scene of many a fashionable wedding.

Before the hotel was taken over by the Navy at the beginning of World War II, in 1942, for flight cadets and later for technicians in electronics, the "sport of kings" had been revived at Del Monte; and steeplechasing was given added thrills by the hazards of the resort's cross-country course. The Del Monte New Year's tournament officially opened the polo season on the Pacific Coast. On Del Monte's professional tennis court championship matches were held annually in midsummer; other championship matches in trapshooting, swimming, and diving were held annually. Stillwater Cove, the yacht harbor at Pebble Beach, is a rendezvous of luxurious craft from all over the world. With the exception of its sand plant near Pacific Grove, Del Monte Properties is a real estate corporation which operates as a gigantic country club. As a strictly commercial venture its management claims that—lavish expenditures being equal to lavish income—the resort earns only a modest profit.

"Just why," asked one of Del Monte's ingratiating advertisements, "does anyone live in a city and pound hard pavements for exercise when he or she can live in the most beautiful place on earth, graced with a climate that has in it what Ponce de Leon sought for in vain, in one of the great hotels of the world, affording the best of facilities for recreation and sports, with charming companions from all parts of the world—a place synonymous with health and happiness?" The question being rhetorical, the advertisement goes on to say that "for $470.00 a month, or $235.00 each, two people can have a sitting room, bath, and double bedroom, with all of the things we have mentioned—including food that is famous among world travelers and gourmets."

At the end of the war the hotel was used as a rehabilitation center for wounded Navy veterans. The hotel properties were considered ideal for a graduate Naval Officers School.

Carmel Mission

As Monterey was the military and civil capital of Alta California, so was CARMEL MISSION *(open daily; offering customary; guide on premises)* the ecclesiastical capital, for it was the home of the *Padre Presidente* of all the missions. Founded by Padre Junípero Serra on June 3, 1770, at its original location in Monterey at La Misión San Carlos Borromeo de Monterey—second oldest of the 21 California missions—it was removed the following year to its present site at the mouth of the Carmel Valley. From this outpost in the wilderness, 500 miles from the nearest settlement at San Diego, Serra undertook his tremendous task of Christianising the Indians and colonizing the territory.

"On the same day, June 3rd, Pentecost Sunday, 1770, on which Governor and Commander Gaspar de Portolá took possession of the Port of Monterey in the name of the king, and began the presidio of San Carlos," wrote Padre Juan Crespí of the mission's founding, "the Rev. Fr. Presidente of all the missions, Fr. Junípero Serra . . . began the new Mission under the title of San Carlos . . ." Beneath an arbor of boughs was placed a table, which served as the altar until a temporary chapel was built. Before the end of the following month two warehouses and several smaller structures had been erected. And on December 26, reported Padre Francisco Palóu, "the first baptism took place in the pagan nation. It was for the fervent and ardent heart of our venerable Father Serra an indescribable jubilee." But Serra, dissatisfied by the mission's proximity to the presidio's soldiers and its isolation from the Indians, set out, with Padre Crespí and a handful of soldiers, in June of the next year, to located a better site. Having found it near the mouth of the Carmel River, he ordered trees cut down for lumber and, living in a little shack on the site, directed his labor force of four Indians supervised by three marines and four soldiers in construction of the first mud-plastered wooden buildings. Before the end of the year, the new mission was ready for occupancy.

By 1772 Serra could thus describe the mission built by Indian neophytes under the padres' supervision: "A stockade of rough timbers, thick and high, with ravelins in the corners, is something more than seventy *varas* long and forty-three wide, and is closed at night with a key, although it is not secure because of the lack of nails. The main house is seven *varas* wide and fifty long. It is divided into six rooms, all with doors and locks. The walls are constructed of rough timbers plastered over with mud, both inside and out. Those of the principal rooms are whitewashed with lime. One of the rooms serves provisionally for a church.

"Near this building, on the outside, is the guardhouse or barracks for the soldiers; and adjoining it, their kitchen. All is enclosed in the stockade. All of these buildings have flat roofs of clay and mud, and for the most of them a kitchen has been made. There are various little houses for the Indians, with straw or hay roofs. Attention was later given to a small garden, which is near at hand, but for want of a gardener, it has made little progress."

"On the 29th day of February, 1772, in the cemetery, which this very day was inaugurated," wrote Padre Serra in the mission burial record's first entry, ". . . I said Mass and gave a solemn ecclesiastical burial to the bones and ashes of Theresa, a little one of about 5 years, or a little more, daughter of gentiles, baptized day before yesterday and burned yesterday by the gentiles . . ." The still unbaptized "gentiles," having recaptured their baptized child, had put her to death, perhaps in the conviction that only thus could they free her from the white man's evil magic.

When Catharina María became the wife of Fernando Malateta on November 10, 1772, the padres recorded the new-grown settlement's first marriage, but by the end of the following year they had 32 more to report. Meanwhile they had baptized 175 converts and buried 11. The community had by this time acquired 47 cattle, 28 pigs, 10 pack mules and 2 riding mules, 4 tamed horses, 4 breeding mares, and 1 stallion. By the end of 1774 a workshop, 30 by 7 *varas*, of adobe and palisades, with a thatched roof, had been put up; houses for the families of the captains of the mission guard, the smith, the surgeon, and two Indian servants had been erected; and a large adobe oven and several smaller ones to bake bread set up near the kitchen. Sometime during the next decade an adobe church was added to the group of structures placed around the mission plaza.

Most of the time Padre Serra was away, traveling from one to another of his new missions, performing the myriad duties of the faith and of his position, supervising the planting and harvesting of mission crops and the schooling of the Indians, compiling records of the progress for the Franciscan missionaries' administrative center in Mexico, the College of San Fernando. When the *Santiago* arrived June 17, 1778, carrying the Pope's grant of official power to confer the sacrament of confirmation, he proceeded to visit every one of his missions within the year, confirming 1,897 persons and registering each name. Meanwhile he was carrying on a determined struggle to uphold the power of the Church against Governor Felipe de Neve, who was striving to introduce some form of self-government for the Indians. Through all these difficult years—despite drought and famine, despite the failure of the supply ships to arrive or the ravages of wild beasts, despite the bitter fued between Church and State—the missions grew in power and wealth. Weakened by his arduous fulfillment of his duties, embittered by his fight with the civil regime, and saddened by the death of his coworker, Padre Juan Crespí, in 1782, Serra still had the satisfaction of having established the missions securely before he died peacefully at Mission San Carlos in 1784. The sailors from the ships in port, the soldiers from the presidio, and the priests from nearby missions came to pay their final tribute in the mission church. He was buried beside his friend Juan Crespí.

When the distinguished French navigator, Jean François de Galaup Comte de la Pérouse, visited the mission in 1786, he and his party "were received like lords of a parish . . . The *presidente* of the missions, in his cope, the holy water sprinkler in his hand, waited for us at the door of the church which was illuminated as at great festivals. He conducted us to the high altar where *Te Deum* was sung." The Comte de la Pérouse observed that "the color of these Indians . . . is that of negroes. Their store houses are built with adobe brick and pointed with mortar; the floor is of earth. The men and women are assembled at the sound of a bell; one of the friars conducts them to work, one to church and to all their other exercises.

"The Indians, as well as the friars, rise with the sun, go to prayers and to Mass; and during this time there is cooked in the middle of the square, in three large kettles, barley meal, the grain of which is roasted, previous to being ground; this species of boiled food, which the Indians call *atole*, and of which they are very fond, is seasoned neither with salt nor butter and to us would be a very insipid mess.

"Each cabin sends to take its proportion for all its inhabitants in a vessel made of bark. There is not the least confusion or disorder and when the coppers are empty, they distribute that which sticks to the bottom to the children who have retained the lessons of catechism.

"This meal continues three quarters of an hour, after which they go to their labors; some go to plough the earth, with oxen; others to dig in the garden; in a word, everyone is employed in different domestic occupations; and always under the supervision of one or two of the friars.

"The women are charged with but little else but the care of their housewifery, their children, and roasting and grinding the several grains. This last operation is very long and laborious, because they have no other means of doing it but by crushing the grains with a cylinder on a stone. M. de Langle, a witness of this operation, made the friars a present of his mill, a greater service could not have been rendered them, as by these means, four women would in a day perform the work of a hundred, and time enough will remain to spin the wool of their sheep, and to manufacture coarse stuffs."

Serra had been dead nine years when, on July 7, 1793, the cornerstone of the third mission church was laid by Padre Fermín Francisco de Lasuén. When Captain George Vancouver visited the mission at this time, he found master mason Manuel Estaban Ruíz directing Indian artisans in the cutting of sandstone slabs from the slopes of Carmel Valley and in the manufacture of mortar from abalone shells. The dedication of the finished structure was celebrated four years later, in September, 1797, with religious ceremonies and a fiesta. Founded on granite and supported by sandstone pillars, it measured 167 feet 4 inches in length, 50 feet 4 inches in width at the north end and 62 feet at the south end. Firmly buttressed, it was surmounted by two belfries, one of them approached by an outside stairway. The massive walls, five feet thick, curved to the ceiling in a parabolic arch. The construction of other buildings—school, dormitories, shops, granaries—proceeded until 1815, when the completion of the mission quadrangle was celebrated with thanksgiving services.

The following year—notable because it was the year in which the padres baptized the State's first American settler, Thomas W. Doak of Boston, as well as its first known oriental settler, referred to only as El Chino—saw an even more festive occasion: the reception of the new governor, Pablo Vicente de Solá. In Hubert Howe Bancroft's description, "the governor with his escort of officers, soldiers, and private persons, repaired to the San Carlos Mission, proceeding by the Calvario road. This road went through a dense forest of pine, about a thousand *varas* from the Mission buildings. In the forest were placed many great crosses, significant of Christ's sufferings. They had not proceeded far, when, behold! a band of holy men appeared, to the number of twenty, all wearing newly washed robes, and attended by a multitude of young Indians, who also had on their dress of acolytes. The vanguard of the acolytes was closely followed by the padres marching in two wings, and in the center, upon a grand platform, was set a crucifix; next came a horde of white-washed savages, to the number of two thousand, each carrying a branch in his hand. The governor was escorted by twenty-five cavalrymen in full uniform. Behind the escort came a goodly number of females of all ages, and all mounted on fine horses. The governor and his officers stopped, alighted, and walked to the center, where the crucifix was presented by the president of the missions. His worship, and the officers one by one, kissed the feet of the effigy, and then repaired to the temple. The acolytes kept burning incense in a large number of silver thuribles. The church ceremony consisted of a sermon preached in Spanish and Indian by the virtuous Fray Juan Amoros."

Despite the demonstration of solidarity, relations between the mission and the government at Monterey grew worse when in 1819 Governor Solá compelled Padre Sarría to provide quarters among his neophytes for 30 of Lieutenant Navarete's ex-convict infantrymen. Since the decline in the mission's neophyte population—which had already fallen from its peak of 878 in 1795 to 397—left extra space in the dormitories, Padre Sarría could not refuse to turn over the keys. The interference of the secular authorities advanced a step farther in 1826, when Governor José María Echeandía declared that all neophytes who had spent 15 years at the mission, who were married and could support themselves, should be permitted to go free. Within two years all but 233 had left, the majority returning to native villages in the hills. When in 1833 the Mexican Republic decreed that all Spaniards must leave her soil, the Franciscan missionaries, who refused to compromise with republicanism by taking the oath of allegiance, were replaced by the native Mexican Zacatecans.

The order of secularization was issued finally on August 17, 1833, turning over all mission lands and properties to civil administrator José Joaquín Gomez. The padres were ousted, the neophytes scattered, the herds confiscated, and the buildings left to fall into ruin.

Valued at $47,000 by the inventory of secularization prepared in 1834, the mission properties had declined so much in value by 1843, when Governor Manuel Micheltorena returned most of them to the Franciscans ,that the padres could not even maintain them—let alone pay the required eighth of their revenue to the State. Even six years earlier, the Frenchman Abel du Petit-Thouars had noted that "the roofs, broken in many places, were already giving way under their own weight." When Governor Pío Pico in 1846 offered the mission for sale at auction, its value was so small that no bids were received. The buildings had crumbled almost beyond repair by October 19, 1859, the date of President James Buchanan's order restoring to the Church a portion of its former holdings.

"It is now a complete ruin, entirely desolate, not a house is now inhabited," noted William H. Brewer in the spring of 1861. Entering the court through a broken adobe wall, he found that "Hundreds (literally) of squirrels scampered around in their holes in the old walls." Of the church, "about half had fallen in. . . . The painting and inscriptions on the walls were mostly obliterated. Cattle had free access to all parts; the broken font, finely carved in stone, lay in a corner; broken columns were strewn around where the altar was; and a very large owl flew frightened from its nest over the high altar." In the sacristy, a "dead pig lay beneath the finely carved font for holy water." And in the next room, as he began to climb the heavy stone steps leading through walls four and a half feet thick to the pulpit, "a very large owl flew out of a nook. Thousands of birds, apparently, lived in nooks of the old deserted walls . . . and the number of ground squirrels . . . was incredible—we must have seen *thousands* . . ."

The owls were still there in 1879, when Robert Louis Stevenson and Fanny Osborne sat among the ruins one moonlit night, talking of ghosts. From directly overhead burst suddenly a horrifying scream. Not until they had reached the crest of the hill did Stevenson realize that the noise was an owl's, not a banshee's.

The ruin of course was haunted—according to all the tale-tellers, who muttered darkly the story told by old Christiano Machado, caretaker, of his having seen, night after night, a light burning in the ruins of the Indian adobe village and then of his meeting, one midnight, a white-clad man astride a white horse on whose forehead burned a light, and of having discovered thereafter a deep hole dug amidst ruins, from which the mysterious rider had no doubt retrieved buried treasure. Others repeated the legend of the padre's lost mine, fabulously rich in silver, where bandit Joaquín Murietta had buried his gold (a legend at least partially confirmed by the discovery in 1940, following a cave-in, of abandoned shafts filled with rusty machinery on ranch property 200 yards from the Mission). It was only to disprove another tale—that the bones of Serra and Crespí had been stolen and distributed as relics—which was still being told although their graves had been opened in 1856 to allay the rumor, that Padre Angelo Casanova on July 3, 1882, had the graves reopened before an assemblage of 400 persons. "The skeletons were in a good state," Father Casanova observed, "the ribs standing out in proper arch, part of the vestment in good order, also the heavy silk stole . . . with the silk fringe to it as good as new."

The restoration of the mission was at last undertaken in 1884 by Padre Casanova, pastor of San Carlos Church in Monterey, with the financial aid of Mrs. Leland Stanford and others; but unfortunately the work was prosecuted with more zeal than accuracy. As restored, the church wore a shingled roof of steep pitch whose lines were quite out of keeping with its original proportions. In buggies and carts, from all the surrounding countryside, people traveled by the thousands—visiting tourists from the newly opened Hotel Del Monte mingling with the descendants of pioneer Spanish families—to witness the consecration ceremonies on August 28, 1884, with Archbishop Joseph Sadoc Alemany officiating.

The roof remained for 52 years until it finally was replaced by one of tiles which restored the church's original appearance. Twelve years earlier the adobe chapel in the wing to the left of the main entrance had been restored as a setting for Jo Mora's Serra sarcophagus. Since 1936 restoration of the mission has gone on, guided by the inventories and reports of the padres, under direction of Harry Downie, skilled cabinet-maker, gardener, carver, painter, mender, and excavator. In reconstruction, the native materials used by the original builders have been used wherever possible and their plans copied with care. During realignment of State Highway 1, scrapers removing top earth from around the crumbling walls of the old mission rectangle uncovered hundreds of square yards of the original dull red tile flooring, buried for more than a century.

Beneath the two belfries with their arched apertures—one larger than the other surmounted by a dome—which flank the steep gable of the tile roof, stands the arched entrance to the mission church, overlooked by an elaborate window in Moorish design. Inside the entrance, to the left, is the baptistry in its covelike chamber beneath the larger of the two belfries, with a vaulted roof of carved stone, in which stands the ancient stone font where the Indians were baptized. Beyond the baptistry, occupying the wing which flanks the entrance, is the modern Mortuary Chapel, a small adobe replica of the chapel which originally stood here. In it lies a bronze sarcophagus (Jo Mora, sculptor), representing Padre Serra on his death bed, with Padre

CARMEL MISSION

Crespí standing at the head and Padres Lasuén and Lopez kneeling at his feet. To the right of the church's entrance a flight of 20 sandstone steps, deeply worn by the feet of padres and neophytes, winds to the choir loft, lit by an irregularly formed star window. The chancel with its arched ceiling leads to the rich altar, before which lie, under the pavement, the graves of Padres Serra, Crespí, and Lasuén (on the left) and of José Antonio Roméu, once governor, and Hermenegilde Sal, once *commandante* of the presidio (on the right). On the founder's grave is a wooden cross, placed there—according to legend —at the time of his death by a devoted Indian, whose grandson removed it when the wall fell in upon the grave and cared for it until he died, after which it was returned to the mission. The pulpit rises on the right from its original base. To the left opens a small chapel; to the right, the sacristy. The ancient beams of the sacristy's ceiling are held in place with wooden nails. Its stone lavabo, of four distinct pieces carved out of sandstone, is one of the finest specimens of mission carving in California. Throughout the church are many of its original paintings and statues, of which the most famous is perhaps the *Pietá,* painted in 1777 by Miguel Rodríguez, founder of the Academy of Fine Arts in Mexico City.

In the old cemetery outside the church, where the gnarled olive trees have grown for a century, neophytes and padres are buried. The wooden cross is the original one from the Corpus in the Church. On the south side, where excavation has brought to light the foundations of shops, storehouses, and dormitories, a rugged stairway of stone leads to the belfry.

At intervals since 1911 the founding of the mission has been celebrated here with pageantry. In 1934, the one hundred and fiftieth anniversary of Padre Serra's death was commemorated by presentation of George F. Marion's *The Apostle of California* on an outdoor stage.

Tours from Monterey

TOUR 1: THE SEVENTEEN-MILE DRIVE

Monterey—Pacific Grove—Pebble Beach—Carmel; *12.8 m.* Seventeen-Mile Drive. Roadbed paved throughout.

Originally 17 miles in length, the celebrated, advertised, talked-about drive around the shores of the Monterey Peninsula—the "Circle of Enchantment"—has been shortened with the years as the vast acres of the Del Monte Properties have been sold and developed. Begun in the eighties, the drive was not completed until 1916. And not until recent years did its starting point cease to be the Hotel Del Monte. But the natural beauty of today's drive remains unchanged: the sand dunes are as white, the water as vividly blue, the cypresses that hug the rocky shore as impressive, the pine forests in the background as darkly fragrant, as when fashionable tally-hos were drawn by high-trotting thoroughbreds along all of its 17 miles.

North from Friendly Plaza in MONTEREY, *0 m.* on Pacific St., which becomes Pacific St. Extension, which becomes Lighthouse Ave.; R. on Lighthouse, which becomes Central Ave. (Pacific Grove); L. on Central; L. on Fountain St.; R. on Lighthouse Ave.; L. on Seventeen-Mile Drive Ave.

South of the Seventeen-Mile Drive's NORTHERN TOLL GATE, *4 m. (automobiles 50c, pedestrians admitted free),* the route lies through a small forest of Monterey pines and scrub oaks.

The dry bed of LAKE MAJELLA, *4.4 m.,* has been filled in and a sand plant constructed here by the Del Monte Properties. This is the Pacific Coast's only plant for washing and steam-drying silica sand. The fine white sand is used on golf courses, children's playgrounds, for sandblasting, and in the manufacture of abrasives.

The route continues southward.*(It is important that the motorist take only right turns; if left turns are taken he may lose his way.)* The trees beside the drive are festooned with streamers of Spanish moss. In the distance to the right lies Moss Beach *(see PACIFIC GROVE: POINT OF INTEREST No. 8).*

The serenity of SPANISH BAY, *5.1 m.,* belies the treacherous currents offshore. Fishermen give this stretch of water a wide berth, for it was here that the *Roderich Dhu* went on the rocks in 1909 and was pounded to pieces.

The route turns seaward toward the rocky coast. In season the

HOTEL DEL MONTE

MONTEREY COAST

CYPRESS POINT GOLF COURSE

EL MONTE LODGE

CARMEL MISSION

MISSION COURTYARD

MISSION TOWER

TOR HOUSE, CARME

white sand bordering the road is carpeted with brilliantly hued flowers. The ocean takes on a variety of colors; sometimes it is a bright jade-green, its white-capped waves breaking far up on the rocks.

Off POINT JOE, 6.2 m., lies the RESTLESS SEA, one of the few places in the world where several conflicting currents meet. Often the foam-topped breakers move in from different directions and clash angrily. Occasional fishing craft and three large boats have gone down here. The latter were the S. S. Cecilia, the St. Paul, and the George F. Buck; their crews and most of their cargoes were rescued. The indigo blue of the water, usually found only at great depth, is due to the presence of a species of algae rare on the Pacific Coast.

The point was named after an old Japanese squatter who lived here for many years, resisting all efforts of eviction. Finally the Del Monte Properties bought out his holdings.

Stretching toward Point Joe are the smooth green lawns of the Monterey Peninsula Country Club (see GENERAL INFORMA-TION). Through here are open meadows and small private residences.

Offshore at 7.4 m. are SEAL ROCK and BIRD ROCK. The former is a nursery and breeding place of countless numbers of sea lions, whose barking can be heard from a great distance; the latter, the haunt of sea gulls, black cormorants, and sea ducks. Each morning these birds fly out to meet the fishing boats; each evening at sunset immense flocks wing their way back to the rocks.

South and east from the little cove sheltering FAN SHELL BEACH, 8.2 m., stretches Cypress Point Golf Course (see GEN-ERAL INFORMATION), rambling through a beautiful grove of Monterey cypresses.

At 9 m. is the junction with a short road.

Right on this road, which forms a "figure 8" and returns to the drive, 0.1 m. to the tip of CYPRESS POINT, the finest lookout on the road. To the southeast is brooding Point Lobos (see TOUR 3); farther east, the Santa Lucia Range. Wrote Bayard Taylor of this spot: "The extremity of the Point is a mass of gray rock, worn by the surf into fantastic walls and turrets. The heavy swells of the open sea, striking their bases with tremendous force, fill their crevices with foaming spray, which pours off in a hundred cataracts as the wave draws back for another shock. In the narrow channels between the rocks, the pent up waters roll inland with great force, flooding point after point and flinging high into the air the purple flags and streamers of seaweed, till they reach the glassy, sheltered pools that are quietly filled and emptied with every pulsation of the great sea without."

At *9.8 m.* is the junction with a short footpath.

Right here *0.1 m.* to MIDWAY POINT, to whose gaunt rocks cling the LONE CYPRESS—aided by wires provided by Del Monte Properties. This single tree has attracted tourist, photographer, and painter to the Seventeen-Mile Drive. Its pictures, good and bad, have graced postcard, calendar, art gallery, and parlor album. Its tenacious hold on the edge of its sheer cliff epitomizes the struggle of its kind against extinction. These trees once covered a large area of the Pacific Coast, but the sea cliffs of the Monterey Peninsula and Carmel Bay mark their last stand *(see THE NATURAL HERITAGE).* Their gnarled and twisted branches, distorted by winds sweeping in from the sea, sometimes assume grotesque forms. To Robert Louis Stevenson they were "ghosts fleeing before the wind."

The drive continues south through the wooded western fringe of exclusive PEBBLE BEACH, many of whose residents have duplicated the luxurious French and Italian villas of the Riviera; their estates are impressive.

At *10.5 m.* is the junction with Cypress Drive; the route turns L. on Cypress.

Right on the Seventeen-Mile Drive. *(This section of the drive is sometimes closed to the public.)* The GHOST TREE (L), *0.1 m.,* is a cypress trunk blasted to gleaming whiteness by wind and spray. The pale branches of the WITCH TREE (R), *0.2 m.,* reach out like long, eerie hands.

PESCADERO POINT, *0.3 m.,* site of an old Chinese fishing village, guards the entrance to STILLWATER COVE. The cove affords anchorage for pleasure yachts and the smart fishing boats of sportsmen. This section of the coast and some of its home have been the background for numerous motion pictures whose scenes have been the coasts of England, France, and Italy. Among pictures "shot" here were *Rebecca* and *Intermezzo.*

This countryside in 1840 was granted as the Rancho Pescadero to Fabian Barreto, and in that year he and his wife, María del Carmen, took possession. A year later Fabian died, and María del Carmen, though by nature neither rancher nor widow, remained on the ranch and added to it another grant, Rancho Canada Honda (deep canyon). In 1844 she married Juan Madariaga. Even with a husband her existence here was too tame for María del Carmen; she desired the social whirl of the capital—a good adobe *casa* in Monterey, where from between the shutters a woman could look out on life and romance. In 1846 María got her wish. She sold the rancho—more than 4,000 good acres— for $500, and purchased her heart's desire: a house in town on a 90-foot lot.

Within a few years the second owner of Rancho Pescadero died, and his widow sold the property for $4,400 to a Mr. Gore from New Jersey. In 1860 Government surveyor William Brewer wrote of the ranch that it had been "formerly owned by an eccentric, misanthropic, curious man [Gore] who lived in solitude and tried to educate two boys, keeping aloof from the world and the rest of mankind. He built a large and very secure loghouse, for fear of robbers. His books are still here—a strange collection of science, art, astrology, romance, infidelity, religion, mystery, etc. He invented a new harpoon, which no one could use."

Already chagrined at the price brought by the second sale of the Rancho Pescadero, María was thoroughly discontented when she learned that Gore

CARMEL VALLEY

had traded the rancho for Eastern property said to be valued at $33,000. Fourteen years after her original $500 sale, María del Carmen Garcia Barreto Madariaga boldly conveyed the same ranch to an agent of David Jacks of Monterey for $200, this time throwing in the Rancho Canada Honda. Jacks promptly paid up the back taxes, fenced the land, and started litigations that lasted for almost 50 years. One by one the legal descendants of Gore battled through the courts and died off, but not until the last claimant lost his life in the San Francisco fire of 1906 did the fight end. María received 12 cents an acre from her original sale; today the Del Monte Properties values single acres at several thousand dollars.

The Seventeen-Mile Drive returns to Cypress Drive at *0.7 m. (see below)*.

From the junction at *10.5 m.* the main route follows Cypress Drive to a junction with the Seventeen-Mile Drive, *10.9 m. (see above);* straight ahead on the Seventeen-Mile Drive, past DEL MONTE LODGE *(see DEL MONTE)*, which overlooks the eighteenth hole of the well-known PEBBLE BEACH GOLF LINKS, one of the finest and most attractive courses in the world, scene of annual championship matches.

At *12.5 m.* is a junction with a paved road.

Left here *1.4 m.* to the PEBBLE BEACH EXIT GATE of the Seventeen-Mile Drive and a junction with State 1, *1.5 m. (see TOURS 2 and 3)*.

The Seventeen-Mile Drive's SOUTHERN TOLL GATE, *12.8 m.*, is at the city limits of CARMEL-BY-THE-SEA *(see CARMEL)*.

TOUR 2: CARMEL VALLEY

Monterey Carmel Valley—Monterey; *37.9 m.* State 1, Carmel Valley Road, Monterey-Salinas Highway. Paved roadbeds throughout.

This route follows State 1 southward from Monterey, climbs a low ridge, and descends to the western end of the little valley of the Carmel River, just east of the Bay of Carmel, into which the stream empties. Eastward the route turns, leaving State 1 to follow the river toward the blue Santa Lucia Mountains into a pleasant agricultural region whose fertile lands produce some of the finest fruits and vegetables in the State. In the chaparral-studded heights far above the valley, range deer, wild boar, coyotes, rabbits, and quail; on the softer slopes below, high-grade Hereford cattle. Today's farms and ranches date from the grants bestowed by early governors: Figueroa, Alvarado, the land-generous Pico. The route leaves the river and its green valley, climbs abruptly over a spur of the Santa Lucia, and winds down to the little hollow that is Corral de Tierra (corral of earth). From here it strikes north through level lands to meet the

163

A GUIDE TO THE MONTEREY PENINSULA

Monterey-Salinas Highway, turns seaward, and returns to Monterey. South from Friendly Plaza in MONTEREY, *0 m.*, on Pacific St. to State 1; R. on State 1.

At *1.5 m.* is the junction with a dirt road.

Left on this road through a fragrant forest of dark pines, part of the Del Monte Properties *(see DEL MONTE),* to the junction with an oiled and dirt road, *1.5 m.*, R. here. Visible from LOOKOUT POINT, *2.2 m.*, are the entire Monterey Peninsula and much of Monterey Bay. East of the lookout the side route follows a one-way road *(impassable in bad weather)* to the SUMMIT OF JACK'S PEAK, 1,080 alt.), *5 m.*, named for David Jacks, pioneer Monterey Presbyterian who acquired through clever real estate manipulations an amazing part of Monterey County. From this distance Monterey Bay, to the north and west, is a miniature, holding its toy fleet of fishing boats daintily between the breakwater and the pier. To the east lie blue mountains and rolling brown hills; to the west stretches the Pacific Ocean. The view is best after nightfall when the moon lays a bright path across the water and whitens the silver oil tanks near East Monterey.

State 1 reaches ahead to the summit *(2 m.)* of the rise known simply as "the Carmel hill." In the days when the trail between Mission San Carlos Borromeo de Carmelo and the *pueblo* of Monterey lay across it this was the Devil's Elbow—a haunted place feared by the Spanish and by the Indians before them, who knew that fog ghosts hid in the little hollow atop the ridge. Here lurked the spirit of La Gallina y Gallinitos (the hen and little chickens), whispered about the length of Alta California—for the blackest luck would befall the person who saw La Gallina, or heard the plaintive cheeping of Las Gallinitos. To this hill a gentle, beloved padre of Carmel was trailed by a *mal hombre* (bad man) who knew that the padre carried in a sack a hen and seven chicks, intended for a sick man in Monterey. Here the *mal hombre* brought his pistol butt down upon the head of the holy man, snatched the sack and hurried away. But when he reached home he found the sack empty. He retraced his steps and was amazed to find the hen and her young scratching diligently in the moist earth beside the padre. Again he collected his booty—and again found the sack empty when he reached home. For the third time he returned to this hillock. The hen and chicks were there, scratching industriously. The *mal hombre* glanced fearfully at the fallen padre. The holy man was dead. The robber raised the pistol to his own head and pulled the trigger.

It was on this swale, according to legend, that a childless couple returning home from a dance at Monterey saw a child weeping disconsolately in the dusty road. The couple picked up the infant, and thanking God for their gift, rode on. But shortly the childish crying was supplanted with laughter—horrible and fiendish. Before the good couples' eyes the child became a squirming red devil. They dropped it and fled—but never again, it is said, did they miss Mass at Monterey.

Just south of the eastern exit of the Seventeen-Mile Drive (R), *2.1 m. (see TOUR 1),* is a junction with Carmel Road, *2.7 m.*

Right here *1 m.* is CARMEL-BY-THE-SEA (220 alt., 2,806 pop.) *(see CARMEL).*

At *4.5 m.* on State 1 is a junction with Carmel Valley Road; the route goes L. here into Carmel Valley, edged on the north by brown foothills, on the south by a blue-green range at whose feet flows Carmel River. At the mouth of the valley lie fields of pale green, feathery artichokes. These lands were part of the vast gardens of Carmel Mission.

The road climbs steadily into low foothills, past fields of artichokes, cabbages, and pumpkins—the latter dotting their vine-covered fields with bright golden orange in autumn.

A San Francisco businessman in 1940 bought the 22,000-acre RANCHO SAN CARLOS, *6.9 m.,* made famous by the Eastern attorney-sportsman George Gordon Moore, who purchased it in 1923 from the heirs of Judge Bradley V. Sargent and spent a million dollars to make it one of the showplaces of the West. Moore built a 57-room hacienda, guest cottages, an airport, a swimming pool, race-track, polo field, golf course, and a game refuge which he stocked with wild Russian boar from his North Carolina estate. The market crash of 1929 wiped away Moore's fortune, and not long after the ranch was sold to satisfy his creditors.

The property consisted of two former grants, El Potrero de San Carlos (the Pasture of St. Charles) and San Francisquito (Little St. Francis), and when owned by the Sargent family was called the Rancho San Francisquito y San Carlos.

The CARMEL STONE QUARRY (L), *7.9 m.,* and ROGER'S QUARRY (L), *9.2 m.,* ship chalk-rock—used as a building material since the days of the padres—to various parts of the State. An old industry is being revived in the valley. Adobe bricks, becoming popular again as building material, are manufactured here, but with the advantages of modern ingenuity: oil is added to the mixture to make the bricks waterproof.

Pear orchards stretch beside the BERWICK RANCH, *10.9 m.,*

owned today by the daughter of Edward Berwick, who came to Monterey from England in 1862, became a successful rancher-farmer—he introduced "winter nellies" (winter nelis, a variety of pear) to California—and onetime mayor of Pacific Grove.

The Berwick ranch is commonly mistaken for the "little goat ranch" on which Robert Louis Stevenson was "nursed back to health by kind mountaineers." Stevenson, who had met Berwick and been invited by the latter to visit his ranch, dropped in unexpectedly late one night with his friend, Jo Strong. Berwick had a houseful of guests and was forced to prepare beds for the two in his hayloft. The next morning Stevenson and Strong rose early and resumed their hike into the Santa Lucia, climbing the 24 per cent grade of Robinson Canyon. During the day they stopped in Rocky Canyon at a small place still called "the goat ranch," continued their walk, and again arrived—again late at night—at Berwick's. Mrs. Berwick got out of bed, bustled into the kitchen, and asked Stevenson, "What can I fix for you—a cup of hot coffee or a whiskey toddy?" Replied the exhausted writer, "I'd like *both*."

Center of social and commercial life for valley ranchers is the CARMEL SOCIAL AND ATHLETIC CLUB (R), *11.4 m.* (also known as the Farm Center). The little white frame one-story building is the scene of Grange and 4-H Club meetings and parties and a market from which farmers sell their products—wholesale and retail —to buyers from the Monterey Peninsula.

Past orchards and neat green fields the road ascends to a junction with Los Laurelles Road, *15.6 m.;* the main route goes L. here.

Straight ahead on Carmel Valley Road to a junction with a narrow oiled road, *13.8 m.;* R. here to a junction with a dirt road, *14.1 m.;* L. here. The founder of JAMESBURG, *16.9 m. (cabins),* John James of North Carolina, came here in 1867 and succeeded in attracting to the tiny settlement a post office and passenger stage—neither of which serve Jamesburg today.

In 1928 a disastrous fire destroyed thousands of acres of forest and chaparral —and most of the rattlesnakes—in this region. Now the trees have their second growth and the snakes are becoming larger and more plentiful each year.

South of Jamesburg the road climbs rapidly, often precariously, to the top of the ridge. The country is wild, offering superb views on all sides. The wooded hills roll down to the Salinas Valley (L) and the blue Pacific (R). Meadowlarks sing in the clearing; roadrunners and quail streak from the paths of oncoming cars.

The road crosses the northern boundary of Los Padres National Forest at *20.4 m.* and continues its steady climb to CHINA CAMP *24.6 m. (campsites, stoves, tables, comfort stations),* one of nine similar camps in the forest. The route southward lies over a dizzily precipitous one-way road. *(Telephone Tassajara Springs from below China Camp to learn whether northbound traffic obstructs road.)* Huge rocks jut from the chaparral; tall yuccas catch the light.

The waters of TASSAJARA (Ind., meat-curing place) SPRINGS (1,700 alt.), *31.1 m. (hotel; baths and plunges, saddle horses),* long have been known for their medicinal qualities. The Indians used these waters long before the Spanish occupation; the huge tub hollowed in rock under a corner of a modern bath house was made with their crude implements. The Tassajara River flows at the base of the mountains, a clear, rapid stream. From boulders along its banks flow the hot springs, containing sulphur, iron, soda, magnesia, lithia, and other minerals. Some of the water is 160° Fahrenheit.

Steep, oil-bound Los Larelles Road winds quickly up the mountain. To the south appear the Santa Lucias, dark with forest and brush; to the east, the brown hills running up to El Toro (the bull); and beyond, the blue Gavilans, looking down on the Salinas Valley, its wide acres of lettuce brightly green the year round. Northward lies Monterey Bay, with Loma Prieta (dark hill) flat and sullen against the horizon. Westward, the hills roll away to rocky headlands: Point Lobos, Cypress, and Pinos.

The summit, *19.5 m.,* offers an excellent view of Corral de Tierra *(see below),* that little bowl of earth about which John Steinbeck wrote *The Pastures of Heaven.* The author described the discovery of the valley, "sometime around 1776," by a soldier from Carmel Mission sent to return "a group of twenty converted Indians [who had] abandoned religion during a night." Atop a ridge, the corporal —"he whose rapacious manhood was building a new race for California, this bearded, savage bearer of civilization slipped from his saddle and took off his steel hat. 'Holy Mother!' he whispered. 'Here are the green pastures of Heaven to which our Lord leadeth us'."

The valley "lay forgotten in its embracing hills. The . . . corporal . . . intended to go back . . . he looked forward . . . to an adobe house beside a stream, and cattle muzzling the walls at night." But Steinbeck's corporal died, and "after a long time a few families of squatters moved into the Pastures of Heaven and built fences and planted fruit trees. Since no one owned the land, they squabbled a great deal over its possession. After a hundred years there were twenty families on twenty little farms in the Pastures of Heaven. Near the center of the valley stood a general store and postoffice, and half a mile above, beside the stream, a hacked and much initialed schoolhouse."

The story moves to the present, to a group of sightseers in a bus which "moved slowly on, up the Carmel Valley—past orchards and past fields of artichokes, and past a red cliff, veined with green creepers. The afternoon was waning now, and the sun sank toward the seaward mouth of the Valley. The road left the Carmel River and

climbed up a hillside until it ran along the top of a narrow ridge . . ."
And the sightseers "climbed stiffly from their seats and stood on the
ridge peak and looked down into the Pastures of Heaven. And the
air was as golden gauze in the last of the sun. The land below them
was plotted in squares of green orchard trees and in squares of yellow grain and in squares of violet earth. From the sturdy farmhouses, set in their gardens, the smoke of the evening fires drifted
upward until the hillbreeze swept it cleanly off. Cowbells were softly
clashing in the valley; a dog barked so far away that the sound rose
up to the travelers in sharp little whispers. Directly below the ridge
a band of sheep had gathered under an oak tree against the night."

Three main land grants covered this territory: the Pilarcitos
(palisades), El Toro, and the Corral de Tierra. Pilarcitos, locally
known as the Chamisal Ranch from the quantities of that brush
growing on the hills, was granted to F. Vasquez in 1835. El Toro
belonged to José Ramon Estrada, *alcalde* of Monterey in 1836. Out
in this country young Tiburcio Vásquez staked a claim but was too
busy avoiding the law to prove up on his land. The large grants have
long since broken up into small holdings, and many commuters now
have suburban homes in the flat regions of the old ranchos most
easily accessible to Monterey and Salinas.

At *22.1 m.* the route turns sharply R. onto a narrow road that
twists downward into CORRAL DE TIERRA.

At *23.8 m.* is the junction with a paved road; the route goes L.
here.

Straight ahead *1.1 m.* to the old WASHINGTON SCHOOL, a grade school
attended by farm children for many years, modernized into a buff-colored,
frame, gable-roofed structure. A tremendous, umbrella-shaped old oak, its
heavy branches growing low and parallel to the ground, stands in the school
yard, an excellent tree for climbing—and as well suited for lynching, if legend
is believed. The tree is reputed to be 4,000 years old. The oldest inhabitants of
the valley played under it when they were children, as do their grandchildren
today.

Beyond the school lies the heart of Corral de Tierra. There are many fine
old farmhouses in the valley, spaced almost exactly a mile apart. These mark
the time when the grants were first broken up for homesteaders; their solid
construction is symbolic of the pioneer spirit which built for more than the
immediate generation. Today these homes have been repainted and modernized.
Besides them stretch fields of pumpkins and squash, tall corn and bright
tomatoes. Above the fields grow many buckeye trees, impressive in winter when
their white trunks and branches, stripped bare of leaves, form patterns against
the brown hills.

The main route continues north to a junction with the Monterey-Salinas Highway, *26 m.*, on which it goes L.

Right on the Monterey-Salinas Highway to a junction with a dirt road, *3.9 m.;* L. here *5 m.* to FORT ORD *(see MONTEREY: POINT OF INTEREST No. 39).*

The main route follows the highway west through flat farmlands edged by foothills.

The 2,180-acre RANCHO LAGUNA SECA (dry lake), *28.5 m.* (R), was granted to Catalina Munras in 1834 and is owned today by descendants of the grantee: Esteban (to Montereyans, "Stevie") Field and his sister, *Excelentisima* María Antonia Field, who was knighted by the King of Spain in 1933. A high picket fence bristling with barbed wire protects the ranch lands; costing thousands of dollars, the fence was built when the Fields planned to make a game refuge of the property.

The route continues west, enters Monterey on Fremont St., which ends at Munras St., goes R. on Munras to Polk St., and L. on Polk to its starting point: Friendly Plaza, *37.9 m.*

TOUR 3: BIG SUR

Monterey—Big Sur; *33.5 m.* State 1. Roadbed paved throughout.

Opened in 1937, after two decades of hard and dangerous labor, the spectacular Carmel-San Simeon Highway (State 1) pierces the Big Sur: a region of lonely grandeur, jealously guarded by the Santa Lucia Mountains—a country slashed by canyons so deep that even its trailmakers had a disheartening task. Its sparkling streams, its ancient, dark redwood trees, its golden pastures 1,500 to 3,500 feet above the sea have been claimed, fought over, and possessed again and again since 1834 when Juan Alvarado claimed the Rancho El Sur as a grant from Governor Figueroa.

The new highway opens the coastal fringe of a region made familiar by the poetry of Robinson Jeffers, to whom this is a somber, brooding country, its isolated people passionate and strange. It poises over gorges carved from rock, dips drunkenly to the sea, spans slim concrete bridges, shoots unexpectedly high above the pounding surf—where men and equipment went into the sea. The hundreds who labored on the road—the catskinners, the bulldozers, the blademen, some free, some convicts—have left behind them a score of stories, some half-legendary, little more than a decade since they have gone.

Few roads were needed more than this. In 1913 a wagon road led south from Monterey about 40 miles, but of it the Salinas *Daily Index* complained "it is a wonder more lives were not lost this year, considering that about 100 drivers were stuck . . . last year. Why not . . . build a Coast road?" Two years later the Salinas *Morning Democrat* protested: "On the Big Sur road, work—what is done— is pick and shovel, and brush overgrows the road until it looks like a cow-path . . . the driver has to yell, 'Low bridge! Look out for hats!' . . . and you bump over loose rocks, stones, and unfilled water- ways, left from last season's rains."

More serious, and more constructive, were the protests of Dr. John Roberts, a young physician who as early as 1897 had traveled the tortuous route by horseback to tend his patients. Roberts fought long and hard for a new road, believing that $50,000 would pay for its construction. He finally appealed to the State Legislature, where he found a staunch ally in Senator Elmer S. Rigdon. To Rigdon goes much of the credit for passage of the bill that in 1919 authorized construction of the highway—which was to cost the lives of men, the loss of equipment, and $10,000,000 before its completion. On June 28, 1937, the new road was opened officially by Governor Frank Merriam, who (said the *Peninsula Herald*) "clipped ribbons, dedicated monuments, set off powder blasts, released pigeons, and posed for photographs all day long." There to watch thousands pour over the highway for the first time were the man who built it, Divi- sion Engineer Lester Gibson, and the man who wanted it built—Dr. John Roberts

South from Friendly Plaza in MONTEREY, *0 m.*, on Pacific St. to State 1; R. on State 1 *(see TOUR 2)*.

At *4.5 m.* is a junction with Carmel Valley Road *(see Tour 2)*.

State 1 continues south past fields of green artichokes at the mouth of Carmel Valley, crosses the concrete span over Carmel River, *5.2 m.*, and turns west to meet the ocean.

The spire-topped, red-roofed, buff-colored stuccoed building atop a knoll (L) at *6.3 m.*, the CARMELITE MONASTERY, was given by Francis Sullivan (one time State Senator) in memory of his wife, Alice, to the Discalced (Lat., barefoot) Carmelite Nuns of Our Lady and Saint Therese. The nuns, vowed to silence, live here in strict se- clusion. Near the monastery is Villa Angelica, rest home for Domini- can nuns.

The tiny semicircular cove (R) known locally as JAP BAY was

once the headquarters for a colony of Japanese abalone fishermen. Before the Japanese a settlement of Chinese was here.

In POINT LOBOS STATE PARK, *7.3 m.*, is POINT LOBOS RESERVE *(pedestrians admitted free; adm. 25c per automobile; no camping; picnic tables; fire permits for use of barbecue pits available from warden)*, on a rocky promontory fringed with wind-blown trees. Purchased by the State in 1932 for $600,000, the park comprises 450 acres extending for 3½ miles along the coast. Fifteen acres were donated as a memorial to A. M. Allen, from whose heirs the property was purchased.

The reserve and point, named Punta de los Lobos Marinos (point of the sea wolves) by the Spanish, comprise one of the most beautiful spots on the California coast. This is the northernmost resting place of the brown pelican, a habitat of the sea lion, and the southernmost stand of the Monterey cypress (a State-maintained station here is devoted to the study and perpetuation of this indigenous tree). Robert Louis Stevenson made visits here in 1879, and some believe that Spyglass Hill in his *Treasure Island* was described with Point Lobos in mind. More recently the poet of this coast country Robinson Jeffers, has captured the dark beauty and passion of the place in his poem *Tamar,* describing:

"... the wind-torn Lobos cypress trunks.
  (O torture of needled branches
Doubled and gnarled, never a moment quit, the northwind
  or the southwind or the northwest.
For up and down the coast they are tall and terrible
  horsemen on patrol, alternate giants
Guarding the granite and sand frontiers of the last
  ocean, but here at Lobos the winds are torturers,
The old trees endure them ..."

Once this was part of the Rancho San José y Sur Chiquito (St. Joseph and the Little South), granted to Marcellino Escobar by Governor Alvarado in 1839, which extended from the Carmel River south to the Little Sur River and "inland as far as the cattle graze." Escobar lost the grant to Captain Castro and nine of his soldiers in a dice game. Castro, who bought out his partners, later sold the ranch to two Americans who discovered coal on the property and organized the Carmel Land and Coal Company. The coal they brought from Mal Paso Canyon by muleback for shipment from Jap Bay. In the seventies, when whaling was an important industry in Pacific waters,

171

a flagman was stationed on Point Lobos to signal fisherman when a whale appeared offshore.

Fashionable CARMEL HIGHLANDS, *8.5 m.*, boasts *an expensive inn* and a number of private estates and homes built on a rocky, forested hillside that slopes steeply into the sea. The coast here often has been compared to that of Cornwall. Highlands residents include playwright Martin Flavin, and marine painter William Ritschel. A wide parking area overlooks Ritschel's gaunt, castlelike home, built of native rock—inside and out—by the artist himself. The gloomy house perches on the edge of the cliff, and to the accompaniment of the waves crashing in the sea-hollowed caverns beneath its foundation, Ritschel paints the photographic marine canvases for which he is famous. The impressive tile-roofed home above Ritschel's also is constructed of native stone. In warm earth tones, it blends into the cliff on which it stands, so that the observer must look closely to detect the rock of the house from that of its foundation.

The deep gorge of MAL PASO (bad crossing) CREEK *10.1 m.*, was named by early travelers who struggled across it with pack mule and wagon. A new concrete bridge now swings gracefully above the rough old wagon trail far below.

Southward State 1 traverses low foothills, smooth and round, cutting an earth-banked path sharply through the hearts of some. Tiny, narrow canyons opening into the sea lose themselves in the distant mountains. Sheltered by the hills are occasional lonely farmhouses whose pastures reach to the water's edge.

Tall redwoods line the watercourse of PALO COLORADO CANYON, *17.1 m.*, the setting for *Roan Stallion*, another of Jeffer's poems. Here his heroine, California, rode the roan stallion across mountain pastures in the moonlight.

Left from Palo Colorado Canyon on a narrow unpaved road *2 m.*, to HOFFMAN'S CAMP *(accommodations; horses available for pack and hunting trips)*, in Los Padres National Forest, a vast recreation area crossed by excellent hiking trails.

Deserted NOTLEY'S LANDING, *17.5 m.*, bears little reminder of the time when it was a thriving village and shipping port for the timber from Palo Colorado and Garrapata (wood tick) Canyons. The timber was brought out by muleback and on clumsy wooden sleds and loaded by cable onto waiting vessels. In 1880 Henry Martin filed a claim on this land. It passed through many hands, finally coming to H. Kron and Godfrey Notley, who founded a small boom town. Tanbark was a lucrative source of income for the landing, but when the supply was exhausted, the town was slowly abandoned. Reputedly Chinese smuggled into California were landed here. Later the spot achieved local notoriety as a rum-running center during Prohibition.

One of the world's highest single-span arch bridges is concrete RAINBOW BRIDGE, *19.3 m.*, over Bixby Creek. Engineering triumph of the road, it is 714 feet long and 285 feet above the sea. The concrete abutments, securely anchored into the sheer rock walls 140 feet above the creekbed, are 330 feet apart; the graceful rings of the open spandrel arch bow above the canyon mouth to carry the deck of the bridge, approximately 260 feet above the creek bottom. Into its construction went 6,600 cubic yards of concrete and 600,000 pounds of reinforcing steel. Unders its slim concrete legs the waves break against a sandy beach in a cove from which shrub-covered mountains rise abruptly from the sea.

It was from this bridge, in March, 1938, that a local man and his wife observed a herd of nearly a hundred strange animals in the creek below. They notified Dr. Walter Fisher of Pacific Grove's Hopkins Marine Laboratories, who identified the creatures for an astonished community and an all but incredulous scientific world as *Enhydra lutris pereis*—E-luk-ke to the Clatsop Indians, *nutria* to the Spaniards, and to nineteenth-century trapper and traders, the otter, bearer of one of the most beautiful and valuable furs in the world. Until the construction of the Carmel-San Simeon highway opened the wild virgin country of the coast region, the wildlife remained unmolested; isolated and protected inlets offered the sorely pressed animals an escape—provided a sanctuary for a pitiful remnant of the species. The dangerous coast with its rocky shoals enabled them to survive, to reproduce every two years their single young and augment the herd.

Particularly proud of the discovery of the herd are the Biological Survey and the Fish and Game Commission, who enforced the international laws of March 4, 1909, forbidding the sale or possession of otter pelts. Before this law went into effect, skins in perfect condition were worth, in St. Louis and other fur centers, from $1,000 to $5,000 each.

The otter is the size of a mastiff dog; "form low and heavy; tail flattened, a foot long; hind feet webbed, paddle-like; front feet adapted for holding food and young; color very dark brown, with grey head and throat. Prime fur or adult is deep and soft," with long, white-tipped hairs scattered through it, giving it the beautiful, frosted appearance that makes it so valuable. Like seals, otters are highly gregarious, congregating always in herds. Early accounts describe them as timid and gentle, unafraid of man, easily killed with clubs and spears. Indian hunters brought down from the North by a Boston whaler in 1805 speared nearly 2,000 in a few months.

In 1805 Lewis and Clarke found their fur worn generally and valued highly by the Clatsop Indians. "One Indian was wearing three very elegant sea-otter skins, which he refused to sell for less than 3 fathoms of *blue* beads for each skin."

On Castle Rock (R) the ruins of BIXBY LANDING stand gaunt on the edge of the cliff, reminder of the days when lime from the mines on three-mile-distant Long Ridge was brought down by cable and loaded here. In 1905 one of the thrilling sights promised vacationers by the proprietor of nearby Hotel Idlewild *(see below)* was the view from the summit above Bixby Creek of the aerial tramway of the Monterey Lime Company. This cable transported the lime in two enormous buckets down to the mouth of the creek, where it was hoisted aboard small coastwise freighters. The lime, never of superior quality, paid well enough until the supply of firewood gave out; then, as it was too expensive to import fuel for the kilns, Bixby Landing was abandoned.

When this country was opened to homesteaders in the 1870's many took up the 640-acre plots offered and struggled to make them pay. Those who remained live far from the new road on isolated ranches, marooned in winter, still living a primitive frontier existence but a few hours' trip from coast and inland cities.

At *25.4 m.* is the junction with a dirt road.

Right on this road *0.5 m.* across a level sandy stretch and up a spiraling precipitous course to the red-roofed buildings of POINT SUR LIGHT STATION *(open Mon., Wed., Fri., 1-4)*, perched on a rocky mesa 450 feet above the booming breakers of the rugged coast. On this lonely height live the families of four lighthouse keepers—about 19 people in all—most of them in a three-story house of native granite, keeping cats, dogs, chickens, and a cow. To reach their eyrie above the sea, the road climbs 364 feet with an average grade of 11.2 per cent—in places even steeper. When the lighthouse was built in 1889, the rock was scaled by 395 wooden steps and a cable to transport supplies. The light flashes a 1,000,000-candlepower beam from its giant lens, visible 26 miles at sea, every 15 seconds. When fog blankets the water, the two diaphone fog signals sound two hoarse blasts every 60 seconds.

From the Big Sur ranches roundabout came the hardy men who labored to construct the lighthouse—its buildings, stairways, water system—taking a fierce pride in their work. When a very special light intended for Pigeon Point, ordered from France brought round the Horn, was sent to Point Sur instead, there was mighty rejoicing in the wild mountain country. Brown old men in their eighties still boast to their grandchildren, "I helped built that light-house." Old Choppy Casuse was the only dissenter; when asked what he thought of the new light, he answered, "Good light—but she no work. Go all the time sad 'Boo-Boo,' but the fog she creep in just the same."

Before the lighthouse was built, Point Sur twice had been the scene of marine disasters. When in November, 1873, the *S. S. Los Angeles* ran aground by the lighthouse, young Dr. Roberts made record time to the rescue. He rode the 30 miles from Monterey in three and one-half hours to find 150 victims, dead or alive, washed up on the beach and clinging to the shore. For three days he labored to save the survivors. In 1879 the *Ventura* went down off Point Sur with a cargo of fine linen and knockdown wagons. From miles around the ranchers came. They furnished their homes with elegant articles all out of keeping with the poverty of their shacks. Some of the wagons still stagger and squeak over the back roads.

On February 13, 1935, Point Sur's lighthouse keeper watched the giant silvery Navy dirigible *Macon* cruise past in the early twilight, escorted by a flotilla of 34 craft of the battle fleet. Only a few miles southward from the point a sudden wind hit the great airship, crumbling up its aft section. When Navy craft answering its "SOS" reached the spot, the *Macon,* badly crippled, was settling into the ocean. Of the 83 men aboard, all but two—radio operator and mess boy—were saved. After weeks of hearings, in which reasons given for the disaster ranged from sabotage to faulty design, a court of inquiry decided that no definite cause could be assigned. This $3,450,000 airship was the last of the Government's large dirigibles.

Its loss recalled an earlier balloon disaster, whose story the *Monterey Peninsula Herald* of February 14, 1935, retold: "Thirty-two years ago an ambitious gas bag flight from San Francisco ended in grief in the wilds inland from the lighthouse when the highly-touted Dr. Greth Mammoth Air Liner crashed. It was not supposed to go anywhere near the coast mountains but to rise majestically from the Market Street Ball Park in San Francisco, circle the Call Building, cruise over Oakland and Berkeley, returning shortly for a triumphant reception. Stock sales in companion ships were to be boosted and air travel generally launched in California.

"Instead of that the ship manned by veteran Tom Baldwin was caught by a freshening north wind as soon as it arose, and blown backward out of sight in the general direction of Mexico. Soon all reports of it ceased and promoters, including Perry Newberry, Carmel editor and writer, took to seclusion.

"After hours of silence a telegram from the Point Sur Lighthouse Keeper told of Baldwin's dishevelled arrival on foot. The promoters still hid, knowing that a much publicized flight, ending with a balloon being blown backward miles off its course would be the laughing stock of the west."

South of Point Sur the highway swings inland up the sycamore-shaded canyon of the BIG SUR RIVER, *27.7 m.*, winding over gravelly bottoms. In the canyon depths is the only place where the sycamore and the redwood grow within the same half-acre, identifying the region as a transition zone between the typical redwood zone and southern arid desert region. In the river bottoms and up the mountainsides grow the redwoods—tall, straight trees, towering upward in immense dignity. Here the great wild country gives way to an intimate resort land, where little cabins are tucked beneath the trees and refreshment stands and barbecue pits face the highway.

Northward stretches the MOLERA RANCH, once known as Rancho El Sur—the "Ranch of the South," so named because it was south of Monterey—from which point and river take their name. Granted to Juan Bautista Alvarado in 1834, the 8,949-acre estate was later confirmed to Juan Bautista Roger Cooper. A shrewd Yankee trader, Cooper acquired many land grants for little or nothing. For many years he sailed to China with otter furs. Since customs duties were high, he schemed to avoid paying them by smuggling ashore at the mouth of the Big Sur and transporting overland to Monterey the merchandise brought back.

Cooper's grandson Andrew J. Molera, inherited the ranch. A giant of a man, Molera rode to Monterey with his long *tapaderos* (stirrup guards) touching the flowers as he passed, his silver-studded bit shining in the sun. At the ranch, his peacocks trailed their feathers beside the rippling waters of the Big Sur River. When Molera was head of it, the Rancho El Sur was famous for its Monterey Jack cheese, of which wagonloads went over the montains to an eager market. The ranch was famed also for its hospitality. Fiestas went on merrily with *cascarón* dances while the population of the coast camped on the Big Sur River banks awaiting for the trading vessel that brought down winter supplies from San Francisco. This annual occurrence was anticipated for months. When the farm produce was loaded onto pack horse or mule, the family stepped forth gaily to make a holiday of exchanging the produce for goods from the city. Campfires and the music of accordion and Spanish guitar brightened one week of their dull lives, and roast bull's head and roast peacock contributed an exotic note to Molera's hospitality.

At *29.3 m.* is the junction with a dirt road.

Left on this road *0.5 m.* to the junction with the narrow, graveled old coast road; L. here on State 1's predecessor, winding downhill and up again, over whose tortuous path Cooper, noted for his recklessness, used to drive his team of small California horses on the run. From the ridge it descends into the sheltered Little Sur Valley, where stands the deserted COOPER RANCH HOUSE, *3.7 m.*, in its haunting old garden. Built under the captain's direction, the house was constructed of lumber brought round the Horn.

On the banks of the Little Sur River is IDLEWILD, *18.2 m. (accommodations)*. At the turn of the century the resort's proprietor, W. T. Mitchell, advertised that "the stage, a light wagon with no canopy, drawn by four horses," left the Pacific Ocean House in Monterey at 8:30 a.m. each Monday, Wednesday, and Friday, arrived at Smith's stage station at the mouth of Palo Colorado Canyon in time for lunch, and reached Idlewild in time for dinner—

COPPER BAS-RELIEF, CARMEL

LOVERS' POINT

PACIFIC GROVE MUNICIPAL POOL

CARMEL VALLEY FARM

HACK IN PALO COLORADO CANYON

RAINBOW BRIDGE, BIXBY CREEK

SANTA LUCIA MOUNTAINS

HOPKINS MARINE STATION

making the 24 miles in about 10 hours. Hotel rates at Idlewild then were quoted at $1.50 a day, family table, "everything included," and a limit of trout was guaranteed the traveler even though he fished from his own tent platform, used a bent pin, and had never fished before.

Thousands of vacationists each year visit the PFEIFFER RED-WOODS STATE PARK *(lodge and cabins; saddle horses; guide)*, *33.5 m.*, 740-acre redwood grove on the banks of the Big Sur River. Amid the giant trees, some of them 1,000 years old and towering more than 200 feet above the crystal-clear stream once known as the Rio Arbolado (river of shady trees), this park is considered one of the most beautiful of the State's 73 recreation areas. It offers complete accommodations for the visitor, including Big Sur Lodge, an outdoor theatre, a swimming pool, and facilities for hunting, fishing, riding, and hiking amid some of the most rugged and least-explored mountain scenery on the California coast.

Originally some 680 acres in extent, the gift of heirs of Michael Pfeiffer of the State Park Commission in 1934, the park was later expanded to its present area by land donated by Monterey County. Value of the Pfeiffer gift was $70,000 and the county contributed $18,000 in cash to match the $76,000 of State park funds provided in 1928. In consideration of the initial owner, the park was named for the pioneer family which had pre-empted a claim in the Big Sur valley. It is now part of the Los Padres National Forest, third largest in the nation and the only national forest with ocean frontage.

With all its modern conveniences, Pfeiffer Redwoods State Park is still primitive in aspect; and it abounds with deer, Russian wild boar, and valley and mountain quail. Among the sheer crags of adjacent mountains bald and golden eagles occasionally are found, and here the American condor, said to be the largest North American bird, is making its last stand.

The Big Sur country was first settled in November, 1869. It was a gray, windy day when the old sidewheeler *Sierra Nevada* pulled out from its wharf at San Francisco, carrying on board Michael Pfeiffer, his young wife, Barbara, and their four small children.

The housing above the paddle-wheel was used as a corral for Pfeiffer's cattle. The trip was a nightmare, waves breaking clear over the boat, while all the seasick passengers hung grimly to the rail. The evening of the second day the little *Sierra Nevada* chugged into the calm waters of Monterey Bay; and young Mrs. Pfeiffer, too ill to stand, had somehow to get her four wan and weeping children ashore and begin to make preparations for the hard part of the journey which was still ahead of them, 40 miles of Indian trail, leading at last to Sycamore Canyon in the untouched fastness of the Big Sur.

A small shelter had been erected and the little Pfeiffer boys, Charlie and John, had already named a spring near the shack "Bears Kill Two Calf Spring" before Mrs. Pfeiffer discovered she had a neighbor. Her husband was out killing grizzly bears the morning that a shadow fell across the rock on which she was rubbing clothes clean, and Barbara Pfeiffer looked up to see a savage-looking Indian. He knew no English, but by signs he made her understand that he had a sick child at his *hogan*. Mrs. Pfeiffer got her precious bottle of castor oil, measured out a dose, and poured it into a little horn cup her husband had whittled out. The Indian took it and vanished.

The Indian, Immanuel Innocente, his wife Francisca, and their four children proved very good neighbors. Peak Immanuel, which rises grandly from the river, is named for this Indian. He and all his family are buried on what was their own land, by a sycamore-sheltered curve of the Big Sur River, not far from the resort lodge. The CCC boys in the Big Sur Camp have built a stone fence, enclosing the Innocente burial plot.

Though game was plentiful, the Pfeiffers found their attempts to raise horses, cattle and hogs on their isolated ranch were impeded by attacks on their stock by grizzly bears, by deer that raided their gardens, and by erosion caused by rainfall averaging 65 to 85 inches per year. Until wiped out by smallpox, a group of Esselon Indians imported from Alaska by a nearby colony of Russian hunters of sea otter aided the Pfeiffers' efforts at farming. To avoid tedious, two-day horseback trips to Monterey the Pfeiffers developed barter trade with small coastwise vessels in which vegetables, meat, milk, and honey were exchanged for staples carried by the boats. Gradually, as their farm became a popular resort for sportsmen, the Pfeiffers saw the establishment of a hunting lodge on their premises and the inauguration of horsedrawn stage service between Big Sur and Monterey. The stage road, impassable today but still visible, followed the coastline and its route over rugged hills providing many a thrill to travelers before construction of State 1.

As the Pfeiffer family's many children grew up, they homesteaded, until in the Big Sur country it was said there was "a Pfeiffer on every hill." By 1880 the land up and down the coast from Sycamore Canyon began to be settled. The Simon Castros; the Josè de la Torres; Edwin Grimes, a bachelor from England, all had ranches. William B.

Post with his wife, a Carmel Indian girl named Anaselma Onesimo, and their family of almost-grown boys and girls settled on land just south of the holdings of Immanuel Innocente.

But it required the advent of the automobile, decades later to overcome the isolation of the Big Sur's fastnesses. As late as 1924 dwellers in these lonely coast mountains were reported never to have seen "anything . . . except something which can be packed on horses or mules." The story is told of two youths, 17 and 19, who were asked how they amused themselves. The younger volunteered, very shyly, that a year before they had been up to Pfeiffer's on the Big Sur River, seen a dance and a lot of people. The older one guessed that, maybe, next year, they might get to make the trip again. Their mother said she had five sons, who were married and were homesteading in the hills. When asked where in the world they found their wives, she laughed, and reported triumphantly that her boys never let a schoolteacher get out of the country! And she added that the latest teacher to be acquired by matrimony in the family had insisted on having a radio. It was the only radio on the coast and everyone spoke of it with awe and deep appreciation. The outside world, the machine-age, was boring in, making an impression.

Barbara Pfeiffer, who had seldom left her Sycamore Canyon home, died in 1930, and had difficulty leaving, even in death. It was winter. Despite slides, washouts, and the swollen stream, a light wagon was got down the steep, narrow road that led into the canyon to the house near the sea. But on the way out with the tiny old lady's body, the wagon overturned, and the body of Barbara Pfeiffer rolled into the stream. It was recovered, but the shock of the gruesome accident was too much for her youngest son, Frank, born in the Sur 60 years before. When he had recovered his shattered nerves, he returned to the Big Sur, vowed to help put a road that was fit to travel into his country. He went to work on the new highway. But in the winter of 1934 a slide that closed the road to travel for more than a month came down at Hurricane Point. It caught Frank Pfeiffer and killed him.

The new highway brings every year a steadily growing number of people to the fringes of the Big Sur country—but only to the fringes. The inner mountain fastnesses—fold after fold of rugged mountains—still guard their lonely isolation, their haughty feet touching the sea, their bold heads lifted proudly above granite cliffs.

The one ballad native to this country has a line which says: "The South Coast's a wild coast, and lonely . . ." And so it will remain.

179

IV. Appendices

A Chronology of the Monterey Peninsula

1542 Nov. 18—Juan Rodríguez Cabrillo sails into the present Bay of Monterey, which he names "Bay of the Pines."

1595 Dec. 8—Juan Rodríguez Cermenho, whose ship *San Augustín* was wrecked in Drake's Bay, sails south along the coast in a small open boat, and sights Monterey Bay, which he calls, "San Pedro Bay."

1602 Dec. 16—Sebastián Vizcaíno anchors in Monterey Bay. The following day, with crew, he goes ashore to celebrate a thanksgiving mass, and formally names the port "Monterey" in honor of Gaspar De Zuniga y Acevedo (Count of Monterey), Ninth Viceroy of Mexico.

1769 Oct. 8—Gaspar de Portolá, en route from San Diego in search of Monterey Bay, passes it without recognition.

1770 May 24—Portolá finally reaches Monterey on his second expedition.
May 31—The *San Antonio*, commanded by Juan Perez and carrying Father Junípero Serra, reaches Monterey, joining the land expedition of Portolá.
June 3—Father Serra founds Misión San Carlos Borromeo de Monterey, second mission to be established in Alta California, named for Carlos Borromeo, Archbishop of Milan and Papal Secretary of State under Pius IV.

1771 Serra moves the mission to the Carmel River, renaming it Misíon San Carlos Borromeo del Rio Carmelo.

1774 May 1—Juan Bautista da Anza, explorer of the first land route from Mexico to Alta California, reaches Monterey.

1775 Aug. 16—The provincial capital is moved from Loreto, Baja California, to Monterey.
Aug. 29—Bruno de Heceta's expedition, coast-exploring, reaches Monterey on its return journey to Mexico.

1776 Apr. 14—Many of the colonists brought by De Anza on his second expedition remain in Monterey.

1777 Feb. 3—Don Felipe de Neve, appointed Governor of California, arrives in Monterey.

1782 Sept. 7—Pedro Fages, former *comandante* of the Monterey Presidio, succeeds Neve as governor.

1784 Aug. 28—Father Serra dies and is buried at Mission San Carlos Borromeo.

1785 Doña Eulalia, wife of Governor Fages, arrives in Monterey. A fashionable lady, she soon tires of provincial life and begins a five-year revolt, marked by scandalous behaviour.

1786   Sept. 14—Jean Francois Galaup de la Pérouse, on a round-the-world trip with a French scientific expedition, arrives in Monterey.

1790   Governor Fages finally succumbs to his wife's will and asks to be relieved of his post.

1791   Sept. 13—John Graham, first American in California, dies in Monterey on the day of his arrival.

1792   Nov. 14—Captain George Vancouver, in the British sloop *Discovery*, makes the first of his three visits to Monterey.

1794   May—Diego Borica becomes Governor of California.

1796   Oct. 29—Ebenezer Dorr, Yankee skipper, brings the *Otter* to Monterey Bay—first American ship in California waters.

1803   June 26—Father Fermín de Lasuén, successor to Serra dies at Carmel Mission.

1804   Mar.—Alta California is divided from Baja California and Monterey named its capital.

1818   Nov. 20—Hippolyte de Bouchard brings two ships of war into Monterey Bay and two days later captures and sacks the town.

1822   Apr. 11—California's allegiance is pledged to the Mexican Empire.
      May 21—California's first general election is held in Monterey.
      Nov.—The first native-born governor, Luis Argüello, is elected.

1825   Mar. 26—California formally becomes a territory of the Mexican Republic. José María Echeandía is sent from Mexico to govern the Californias.

1826   The population of Monterey is estimated at 114 civilians, exclusive of army personnel.

1827   Oct. 29—Captain Frederick William Beechey, R. N., in H. M. S. *Blossom*, while mapping and exploring Pacific routes, returns to Monterey for a two-month's stay.

1828   Monterey soldiers revolt against Echeandía.

1829   Nov. 12—Monterey soldiers again revolt.

1831   Jan.—Echeandía turns over the governorship to Manuel Victoria.

1832   Jan.—The provincial legislature elects Pío Pico Civil Governor.

1836   July—Governor Mariano Chico, who appeared in public with a known adulteress, is forced to return to Mexico.
      Nov. 3—Don Juan Bautista Alvarado and José Castro lead a revolt against the Mexican government.
      Nov. 8—The California *diputación* issues a declaration of Independence. California remains a free state for eight months.
      William S. Hinckley forms a business partnership in Monterey with Nathan Spear and Jacob Leese.

1837   Oct. 18—Captain Abel du Petit-Thouars, commanding the French frigate *Venus*, engaged in investigating the whaling industry in the north Pacific, arrives in Monterey.

1838   The *Beaver*, first steamship in Pacific waters, enters Carmel Bay.

1840   Mar. 10—California's first Supreme Court, the *Tribunal de Justicia*, is formed.
      Apr. 7—All foreigners (47) not married to California women are imprisoned.

A CHRONOLOGY OF THE MONTEREY PENINSULA

1841   May 12—The *Ninfa* arrives in Monterey, carrying French emissary Eugene Duflot de Mofras, sent to investigate the possibilities of French-Mexican trade.

1842   Oct. 19—Believing the United States to be at war with Mexico, Commodore Thomas Ap Catesby Jones, U.S.N., seizes Monterey and raises the United States flag. Two days later he apologizes and withdraws.
Dec. 31—The rule of Civil Governor Alvarado and Military Governor Vallejo ends, leaving 25c in the treasury.

1843   Governor Micheltorena and his army march on Monterey.
May 1—Thomas O. Larkin, pioneer merchant, is appointed the first and only United States consul to California (1843-46).

1844   Nov. 14—Californians revolt, forcing Governor Micheltorena's abdication.

1846   Jan. 27—Captain John Charles Frémont arrives in Monterey to consult with Larkin on formation of an independent Republic of California.
Mar. 6—Frémont raises the United States flag at Gabilan Peak, near Monterey. Ordered to leave California, he retreats on the third night to Sutter's Fort, Sacramento.
May 13—War between the United States and Mexico is formally declared.

1846   July 7—Commodore John D. Sloat raises the American flag at Monterey and declares California a possession of the United States.
Aug. 15—The first issue of California's pioneer newspaper, the *Californian*, is published in Monterey.
Sept. 4—*Alcalde* Walter Colton impanels the first jury called in California.
Sept. 6—General Stephen W. Kearny defeats the Californians at the Battle of San Pascual.

1847   Jan. 9—The final battle between United States forces and Californians is fought at La Mesa. Articles of capitulation are signed four days later.
Jan. 19—Commodore Stockton appoints Captain John Charles Frémont first American Governor of California under military rule.

1847   Mar. 1—General Stephen W. Kearny is appointed civil and military head of California Territory, displacing Frémont, who is later court-martialed for aggressive action in California.

1848   Feb. 3—A treaty of peace is signed between Frémont's forces and the Californians.
Nov. 21—The first United States Post Office in Monterey is established.

1849   Feb. 28—General Persifer F. S. Smith is appointed Military Governor.
Apr. 12—General Bennett Riley is appointed Military Governor, serving until the organization of the State government in December 1849.
Sept. 1—Forty-eight delegates convene in Colton Hall, Monterey, to draft a State constitution. It is adopted on October 10, signed October 13, ratified November 13. The State capital is transferred to San José.

1850   Walter Colton resigns in favor of a town council—the "Common Council of Monterey."
Feb. 18—California's 20 original counties, including Monterey, are created by the State Legislature.

1854   Captain J. D. Davenport organizes whaling operations in Monterey Bay.

A CHRONOLOGY OF THE MONTEREY PENINSULA

1859   Feb. 9—The town council, for the sum of $1,002.50, deeds all town lands to David Jacks and D. R. Ashley, in payment of debt. Subsequently the council adjourns, not to convene again until 1865.

1860   The eighth United States Census sets Monterey's population at 1,653.

1872   Dec. 25—The rapidly growing town of Salinas becomes county seat. The Central Pacific Railroad completes its line to Salinas, with plans to continue southward.

1874   Feb. 12—San Benito County is set apart from Monterey.
Oct.—The first railroad to Monterey, later sold to the Southern Pacific Railroad Company, is built by David Jacks and C. S. Abbot, with the financial aid of several prominent citizens.

1875   June 15—The Pacific Retreat Association establishes the "Christian Seaside Resort" (Pacific Grove) next door to Monterey.

1879   Sept. 1—Robert Louis Stevenson comes to Monterey for a three month's stay.

1880   June—The Hotel Del Monte is opened.
The tenth United States Census sets Monterey's population at 1,396.

1883   Mar. 31—The Pacific Improvement Company purchases Los Laurelles Rancho and water rights in the Carmel River.
The Pacific Improvement Company builds a dam at the junction of the Carmel River and San Clemente Creek to furnish water for Hotel Del Monte, thus beginning the Monterey County Water Works, later to furnish the first public water service to the people of Monterey Peninsula.

1887   Mar. 31—A disastrous fire sweeps Hotel Del Monte; rebuilding commences immediately with even more lavish plans.

1889   Mar. 16—Monterey is finally incorporated as a city. (Three former acts of incorporation, in 1850, 1851, and 1853, were repealed after enactment.)

1890   The eleventh United States Census sets Monterey's population at 1,662, Pacific Grove's at 1,336.

1896   The U.S.S. *Philadelphia* visits Monterey during the celebration of 50 years of American rule.

1900   The twelfth United States Census sets Monterey's population at 1,748, Pacific Grove's at 1,411.

1902   Establishment of the Booth Cannery starts a new industry, which eventually will make Monterey renowned as the "sardine capital of the world."
A United States Army Post is established at Monterey.

1906   The town plan of Monterey is redesigned by City Engineer Howard Sevarance.

1910   The thirteenth United States Census sets Monterey's population at 4,923, Pacific Grove's at 2,384.
First outdoor community theatre in California—The Forest Theatre—established in Carmel.

1915   The Seventeen-Mile Drive is completed and opened to the public.

1916   Nov.—Carmel-by-the-Sea, settled in the early 1900's by artists and writers, is incorporated as a town.

1920   The fourteenth United States Census sets Monterey's population at 5,479, Pacific Grove's at 2,974, Carmel's at 638.

1924   Sept. 27—The Hotel Del Monte again is swept by fire and rebuilding commenced.

1925   The Del Monte Country Club was opened—instead of an initiation fee, eligibles were required to purchase a house lot in the forest.

1926   Municipal Wharf No. 2, extending 1,750 feet into Monterey Bay, is built by the Southern Pacific Railroad Company.

1930   The fifteenth United States Census sets Monterey's population at 9,141, Pacific Grove's at 5,558, Carmel's at 2,260.

1932   Monterey's breakwater is completed.

1936   The year's total value of field crops for Monterey County is $18,455,909.

1937   June 28—The scenic Carmel-San Simeon Highway, a secondary link in the plan for a coastal highway running from Canada to Mexico, is opened to the public.

1938   Monterey's reduction plants are producing annually 12,000,000 gallons of sardine oil and more than 50,000 tons of sardine meal.

1940   The sixteenth United States Census sets Monterey's population at 8,531, Pacific Grove's at 6,249, Carmel's at 2,837.

1941-5 World War II—Monterey Peninsula one of the largest training centers.

1946   Centenary of American Occupation.

Glossary of Spanish Names and Words

Adobe. On a wet roadbed this sticky-claylike soil is a nightmare to travelers; processed and baked in the hot sun, it is a boon to builders. Most of the historic houses of California are made of adobe bricks.

Adiós. One of the most musical ways of saying goodbye.

Aguárdiente. Native high-proof brandy, powerful and popular. An old California recipe advises that a glassful of sugared water mixed with a like quantity of *aguardiente* gladdens the heart, purifies the blood, benefits the head and stomach, cleanses the spleen, and opens the appetite.

Alcalde. The high official of the town: mayor, justice of the peace, and police judge. He carried a wand of office to prove the point.

Alférez. Ensign.

Alisar (or *aliseda*). A grove of alder trees.

Arroyo. A creek, or stream, preferably a creekbed dry most of the year.

Arroyo Seco. Dry creek.

Asilomar. From *asilo,* meaning asylum, or shelter, and *mar,* meaning sea.

Ayuntamiento. A city council or board of aldermen.

Baile. Dance; any dance, but in early California usually a ball lasting from one to three days.

Baja. Lower.

Brasero. Brazier. A metal vessel in which charcoal was burned to produce heat for warming or cooking. This furnished the only heat in the homes of the first pioneers.

Bota. A goatskin winebag. In these sacks, common in Spain and the Basque region, the hair side is inside. A new bag is treated with brandy to absorb the more pungent odors and tastes. Drinking from a *bota* is a fine art in itself, for the bag is held well above the head, allowing a small stream of wine to run into the open mouth.

Caballero. Horseman; also gentleman.

Calabozo. Prison.

Calle. Street. *Calle Principal:* Main Street.

Calzoneras. Short pants. The traditional type of trouser worn by the early settlers that finally gave way to long pantaloons.

Camino. Highway or road. *El Camino Real:* The King's Highway. The main road between San Francisco and Los Angeles was the royal highway of California; once a trail beaten by the dusty feet of gray-robed missionaries, it has become U. S. Highway No. 101.

Cañada. A canyon or hollow.

Carmel. Gardenland.

Carreta. The primitive and highly uncomfortable means of transportation prevalent in the early California era, made of rawhide stretched tight on a frame suspended on two large wooden wheels, without springs of any type. Occasionally a canopy shaded the occupants or merchandise on long trips. *Carretas* were pulled by oxen and accompanied by the agonized noises of screeching axles.

Casa. House. The word *casa* as applied to most of the adobe houses in Monterey means "home."

Cascarón. Shell. The pleasure-loving Californians usually meant that of the egg. Any fiesta or ball was incomplete without a vast collection of eggshells in which the original contents had been replaced by perfume or confetti. Each guest was supplied with a number of these bombs. The object of the game was to approach an unsuspecting victim and crack the shell over his head. The perfume was hard on the eyes, but made the confetti stick more easily.

Castillo. A small fort; also a castle, or pretentious residence.

Celador. Overseer, monitor, or warden.

Chamizal. A thicket of wild cane or weeds, low brush or shrubs.

Chaparral. A tangle of dwarf oak or low thorny shrubs. This type of growth is prevalent throughout California; the Santa Lucia Mountains are so covered with chaparral that they remain green all year.

Comandante. Commander, or commandant. The highest military title awarded by the Spanish in California.

Compañia Estranjera. Foreign legion. Especially, that group of foreign-born residents in Monterey who banded together under the leadership of Agustín Zamorano for the defense of the city during the Solís revolt.

Contradanza. Quadrille.

Cuartel. A jail, prison, or soldiers' barracks.

Diputación. Assembly or delegation. *Diputado:* delegate. The man elected *premier vocal* of the *diputación* was the senior member, next in rank to the governor.

Don, Doña. Courtesy titles (masculine and feminine), similar to "Honorable," usually given only to persons of prominence. Also used in formal address.

Estero. An estuary or outlet.

Excelentísima. Most excellent.

Fazada. The section of meat just over the ribs. This was considered a great delicacy by the *vaqueros;* they removed it from the freshly slaughtered carcass, roasted it over the coals, sprinkled it with salt, and ate it half-raw.

Fiesta. A feast or celebration, usually in honor of a saint.

Flores. Flowers.

185

Frijoles. Red beans, the national dish of the Californians and Mexicans. The preparation of this dish usually calls for quantities of thyme, chili peppers, onions, garlic, and tomatoes. There are hundreds of recipes, however.

Gavilán. Sparrow hawk, a bird of prey. A suitable name for the peak from which Frémont, encamped, looked down on the "hornets gathering in San Juan."

Gobernador. Governor. *Gobernadora:* the governor's lady.

Grande. Large or great. A Spanish nobleman or officer. The recipient of a grant of land from the Spanish crown or a Mexican governor.

Gringos. Term applied to Americans by Mexicans.

Jefe. Chief. *Jefe de politico:* political chief.

Juez de campo. Judge of the country, applied to a judge or *alcalde* holding court away from his office. During the *rodeos* on the ranches a *juez de campo* was always present to count the cattle and see that they were properly segregated and branded.

Laguna. Lagoon or lake. *Laguna seca:* dry lake.

Laureles. Laurels, or bay trees.

Mal. Bad. *Mal paso:* bad crossing; *mal hombre:* bad (or sick) man.

Matanza. The annual killing or slaughtering of beef.

Mantilla. The rectangular lace shawl that the women of California wore over their heads. This usually was draped over the high combs; often it was held in place by flowers. A flattering head covering indispensable to the well-bred young lady; especially useful in attending church, and for flirtations.

Merienda. Party or picnic. The woods were full of them in the days of Mexican and Spanish rule. Monterey's birthday party is celebrated each year with a *merienda.*

Padre. Father or priest.

Paisano. Countryman, native son. In common usage in modern California, a Mexican.

Pájaro. Bird.

Palo colorado. Redwood. The Portolá expedition discovered redwood trees in 1769.

Palomino. A cream-colored horse with white mane and tail. The original Spanish name of the horse was *palamilla,* a word the immigrants evidently found hard to pronounce. (A literal translation means dove droppings.)

Pancho. Colored shirt (Mexican).

Pastores. Shepherds. *Los Pastores:* Christmas play, full of fun and allegory.

Pescado. Fish. *Pescadero:* fisherman or fish dealer.

Peseta. A Spanish and Mexican coin worth two *reales,* the commonest coin in circulation in early California.

Pico. Peak.

Pilarcitos. Little pillars.

Playa. Beach. *Playa de Los Insurgentes:* beach of the insurgents (so named from the landing of the pirate Bouchard in 1818).

Poblodore. Founder or settler.

Potrero. Pasture.

Pronunciamiento. A legal publiciation. Every change of government was heralded by wordy *pronunciamientos* composed by the winning side. Juan Bautista Alvarado developed a fine technique from experience.

Pueblo. Chartered town.

Punta. Point. *Punta de Pinos:* point of pines. *Punta de los Lobos:* point of the wolves.

Ranchero. Rancher.

GLOSSARY OF SPANISH NAMES AND WORDS

Rancho. A large ranch, much greater in area than a *hacienda.* Granted with a lavish hand by the Spanish and Mexican governments, the ranchos formed the core of the economic and social life of the Spaniards. *Rancho del Rey:* Ranch of the king; on this land the horses and cattle of the crown were kept to provide food and transportation for the soldiers. Sometimes this land was called *El Rancho Nacional:* the national ranch.

Reata. Lasso of braided rawhide used by the Californians as a defensive and offensive weapon. One end was furnished with an *honda,* a loop of metal through which the other end of the rope passed to form a slip noose. This was held just so and whirled over the head to gain momentum. The rider threw the loop, allowing the rest of the rope to slip through his hands to the required length. Once the loop slipped over the head of his prey, the *vaquero* slid his horse to a quick stop and twisted the *reata* around the pommel of his saddle. A good roper must have a perfect sense of speed, distance, and timing.

Rebozo. The scarf of silk or wool used as a head and shoulder covering by the women of California *(see mantilla)*

Refugio. Refuge, shelter or protection; also a common Christian name.

Regidor. Petty official, such as alderman or district governor.

Remuda. A group of gentle horses kept near the ranch or driven with travelers for relay riding.

Rio. A river, sometimes a creek or minor stream.

Rodeo. The round-up of cattle on the ranches. It comes from the verb *rodear,* meaning to encircle, to surround. The Americans adapted this into common usage until today it applies not only to working cattle but to the celebrations and contests in which cowboys show their skill in riding, roping, bulldogging, and similar feats.

Sala. Ballroom or room.

Salinas. Salt marshes. One group of Indians of the region were known as Salinans.

San Carlos. St. Charles.

San Francisquito. Little St. Francis.

San José St. Joseph.

San Simeon. St. Simon.

Señora Gobernadore. Governor's wife.

Siesta. The rest period at noontime, sacred to Latins. In California it frequently extended from noon to midafternoon.

Sindico. Petty official under the Mexican regime.

Soldados de cuero. Soldiers of leather. The troops who came overland with the Portolá expedition wore heavy coats of cattlehide or horsehide to protect themselves against Indian arrows.

Sombrero. Hat. In California, the high-crowned wide-brimmed felt or wool hat introduced by the Spanish and retained by the cowboys and cattlemen.

Sur. South.

Tapaderos. The long and highly ornamented foot coverings on the stirrups of Mexican stock saddles. Still used by the modern cowboy.

Tecolero. The master of ceremonies at dances. No party was complete without him.

Tierra. Land, soil, earth.

Toro. Bull.

Tortilla. Mexican bread. It is made of flour, salt, and water, and flattened with the hands into a thin cake (like a pancake) and cooked on hot stones. It is a pleasure to see and hear an expert flip the cakes from one hand to another to obtain the right degree of thinness.

Tule. A marsh reed. These were used by the Indians to make baskets and thatch their huts. The first buildings in the State were roofed with them.

Tularcitos. Little tules, or little rushes.

Vaquero. Cowboy, cowpuncher, or just puncher. Obsolete form: cowherd.

Vara. A lineal measure of 33 inches. A twig, rod, or wand.

Visitador-general. General inspector; an investigator sent from the seat of government.

Bibliography

Andresen, Anna Geil. *Historic Landmarks of Monterey* (Salinas: Salinas Index Press, 1917).

Atherton, Gertrude. *California, an Intimate History* (New York: Boni, Liveright, 1927).

Austin, Mary. "George Sterling at Carmel," *American Mercury, 2* (May, 1927), 65-72.

Bancroft, Hubert Howe. *History of California,* in *History of the Pacific States of North America,* vols. 13-19 (San Francisco: The History Co., 1884-1890).

Barrows, H. D. and Ingersoll, L. A. *A Memorial and Biographical History of Counties of Central California* (Chicago: Lewis Publishing Co., 1893).

Bedell, Clyde O. *Fulfillment* (Monterey, n.p., 1930).

Bolton, Herbert E. *Outpost of Empire* (New York: Knopf and Co., 1931).

Bostick, Daisy. *Today and Yesterday* (Carmel: The Seven Arts, 1945).

Brewer, William H. *Up and Down California in 1860-1864* (New Haven: Yale University Press, 1930).

Brown, Wallace., ed. *Historic Monterey and Surroundings* (Monterey: Monterey Cypress Publishing Co., 1899).

California. Department of Public Works: "Mission San Carlos Borromeo," *News Bureau Release,* No. 16. (Sacramento, 1937).

California. Division of Fish and Game. *Laws Relating to Fish and Game, 1931-33* (Sacramento, 1938).

California. Division of Parks. *Pfeiffer Redwoods State Park Pocket Guide* (Sacramento, 1938).

California. State Mineralogist. *Mines and Mineral Resources of Monterey, San Benito, San Luis Obispo, Santa Barbara, Ventura Counties* (Sacramento, 1916).

Carmel. Board of Councilmen. *Minutes* (May 27, 1936).

———— *Ordinances,* Nos. 6, 38, 43, 44, 63, 68.

Carmel *Pine Cone,* July 8, 1932; Nov. 16, 1934; Feb. 7, May 27, 1936.

Caughey, John Walton. *California* (New York: Prentice-Hall, 1940).

Chapman, Charles E. *A History of California. The Spanish Period* (New York: Macmillan, 1921).

BIBLIOGRAPHY

Chase, J. Smeaton. "Exploring the Santa Lucia Sierra of California," *Overland Monthly,* n.s. 42 (Dec. 1913). 595-602.

Cleland, Robert Glass and Hardy, Osgood. *California, March of Industry* Los Angeles, San Francisco: Powell Publishing Co., 1929), vol. 7.

Clements, E. S. *Flowers of Coast and Sierra* (New York: H. W. Wilson Co., 1932).

Colton, Walter. *Three Years in California* (New York: A. S. Barnes, 1854).

Dana, Richard H. *Two Years Before the Mast* (Greenwich, Conn.: Appleby and Co., 1939).

Davis, William Heath. *Sixty Years in California* (San Francisco: A. J. Cleary, 1889).

Dawson, William Leon. *The Birds of California* (San Francisco: South Moulton Co., 1923).

"Del Monte," *Fortune,* 21 (Jan. 1940), 59-67, 104, 106, 107.

Drury, Aubrey. *California, An Intimate Guide* (New York: Harpers' 1935).

Eldredge, Zoeth Skinner. *History of California* (New York: Century History Co., 1915). 5 vols.

Englehardt, Fr. Zephyrin. *Mission San Carlos Borromeo* (Santa Barbara 1934).

———— *Missions and Missionaries of California* (San Francisco: The Barry Co., 1908-1916). 4 vols.

Forbes, Mrs. A. S. C. *California Missions and Landmarks* (Los Angeles: Wetzel Publishing Co., 1925).

Ford, Tirey L. *Dawn and the Dons* (San Francisco: A. M. Robertson, 1926).

Guinn, James Miller. *Historical and Biographical Record of Monterey and San Benito Counties* (Los Angeles: Historic Record Co., 1910).

———— *History of the State of California, and Biographical Record of Coast Counties* (Chicago: Chapman Publishing Co., 1904). 12 vols.

Handbook of Monterey and Vicinity (San Francisco: Bacon and Co., 1873).

Hannaford, Donald R. and Edwards, Revel. *Spanish or Colonial Adobe Architecture of California 1800-1850* (New York: Architectural Book Publishing Co., 1931).

Hardy, Lady Duffus. *Through Cities and Prairie Lands* (Chicago: Belford, Clarke and Co., 1882).

Harrison, E. S. *Monterey County* (Salinas, Calif.: the author, 1888).

Hittell, John S. *The Resources of California* (San Francisco: A. Roman and Co., 1874).

Hittell, Theodore H. *History of California* (San Francisco: N. J. Stone, 1885-1897). 4 vols.

Hoover, Mildred Brooke. *Historic Spots in California, Counties of the Coast Range* (Stanford University: Stanford University Press, 1937).

Hunt, Rockwell D. and others. *California and Californians* (Chicago and New York: Lewis Publishing Co., 1926). 5 vols.

———— and others. *California the Golden* (New York: Silver, Burdette, 1911).

———— and Ament, William Sheffield. *Oxcart to Airplane* (Los Angeles: Powell Publishing Co., 1929).

189

A GUIDE TO THE MONTEREY PENINSULA

Illustrated History of Monterey County, Scenery, Farming, Business, Houses, etc. (San Francisco: Elliott & Moore Publishing Co., 1881).

James, George Wharton. *In and Out of the Old Missions* (New York: Little, Brown Co., 1905).

Jeffers, Robinson. *Roan Stallion, and other Poems* (New York: Horace Liveright, 1925).

Jepson, Willis Linn. *The Silva of California* (Berkeley: University of California Press, 1910.)

Jochmus, A. C. *The Circle of Enchantment* (Pacific Grove: Chamber of Commerce, 1931).

———— *Monterey: All of It Between Two Covers* (Pacific Grove, Calif.: n.p., 1930).

Lawson, Andrew Cowper. *Geology of Carmel Bay,* University of California Publications in Geology, Vol. 1, (Berkeley: University of California Press 1893).

Los Angeles *Times,* Nov. 27, 1929.

MacFarland, Grace, *Monterey, Cradle of California's Romance* (Monterey: W. T. Lee, 1914).

Markham, Edwin, *California the Wonderful* (New York: Hearst International, 1914).

Monterey. City Planning Commission. *The Master Plan of the City of Monterey* (Monterey, 1939).

Monterey. County Recorder. *Deeds of Monterey County,* Book A (1851), Book 2 (1860).

———— *Translations of Spanish Documents,* vol. 1.

Monterey *Argus* (Monterey), July 8, 1886; Jan. 31, 1882.

Monterey County Post (Salinas), June 28, 1929.

Monterey *New Era* (Monterey), Jan. 8, 1896; Sept. 5, 1900; Jan. 16, 1901; May 27, Aug. 20, Sept. 10, 1902; Aug. 20, 1906.

Monterey Peninsula Herald (Monterey), Aug. 19, 1921; Feb. 10, 1924; Mar. 30, Sept. 13, 1928; May 24, 1929; Jan. 25, June 21, 1935; Feb. 13, 19, 21, Apr. 4, May 13, June 26, Aug. 14, 22, Nov. 24, 1936; Apr. 2, June 25, July 19, 1937; Feb. 4, Mar. 12, 14, 25, May 25, Oct. 11, 28, Nov. 3, 1938; Nov. 10, 1939.

Monterey *Trader* (Monterey), May 29, 1936.

Newcomb, Rexford. *The Franciscan Mission Architecture of Alta California* (New York: Architectural Book Publishing Co., 1916).

Oakland *Tribune,* Feb. 8, 1931.

Older, Mrs. Fremont. *California Missions and Their Romances* (New York: Coward-McCann, 1938).

Osterhout, W. J. V. "Jacques Loeb, Biographical Sketch," *Journal of General Physiology,* 8 (Sept. 15, 1928), ix-lix.

Pacific Grove. City Council. *Ordinance No. 284* (Apr. 21, 1932).

Pacific Grove *Tribune,* Jan. 23, 1936.

Parsons, Mary E. *Flowers of California* (San Francisco: Cunningham, Curtiss and Welch, 1907.)

GLOSSARY OF SPANISH NAMES AND WORDS

Phillips, C. A. *The Manufacture of Monterey Cheese.* California Agricultural Extension Service, Circ. 18. (Berkeley: University of California Press, 1933).

Powers, Laura Bride. *Old Monterey California's Adobe Capital* (San Francisco: San Carlos Press, 1934).

Reed, Ralph Daniel. *Geology of California.* (Tulsa, Okla.: American Association of Petroleum Geologists, 1933).

Richman, Irving B. *California Under Spain and Mexico* (Boston: Houghton Mifflin, 1911).

Royce, Josiah. *California:From the Conquests in 1846 to Second Vigilance. Committee* (Boston: Houghton Mifflin, 1886).

Salinas *Daily Index,* Sept. 8, 1913.

Salinas *Morning Democrat,* June 20, 1915.

Salinas *Morning Post,* June 16, 1936.

Sanchez, Nellie Van de Grift. *Spanish Arcadia* (San Francisco, Los Angeles, Chicago: Powell Publishing Co., 1929).

San Francisco *Bulletin,* May 14, 1938.

San Francisco *Chronicle,* Aug. 21, 1900; June 20, 1936; Mar. 11, 1940.

San Francisco *Examiner,* Aug. 31, 1900; Nov. 3, 1905; Oct. 27, 1927; Jan. 14, 1936.

Scammon, C. M. *Marine Mammals of the Northwest Coast* (San Francisco: J. J. Carmody, n.d.).

"Sea Otter Herd Viewed from New Coast Highway," *Motor Land,* 42 (May 1938), 23.

"The Sea Otter Returns," *California Monthly,* 40 (June 1938), 7, 36.

Sherman, William Tecumseh. *Memoirs of W. T. Sherman* (New York: D. Appleton, 1875). 2 vols.

Shepardson, Lucia. *Monterey Adobes* (Monterey: The Monterey Press, 1935).

Smith, Mrs. Sarah H. *Adobe Days* (Los Angeles: Jake Zeitlin, 1931).

Staiger, J. Dana. "Pfeiffer Redwoods State Park is Vacation Mecca for Thousands," *California Conservationist,* 5 (Aug. 1940). 17, 21.

Steele, J. K. *Monterey Peninsula Country Club* (San Francisco: Carlisle and Co., n.d.).

Steinbeck, John. *Tortilla Flat* (New York: Covici, Friede, 1935). *Cannery Row* (New York: The Viking Press, 1944).

Stevenson, Robert Louis. *Across the Plains, 1883-1894* (New York: Scribners, 1905).

The Story of Beet Sugar from the Seed to the Sack (Saginaw, Michigan: Farmers and Manufacturers Beet Sugar Assn., 1933).

Swasey, W. F. *The Early Days and Men of California* (San Francisco: Pacific Press, 1891).

Symons, Henry H. *California Mineral Production for 1934* (Sacramento, 1935).

Tavernetti, A. A. *Production of the Globe Artichoke in California.* California Agricultural Extension Service Circ. 76 (Berkeley: University of California Press, 1933).

Tide (Pacific Grove), July 24, 1936.

Taylor, Bayard. *Eldorado, or Adventures in the Path of Empire* (2d ed; New York: Putnam, 1850).

Underhill, Reuben L. *From Cowhides to Golden Fleece* (Stanford University: Stanford University Press, 1939).

U. S. Bureau of the Census. *Eighth Census of the United States, 1860* (Washington, 1864).

Vancouver, Captain George. *A Voyage of Discovery to the North Pacific Ocean* (London: J. Stockdale, 1801).

Vansell, G. H. *Nectar and Pollen Plants of California,* University of California Experiment Station Bull. 517 (Berkeley: University of California Press, 1931).

Voorhies, E. C. and others. *Economic Aspects of the Bee Industry,* Giannini Foundation of Agricultural Economics, Bull. 555 (Berkeley: University of California Press, Sept. 1933).

———— *Honey Marketing in California.* Giannini Foundation . . . Bull. 554 (Berkeley: University of California Press, 1933).

Ware, Lewis S. and others. *The Sugar Beet* (Philadelphia: Henry Carey Baird, 1880).

Watkins, Major Rolin C. *History of Monterey, Santa Cruz, and San Benito Counties* . . . (Chicago: S. J. Clarke Publishing Co., 1925). 2 vols.

Wheelock, I. G. *Birds of California* (Chicago: A. C. McClurg and Co., 1904).

White, Mary L. "Over the Santa Lucia," *Overland Monthly,* n.s., 20 (Nov. 1892), 449-468.

Works Progress Administration, Project 4080. "Adobes and Old Buildings in Monterey," manuscript, Monterey, 1937.

Index

abalone, 68; song, 143
Abrego, José, 77, 118
Abrego, Julia, 118
adobe brick, 80
agar-agar, 133
Agassiz Laboratory, Pacific Grove, 129
airport, Monterey, 11, 61
albacore fishing, 101
Alemany, Joseph, 93
Alexander, Cyrus, 126
Allen, A. M., 171
Allen, George, 116
Alvarado, Juan Bautista, 44, 45, 82, 85, 90, 104, 105, 111, 169, 176
Alvarado street, 65
American condor, 177
American Can factory, 127
American occupation, 46
Amesti, José, 82
Amoros, Juan, 156
Anza, Juan Bautista de, 32
architecture of Monterey, 73
Argüello, Concepción, 94
Argüello, José, 102, 104
Argüello, Louis, 40
Ariss, Bruce, 72
Army headquarters, Fort Ord, 99
Arrillaga, José Joaquín de, 35, 103
art in Monterey, 71
art collections and museums, 14; Carmel, 141
artichokes, 60
artists and writers, 55
Arts and Crafts Theater, Carmel, 139
Ashley, D. R., 52
Asilomar, 124
Atwood, Thomas, 109
Austin, Mary, 58, 135, 138

Bach Festival, Carmel, 139
Bacon, Ernst, 139
Baker, Ray Stannard, 136
"Bandit House," 92
"Barbizon of California," 29
Baretto Adobe, 112
Baretto, Fabian, 162
Baretto, María del Carmen, 146, 162
Baseball park, Pacific Grove, 127

Bautista, Juan, 81
Bay of Monterey, 22, 30
beach pine, 25
bear and bull fights, 38
Bear Flag Republic, 46
Beaver, 44
Bechdolt, Fred, 58
Belcher, Louis, 109, 119
Belcher-Roach vendetta, 119
Bellows, George, 138
Benet, William Rose, 59, 136
Berwick, Edward, 166
Big Sur, 169; Lodge, 176; River, 175; Tour, 169
Bird Rock, 161
Bishop pine, 25
Bixby Canyon, 59
Bixby Creek, 173
Bixby Landing, 174
Black Hills, 134
Blanding, Don, 138
Bohemian Club exhibit, 106
Bonifacio, Giovanni, 112
Bonifacio, María, 110, 112
Booth Cannery, 60, 102, 121
Booth, F. E., 60
Borica, Diego, 35
Boronda, Manuel de, 111, 116
Botke, Cornelius, 138;—Jesse, 142
Bouchard, Hippolyte de, 10, 99, 103, 114
Boundy, Burton, 72
boy's school, first, 116
breakwater, Monterey, 70
Brewer, William H., 51, 157, 162
Brick House in California, first, 96
Brown-Underwood Adobe, 89
Browne, Maurice, 139
Buelna, Antonio, 111
Bull and Bear Pit, 79
bull fights, 38
Burnett, Peter H., 50
butterfly collection, 130; trees, 132

Cabrillo, Juan Rodríguez, 20, 27, 30, 128
Cabrillo Point, 124, 129
California Battalion, 84

193

INDEX

195

INDEX

marine algae collection, 130
marine life, 22
Marion, George F., 139, 159
Mason, Richard B., 48, 86
Master Plan, Monterey, 73
Maybeck, Bernard Ralph, 142
Mays, Paul Kirkland, 138
McAuley, Martin, 117
McGowan, J. S., 93
McKinley, Santiago, 82
Memorial Library, Carmel, 142
Memory Garden, 107
Merriam, Frank, 170
Merritt House, 94
Mervine, William, 46, 101
Mestres, Father, 109, 144
Methodist community, Pacific Grove, 126
Michaelis, E., 56
Micheltorena, Manuel, 45, 82, 91, 105, 156
Midway Point, 162
Milton Little Ranch House, 122
Mission Inn, 79
Mission Point, 134
Mission San Carlos Borromeo, 31, 32, 34, 36, 100, 113, 116, 134, 141, 152-159, 167
Mitchell, W. T., 176
Moerenhaut, J. A., 108
Molera Ranch, 176
Monarch butterflies, 25
Montague, Mrs. Nellie, 143
Montenegro, Eugenio, 119
Monterey Argus, 53, 56
Monterey Art Gallery, 71
Monterey Bay, 20
Monterey Boat Owners Assn., 121
Monterey Chamber of Commerce, 77
Monterey cypress, 24, 176
Monterey Foundation, 85
Monterey History and Art Assn., 73
Monterey Jack Cheese, 176
Monterey Lime Co., 174
Monterey Master Plan, 73
Monterey, naming of, 31
Monterey Park and Playground Com., 87
Monterey pine, 25
Monterey Planning Com., 74
Monterey Peninsula Country Club, 21, 150, 161

Monterey Presidio, 98
Monterey-Salinas Highway, 169
Monterey Whaling Co., 97
Monterey Women's Civic Club, 86
Montgomery, Capt. John B., 46
Moore, George Gordon, 165
Mora, Jo, 138, 141, 158
Morgan, De Neale, 72
Morris, Gouverneur, 111
Morse, Samuel F. B., 149
Moss Beach, 132, 160
Mount Toro, 64
Municipal Baseball Park, 127
Municipal Beach, Pacific Grove, 131
municipal ordinances, Pacific Grove, 125
Municipal Wharf, 71
Munras Adobe (Cooper House), 80
Munras, Catalina, 169; Estaban, 117
Murietta, Joaquin, 157
Murray Hacienda, 130
Museums: Custom House, 106; Pacific Grove, 130
"My Attic," 80

Natalie, ship, 106, 118
Native Sons of the Golden West, 106
Navarete, Lieutenant, 156
Neuhaus, Eugen, 71
Neve, Felipe de, 154
Newberry, Perry, 137, 139
New Monterey, 66, 124
newspapers: 14; in Carmel, 138; first in State, 43, 47
night clubs, 13
Ninth Coast Artillery Dist., 99
Ninth Corps Area, 99
Norton, Mary E. B., 131
Notley's Landing, 172

Oak Grove, 66
O'Connel, Daniel, 112
Okies, 69
"Old Company," 97
Old Custom House, 102
Old Monterey, 65
Old Whaling Station, 97
Oliver, Myron, 92
Onesimo, Anaselma, 179
Ord, Fort and Camp, 99
Osborne, Fanny, 157
O'Shea, John, 72

197

INDEX

199